p.195

Kuznets - Curve

p.41 | Rev.

11/29 - 2-4
12/6 - 5-7

Structural Contexts of Opportunities

PETER M. BLAU

STRUCTURAL CONTEXTS OF OPPORTUNITIES

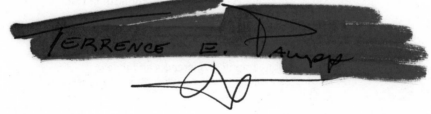

THE UNIVERSITY OF CHICAGO PRESS
CHICAGO & LONDON

PETER M. BLAU is the Robert Broughton Distinguished Research Professor at the University of North Carolina and the Quetelet Professor Emeritus of Sociology at Columbia University. He is the author of numerous books, including *The Dynamics of Bureaucracy: A Study of Interpersonal Relations in Two Government Agencies,* published in 1955 by the University of Chicago Press.

The University of Chicago Press, Chicago 60637
The University of Chicago Press, Ltd., London
© 1994 by The University of Chicago
All rights reserved. Published 1994
Printed in the United States of America
03 02 01 00 99 98 97 96 95 94   1 2 3 4 5

ISBN: 0-226-05729-1 (cloth)

Library of Congress Cataloging-in-Publication Data

Blau, Peter Michael.
    Structural contexts of opportunities / Peter M. Blau.
        p.   cm.
    Includes bibliographical references and index.
    1. Macrosociology.   2. Social structure.   3. Intergroup.
    I. Title.
HM24.B554   1994   94-10313
305—dc20   CIP

∞ The paper used in this publication meets the minimum requirements of the American National Standard for Information Sciences—Permanence of Paper for Printed Library Materials, ANSI Z39.48-1984.

To the memory of

PAUL L. LEHMANN

and to

ROBERT K. MERTON

two eminent scholars and teachers

who have greatly influenced my life and work

CONTENTS

PREFACE

WHEN ONE REACHES THE AGE at which one can look back over three-quarters of a century of one's life and one-half of a century of academic work as a sociologist, it is appropriate to consider how the various major topics on which one has worked fit together. This is particularly the case when a person's scholarship and research have involved quite diverse topics in sociology, as has been true for my work.

I shall dispense with talking about the first quarter century, although it involved two most important events for my future academic career—my immigration to the United States and my majoring in sociology in college. (Indeed, I did not know what sociology was—not even the term—when it was first suggested to me as a possible major.) After all, this is a preface to a particular book, not an autobiography of one's life and personal experiences. What I do in this preface is indicate how a number of subjects I discuss in this book represent areas in which I have worked in the course of my career.

This was not the objective I had for the book when planning it and working on it. My objective was to broaden a macrosociological theory I developed in the late seventies by applying it to new subject matters, as described in the introductory chapter. The original theory dealt with influences of population structures on intergroup relations. My plan for this book was to show that the theoretical scheme can be used in the analysis of such other sociological problems as macrosociological influences on career opportunities, social mobility, and formal organizations. But as I look back over the topics by which I illustrated the theory's wider applicability, I realize that many of the topics, though by no means all, deal with subjects on which I had worked extensively during my career.

ix

Let me elaborate by introducing an, admittedly somewhat over-simplified, dichotomy into which the diverse theoretical views and orientations in sociology can be divided. The issue is whether the domain assumption stipulates that the starting point of the theoretical analysis refers to actors or to systems. The first assumption asserts that since sociology studies people, its starting point must be an analysis of actors. This may lead to various sociopsychological approaches, or to that of exchange processes, or to theories of rational choice. But it may also lead to system theories, as illustrated by Parsons's theoretical analyses, or to the study of social ties between individuals and the networks they create, which become connected by bridging ties into increasingly encompassing structures of networks. The conception of microfoundation of macrosociology represents this view.

The opposite domain assumption is that sociology, since it studies societies or other collectivities, must start to distinguish the various subunits and corresponding social positions into which all populations—though to varying degrees—are divided. What divides them are the population members' affiliations with various groups and strata, which are manifest in the different rates of ingroup and outgroup relations. Social relations hold groups together in two ways. Ingroup relations make a group's members cohere, express their group solidarity, and draw the boundaries among groups, whereas intergroup relations express the community's or society's solidarity by providing social bonds among the various groups. The macrostructural perspective represents this assumption.

The macrosociological conception of social structure defines it not in terms of the network of social ties between individuals but in terms of the different groups and strata composing the population, whether a community, a region, or an entire society. To be sure, groups or strata can be distinguished on the basis of many dimensions, for example by the population's distribution in age, education, social class, and ethnic affiliation. Any one of these differences among people is an aspect of the social structure, and the degree to which various differences are related is a particularly important structural attribute. For instance, structural attributes are a population's ethnic heterogeneity, socioeconomic inequality, and the extent to which ethnic and socioeconomic differences are related. The theory stipulates how these and other forms of differentiation influence intergroup relations, which must be tested by comparing populations.

My major sociological interest and work have gradually changed from a concern with the social processes that govern the interpersonal

From group (micro) to macro

relations in networks of small groups to a focus on macrostructural influences on patterns of social relations. Most of my early research was on networks of social relations in work groups, notably those in government bureaus and public welfare departments. This research on the social processes in social networks of small groups led to a theory of interpersonal exchange—*Exchange and Power in Social Life* (1964).

My next major project was a large study, coauthored with Otis Dudley Duncan, on the social stratification and mobility of American men, the first such study in this country based on a national representative sample (*The American Occupational Structure*, 1967). Although this study dealt with socioeconomic status and intergenerational mobility in a large society, it was a case study of one society and the analysis centered attention not on structural influences but on the influence of attributes of individuals on occupational achievements.

I spent more than a decade during the 1960s and 1970s on studies of *meso*-structures, which involved a series of quantitative studies of formal organizations. Whereas research on organizations had heretofore largely entailed case studies, I and a few others, mostly in England, started to conduct quantitative research on organizations, based on enough cases to permit statistical analysis of their administrative structure. The projects of my research team included a study of all state employment security agencies and their local offices in the United States, another of 416 public finance departments, one of 126 department stores, and one of 115 universities and colleges.

Finally, in the mid-1970s I developed a macrosociological theory of the influences of population structures on intergroup relations—*Inequality and Heterogeneity* (1977)—the implications of which were later tested in research conducted in collaboration with Joseph E. Schwartz (*Crosscutting Social Circles*, 1984). To be sure, my work did not exhibit the simple linear trend from a focus on microprocesses to one on macrostructures that the present summary seems to imply. My dissertation on work groups in government bureaus (*The Dynamics of Bureaucracy*, 1955) indicates an early interest in formal organizations, stimulated by Merton's lectures on bureaucracy, and in graduate school I was already concerned enough with structural effects to write a paper on them a few years later (1960).

The sequence of chapters in this book does not follow the chronological changes in my academic orientation. It is not determined by the shifts in my scholarly and research interest but by my initial objective to apply the theory formulated to explain macrostructural influences on intergroup relations to the analysis of these influences on other aspects of social life. A secondary objective is to establish a connection between the theory of exchange processes in interpersonal relations and the theory of the macrostructural influences on these relations. (This objective conflicts with an earlier claim of mine that these two theories could not be connected in a single scheme.) Such a theoretical connection must not only acknowledge these macrostructural influences, which the conception of the microfoundation of macrostructures denies, but specify the conditions on which the population structure's effects on interpersonal relations depend. This is the purpose of multilevel structural analysis.

After the introduction (chap. 1), I present a somewhat revised formulation of the original theory of the effects of differentiation in a population on intergroup relations in chapter two. Several tests of the major theorems, based on empirical comparisons of the 125 largest American metropolitan areas, are described in the next chapter (chap. 2). Chapter 4 applies the theoretical scheme to the analysis of the influence of occupational structure on career opportunities. It uses a refinement for estimating the extent of structural mobility, and it examines the effects on occupational chances of differences in education and the paradoxically opposite effects of aggregate changes in education.

Formal organizations are discussed in chapter 5. I first present an analysis of influences of the multidimensional social space of the population structure on the growth of voluntary associations and other organizations and then discuss two theories of organizations. The last part of the chapter reports studies of recent changes in corporations and their consequent intersection with markets. After reviewing exchange theory in chapter 6, I attempt to link it with macrostructural theory. To do so, I treat interpersonal relations as the ultimate expression of the macrostructure, not as its foundation; specify conditions that can prevent macrostructures from affecting intergroup relations; and distinguish two forms of power—interpersonal influence and economic or political domination.

The last chapter raises the question of what historical conditions influence population structures. The effects on population distributions of demographic trends are examined first. The rest of the chapter centers attention on the influences on them of industrialization, the division of labor, and economic growth or decline. The economic growth at accelerating rates we experienced following the Civil War furthered structural mobility and career opportunities. A reversal has occurred in recent decades, however. The major reason for this reversal is in all likelihood the large shift of the labor force from manufacturing to mostly low-skilled jobs in service industries, where productivity is much lower than in manufacturing. In closing, I speculate about future developments in mobility opportunities and in class conflict, and discuss whether advances in information technology will raise productivity in services.

I am enormously indebted to a number of colleagues who read an earlier draft of the manuscript and made comments that enabled me to greatly improve the monograph, among them Craig J. Calhoun, Herbert J. Gans, Michael Hechter, Guillermina Jasso, Arne Kalleberg, and Rachel A. Rosenfeld. Two colleagues deserve to be singled out for the special contributions they made: Steven Rytina, who sent me an article-length set of comments with some suggestions for virtually every page, and my colleague and spouse, Judith R. Blau, who made important suggestions for revisions on three drafts she read completely, protected me from external demands, and provided encouragement and continual social and emotional support.

I also owe thanks to my research assistants, who helped with the quantitative analysis and in many other ways: Andrey Lukashov, Ritch Milby, and Jim Moody. Finally, I want to express my appreciation to Douglas Mitchell, my editor at the University of Chicago Press, for his support and advice and to Jennie Lightner, the manuscript editor, for her excellent editing.

ONE

MACROSTRUCTURAL
CONCEPTS

T HIS BOOK PRESENTS A macrosociological analysis of influences of
forms of differentiation in population structures on people's life
chances. Macrostructural concepts refer to people's distribution
in various dimensions and the degrees to which these dimensions of social
differences among people are related. Macrosociology is concerned primarily with large populations—composed of many thousands or even
millions of persons. My endeavor is to develop a systematic theoretical
scheme for the study of macrostructures and their impact on social life.
For this purpose, population structures are conceptualized in terms of a
few generic concepts abstracted from their diverse empirical contents (in
Simmel's [1923] sense). These theoretical concepts are employed in the
study of macrosociological influences on social relations, occupational
opportunities, social mobility, and organizational growth. I conclude by
discussing some historical trends.

Whereas the macrosociological study here is confined to effects of
the population *structure* on social life, I do not want to imply that structural influences are the only or only important influences on people's
lives and life chances. Many sociologists adopt other theoretical orientations—cultural, institutional, evolutionary, to name a few—and I acknowledge that these other approaches may be more appropriate for
the study of some issues than is the structural one. However, I do think
that the analysis of the effects of the objective conditions of population
compositions and structures has much to contribute to sociology and
that it has been greatly neglected, particularly in recent decades. By
adopting the structural approach, I want to rectify the past imbalance
by complementing the prevalent cultural and institutional orientations in
our field.

I

The theoretical analysis in this monograph is an expansion of one originally developed to study structural influences on interpersonal relations among members of different groups (Blau 1977; Blau and Schwartz 1984). The next two chapters present a somewhat revised formulation of this theory and empirical tests of its implications.[1] Whereas this theory of intergroup relations is couched in formal terms—with theorems, deduced from a few assumptions, having empirically testable implications—its application to other subjects is not, because here I wish to expand the scope of the theoretical scheme even when I cannot formulate rigorous theories. Thus, the rest of the chapters present various substantive analyses that merely apply the theoretical scheme, whenever appropriate, without advancing formal theories.

The fourth chapter centers attention on occupational opportunities and social mobility, with emphasis on the effects of variations in such structural conditions as the division of labor, the level of education, and labor demand, concluding by contrasting structural and circulation mobility. The structural context of society's population is far removed from the various organizations and other substructures where people live and work and their daily social lives take place, which is the subject of multilevel structural analysis. The significance of society's structural context for organizations is examined in chapter 5, and so are the interrelations of firms and their markets. Chapter 6 is devoted to the processes of direct social interaction and exchange, which are the ultimate expressions of macrostructural influences on interpersonal relations that integrate individuals through increasingly encompassing social circles in society. This chapter also contrasts power in face-to-face relations with the power to dominate entire segments of society.

The preceding analysis of social consequences of different macrostructural conditions takes these conditions as given. The final issue addressed is what the antecedents are that influence the conditions of the population structure. The last chapter explores historical antecedents, such as demographic trends and industrial and economic developments, that have helped shape the structure of society. It also examines recent structural changes that adversely affected occupational opportunities, and it concludes with some conjectures about future prospects.

---

1. The core of the original theory (recapitulated in chap. 2) is a formal theory influenced by the methods of theorizing of Braithwaite (1953) and Popper (1959).

POPULATION STRUCTURES

The term *population* is used for large social units of any kind—societies, regions, metropolitan areas, communities, and so forth—and by *population structure* I refer to a population's composition. Specifically, population structure is reflected in people's distribution among social positions in various dimensions and the degrees to which these differences among people along various lines are correlated. Thus, distributions and their correlations are used not merely as procedures for analysis but initially to formulate concepts and measures indicative of aspects of social structures. An analysis of these structural influences cannot, of course, be derived from the study of a single population but requires the comparison of many.

Broadly defined, a social position (in a single dimension) is any difference among people in terms of which they make social distinctions among themselves in social intercourse. A narrower but more specific criterion of social position is an excess of ingroup (or proximate) over outgroup (or distant) social associations. If friendships, for example, are disproportionately infrequent between persons who differ substantially in age or in education and between those who do not have the same religious or ethnic affiliation, these differences refer to socially significant distinctions in social positions.[2] Any attribute distinguishing people for which such differential associations occur is considered a social position in my terms, even if it is not conventionally called a position.[3]

These criteria indicate positions in a single dimension. People belong to multiple groups, however, particularly in complex modern societies. (The terms *ingroup* and *intergroup,* though strictly applicable only to categorical differences, are used for convenience when reference is to both categorical differences and those by degree.) Thus, a woman not only is female but also may be an affluent Catholic lawyer of Italian descent. Of course, not all common group memberships are equally meaningful and important. The preponderance of ingroup over outgroup relations indicates the strength of attachment of group members—how

2. It is evident that the first two examples pertain to continuous and the second two to discrete differences. This distinction affects the analysis, as discussed below.

3. This is a very broad definition of social position, but it is not all-encompassing. It includes only those differences in people's attributes that affect their social relations, notably the likelihood of ingroup associations. This provides a criterion for empirically testing whether some attribute of interest to the investigator—say, being or not being a member of the ACLU—actually influences social intercourse.

closely knit they are and how great the group's salience is for them. Ascribed positions tend to be more salient than achieved ones—possibly, at least in part, owing to the longer duration of most ascribed relations.

The study of multiple social affiliations is at the core of the theory to be presented. Although various social differences must first be analytically distinguished, they must be analyzed together to discern their separate and combined influences. For instance, ethnic ingroup associations are affected not only by ethnic preferences but also by education and socioeconomic status, which tend to differ among ethnic groups. To clarify the observed degree of ethnic ingroup relations, the influences of these two (and other) correlates of ethnic affiliation must be separated from the (residual) influence of ethnic affiliation itself.

. . .

The most important theoretical reason for the analysis of the influences of multigroup affiliations, however, is that it can account for people's interpersonal choices that are contrary to their interests and preferences. If people tend to prefer to associate with others like themselves—and much evidence indicates that they do—multigroup affiliations imply that they are constrained to choose among their various ingroup preferences, for others are unlikely to have the same multigroup affiliations they do. Notwithstanding the prevalence of ingroup preferences, therefore, people's very ingroup choices in some respects often involve them in intergroup relations in others. Hence, multigroup affiliations make some intergroup relations likely if not inevitable, even if all persons were to prefer ingroup associates in all respects, and they make the probability of intergroup relations dependent on structural conditions.

Social structure can be conceptualized as a multidimensional space of social positions among which a population is distributed. This conception takes multigroup affiliations into account, and it also implies that opportunities for ingroup and intergroup relations depend on conditions in the social structure, for proximity in social space, just as physical proximity, makes social relations more likely. The axes in this social space are the dimensions of social differences among people. Persons alike in one respect, such as education, are the same distance from the origin on one axis, though not on others. Those proximate in one dimension, such as age, are closer than distant persons on that axis. Persons who have the same nominal position in one dimension are considered a group, even if it involves a large number, such as an ethnic or religious group.[4] The more two dimensions, such as education and occupational status, are correlated, the greater is the probability that individuals will have the same or similar positions in these two dimensions.

The degree to which social differences in one respect are related to those in several others has particularly important implications for opportunities and their limits, such as occupational chances and mobility, and ingroup and intergroup relations. Strong correlations consolidate group boundaries and hierarchical differences. Weak correlations indicate that social differences intersect, which implies that many people who differ in some respects are alike or similar in others. Such intersecting differences often become dialectical forces that counteract the influences of the specific structural differences, as we shall see.

Population structures entail not only multiple forms of social differentiation but also multiple levels of structure. For example, a nation is composed of provinces, which consist of counties, whose subunits are cities and towns, which contain neighborhoods. Similarly, the labor force can be divided into manual and nonmanual workers, who, in turn, are divisible into major occupational groups, whose subunits are detailed occupations, which are composed of increasingly narrow specialties. The larger population has a social structure, and the subunits on successive levels have their own social structures. The macrosociological approach to analyzing these multiple levels is not to aggregate from smaller to increasingly larger structures but to disaggregate from the most encompassing structures to increasingly smaller substructures. The question is how much any form of differentiation in the encompassing structure penetrates into the substructures on successively lower levels rather than finding expression in differences among the substructures[5] (which multilevel structural analysis is designed to answer). Only the former promotes intergroup relations; the latter entails segregation that limits them.

. . .

4. This use of *group* seems to conflict with the usage that confines the term to persons in direct social interaction. But unless the term *group* is considered synonymous with a small face-to-face group, it is unlikely, if not impossible, even in fairly small groups—a few hundred, say—for all members to have direct social ties with all others. An appropriate macrosociological conception of group, therefore, is that the likelihood of ingroup rates of social associations exceeds that of outgroup rates, which is the definition adopted.

5. How much of the ethnic heterogeneity or income inequality in this country, for example, penetrates into states, into cities, and down into neighborhoods.

Before distinguishing two forms of macrostructural influences on people's opportunities and constraints, the conception of macrostructure
adopted should be compared with that of microstructure in network
analysis. The two have important assumptions in common. Both center
attention on the links between different positions or roles, which in network analysis are referred to as ties between nodes.[6] Both abstract the
pattern of links (ties or intergroup relations) and the points they con-
nect (nodes or social positions) from persons' attributes—their culture
as well as their personal characteristics—and from the nature of the
links: whether they are interaction frequencies or friendship choices,
for example. But the assumed causal nexus between persons or groups
and their social links is opposite in microstructural and macrostructural
analysis.

Macrosociology assumes that the distributions of people's positions
and their nexus—the degrees of their various similarities and differences,
and how closely related the various dimensions are—govern people's
social relations and life chances. Hence, social structure is defined in
terms of a population's differences in various dimensions and the relationships of the various differences, which corresponds to the usage in speaking of a population's age structure, occupational structure, and class
structure or how closely ethnic background is related to occupational
status.

However, network analysts (for instance, Wellman 1988) define social structure not in terms of some differences between persons ("nodes")
but on the basis of the pattern of ties, the network structure. In short,
networks constitute the social structure and the assumption is that this
network structure determines the roles of individuals—"nodes"—in the
group, whether the roles are defined by interaction process profiles (Bales
1950) or structural equivalence (Burt 1982). These procedures require
knowledge of the social links between all possible pairs in a group and
hence are necessarily confined to fairly small groups.[7]

Implicit in this microsociological assumption that social relations

6. Represented, for instance, by Burt (1982, 1992) and Wellman (1988), as well as by
their sociometric predecessors, notably Moreno (1934), Bavelas (1950), and Cartwright
and Harary (1956).

7. Although some network analyses have been carried out on matrices of several hundred persons, this is still a small population compared to that of a country or large city.
Network analysis has also been applied to the study of the links among "collective actors," such as economic sectors and firms (Burt 1983), and even to entire societies (Snyder
and Kick 1979). In this case, it deals implicitly with large populations, but the analysis

determine positions and roles is another assumption that is still more questionable, namely that the only positions or roles that affect social relations are those generated by the group's social interaction. One may think this implicit assumption may be justified for small groups in laboratory experiments, though even there research evidence shows it to be incorrect. One study of experimental juries (Strodtbeck, James, and Hawkins 1958), for example, found that the occupation and social class of jurors influenced their likelihood of becoming foremen, participating in deliberations, and various postexperimental sociometric choices (such as being wanted as a juror in one's own trial). Thus, there can be little doubt that social associations in laboratories as well as in natural situations are affected by people's social positions and the experiences associated with them.

Even if it were the case that a person's outside positions exerted little influence on social interaction in artificial laboratory experiments, the primary direction of influence outside the laboratory is undoubtedly from differences among people, and the structural conditions engendered by these differences and their correlations, to social relations. To be sure, there may be some feedback, since differential fertility and migration of diverse groups can alter the population composition in the long run, but it is very rare for some agents' actions, even very powerful ones, to effect changes in the composition of the population, genocide being a fortunately rare exception.

This is the reason that I disagree with the view—represented notably by Giddens (1986) and Coleman (1990a)—that the analysis of the structure's influence on social relations needs to be complemented by an analysis of how agents' actions produce social structure. The population structure, as I conceptualize it, is not produced by the deliberate actions of individual members of the populations, at least not of its present members. To be sure, historical developments that affected the existing population structure resulted from actions of individuals in the past, such as differences in fertility among persons affiliated with different ethnic groups or social classes. Indeed, the population composition of a country as a whole is the result of the actions of millions to get married and have children and move from one place to another. But this is not what is usually meant by the acts of individ-

also needs to be confined to the relations among a small number of "collective actors." Some questions about such treatment of large collectivities as "actors" are raised in chapter 5.

ual agents and by assuming a complementarity of structure's influence on agents and their actions creating structure.

OPPORTUNITIES AND CONSTRAINTS

The multidimensional space of social positions among which a population is distributed is a matrix of life chances. It circumscribes people's chances of occupying various positions and of establishing social relations with various other people. By circumscribing social opportunities, the population structure supplies them and simultaneously limits them. In the case of favorable opportunities, the number of persons aspiring to take advantage of them typically exceeds the available supply, which means that many people are constrained to resign themselves to choose other positions or social relations than those they prefer.

To give a few illustrations: If medical schools accept fewer applicants than the number applying to them, some of the applicants are forced to find other careers. When the majority of young immigrants to a country are male, some will be constrained to set aside their ingroup preferences and marry a woman of different nationality. The greater demand for professionals in highly industrialized than other countries improves people's chances to become professionals in the former. Yet rising expectations have undoubtedly increased the numbers aspiring to become professionals in Western societies even more than the demand for them, so that many persons who want to become professionals must choose other occupations. The smaller a religious denomination's proportion of a city's population, the more likely are its members to marry outside their own religion, despite the well-known preference for marrying coreligionists, as shown by numerous studies (Thomas 1951; Locke, Sabagh, and Thomes 1957; Barnett 1962; Bealer, Willits, and Bender 1963, to name a few).[8]

Structural opportunities and constraints are complementary,[9] and

---

8. Distributions change over time, which must be taken into account. Thus, occupational chances depend on the occupational distribution at the time of entry into the labor force (and other conditions that influence these opportunities), and the chances of religious inmarriage depend on the religious distribution at the time of marriage (and other influences).

9. Giddens (1986: 169) criticizes "structural sociology, from Durkheim onwards," for stressing social structure's "constraining influences over action." He contrasts this with the view of his structuration theory that "structure is always both enabling and constraining."

both can be subsumed under probabilities or expected chances. Of course, the opportunity structure does not determine in which position or with which associates a given person ends up, only the probability or likelihood that a member of this population occupies certain positions and has certain associates. Differences among individuals govern which ones achieve their preferred positions and establish their preferred social relations, though again only the probability that they do so. Yet the probable effects of macrostructures (and of individual differences) have real impact on people's lives.

. . .

Opportunity structure has been defined in terms of the multidimensional space of social positions among which a population is distributed. Although this definition of macrostructure appears to clearly distinguish the people who occupy social positions in various dimensions from the positions they occupy, the above illustrations of opportunities confound the distribution of people and that of their positions.[10] The opportunities to establish social relations with certain associates and the opportunity to enter a given occupation or get a particular job depend on different aspects of the population structure.

The opportunity to establish ingroup relations, for instance, to marry a spouse whose religion is the same as your own, depends on the distribution of *people* in the place where you live. In the example, it is contingent on the proportion of unmarried persons of the opposite sex, of the right age, and with other appropriate attributes, as well as with the same religion as yours, relative to the proportion of your own sex with these attributes (except for the conventional age difference). If there are very few Muslim women in a community with the proper other attributes but many Muslim single men, the chances of a given Muslim man's finding an appropriate Muslim bride are slim.

The earlier illustration that the expansion of professional workers in this century improved opportunities for becoming a professional is quite

---

I too have emphasized structural constraints in the past, because they center attention on the more unexpected effects of structure. However, I fully agree with Giddens that structure is enabling as well as constraining and that a theory should deal with both, as my analysis of opportunity structures in this book indicates.

10. I am grateful to an anonymous reader for calling attention to the need for clarifying the distinction between persons and positions, which made me realize that the distinction I had considered unambiguous needs refinement for the analysis of opportunities.

a different case, which does not indicate that the improved opportunities depend on the proportion of people who are in professional positions. Those who already occupy professional positions and satisfy the existing demand for services preempt rather than furnish opportunities for entering these positions. Only when these people retire or die or for other reasons discontinue working as professionals do they create unmet demand for professional services and thereby opportunities for becoming professionals. Another important source of professional opportunities has been the expanding demand for professional services, but it too depends not on more people working as professionals but on more persons needed to provide professional services, which tends to be reflected in a growing number of professionals.

The restraints on opportunities exercised by distributions of people contrast with those exercised by distributions of *positions,* as is most readily apparent in formal organizations, like the army, which have a table of organization with designated formal positions. The possibility of occupying a position in such an organization is completely contingent on there being a vacancy in this position (see White 1970). A private cannot become a corporal or sergeant unless there are vacancies for these grades. Since there were many more such ranks in the air force than the military police in World War II, the opportunity to become a noncommissioned officer was much greater in the former than in the latter service. The distribution of filled positions reflects approximately the likelihood of vacancies and hence the chances of moving into a position.

National labor markets—in contrast to bureaucracies like the army—have no tables of organization with designated formal positions that are either filled or vacant (see chap. 4). Since no measure of vacant professional positions exists, changes in the proportion of professionals were used as a rough indication of the changes in demand and vacancies that have increased opportunities for professional careers. This approximate expression of the likelihood of finding a position takes into account the influences on opportunities of both departures of older professionals and expansions of demand for professional services. (The use of the proportion of professionals as a crude indication of expected professional vacancies, although the vacancies do not exist until the professionals have left their positions, resembles the figure-ground effect. You cannot see the shape in the background until you take the figures out.)[11]

---

11. I am indebted to Eviatar Zerubavel (1991) for this analogy of occupational distributions and opportunities and the figure-ground effect (see esp. his pp. 97–102).

In short, there is a sharp distinction between what produces the opportunities and constraints in ingroup and intergroup associations, including marriage, and what determines the likelihood of moving into various positions, including occupations. The former depends on the distribution of the individuals composing the population itself. The latter depends on the available positions in a formal organization or a social system that is not formally organized, and comparisons or changes in the population distribution are used in the latter case only as reflections of the likelihood that positions become available.

EMERGENT STRUCTURAL PROPERTIES

The terms by which social structures are characterized are not the same or simply aggregates of the characteristics of their subunits. The concepts of emergent structural properties centers attention on this crucial point and analyzes not the common culture or average characteristics of a population but its diversity in various respects. Thus, in studying the religious composition of Spain and Norway, structural analysis does not treat the two countries as contrasts—one being largely Catholic and the other largely Lutheran—but as similarly homogeneous, in contrast to the great religious diversity in the United States, for example.

Neither are average population characteristics of primary interest (some exceptions will be noted presently). A population's income structure is reflected by the distribution of or differences in income, not by the average income. Thus, a population structure cannot be derived by aggregating or averaging attributes of individual members, as even Coleman (1990a: 19–23, 300–313), whose theory considers rational choices of individuals the foundation of macrostructure, recognizes. In fact, Lieberson (1987: 107–10) points out that the properties on one level of social structure cannot be inferred from those on any other level.[12] This implies that every structural level has its own emergent properties.

12. Lieberson (1987: 110–11) illustrates this point by noting that it is ignored in a paper I coauthored (J. R. Blau and P. M. Blau 1982) in which we introduce research on influences on differences in crime rates among American metropolitan areas by posing as a paradox that the rich United States has one of the highest crime rates. He is admittedly quite correct that this paradox about national differences was a poor rhetorical device for introducing a study on differences within a nation, which cannot clarify international differences. It is ironic that I did not realize how malapropos the introductory paradox is, as I have been for a long time interested in the distinctiveness of structural properties and their influences (e.g., Blau 1960).

What are the various types of emergent properties? It is important to realize at the outset that not all emergent properties are structural ones and that not all structural characteristics refer to properties of the population structure. The two most important emergent attributes of societies that are not structural are undoubtedly the common cultural heritage, which governs people's values, norms, personalities, and motivation, and the historical development of the society, which has shaped its present character. Society's institutions, which combine cultural, historical, and structural elements, are another major emergent property. I consider institutions organized arrangements and structures that are culturally legitimated and historically perpetuated for generations. A prototype is society's political system.

Two related historical trends of great significance for a country's welfare are its stage of industrial development and its stage of economic development (which tend to be closely related). These are usually measured per capita (by energy consumption and by gross national product per capita, respectively), which makes them, in fact, averages. However, since they are used in macrosociology to study not individuals' average standard of living but society's stage of development, I consider their use admissible—indeed, essential—in comparative macrostructural analysis. They are a conceptually justified exception to my earlier admonition that individual averages are not really emergent properties.

What Lazarsfeld termed "global properties" (Lazarsfeld and Menzel 1969: 505), which includes some of those mentioned above, refers to attributes that characterize a society or organization as a whole rather than its members or their distribution. An illustration is that only nations have armies and can be characterized by the size and strength of their military forces. Other illustrations of global properties are the dogmas and rituals of religious denominations, the extent of automation of a factory, and the assets of a corporation. As the illustrations indicate, global properties differ generally by type of organization.

The formal structure of organization, as reflected in the organizational chart with multiple levels and subunits, is an emergent property that is structural without referring to population distributions. (Actually, it involves distributions of employees, but in contrast to emergent population structures those in organizations are based on predetermined formal positions.) Thus, the executive branch of the American and, indeed, most governments consists of a substantial number of departments with a multitude of substructures on different levels and in different parts of the country. Similarly, the judicial branch of a government comprises courts on several levels dispersed throughout the nation. Large private firms also are composed of complex administrative structures with several levels and numerous subunits.

Finally, we turn to the major emergent structural properties of concern. One refers to the social relations between individual or groups. In microstructural studies, it involves the network of social ties between the individuals in a group. In the macrosociological analysis here, it refers to the rates of intergroup or ingroup relations of the members of various groups. A second pertains to the distributions among social positions in any given dimension, which is an emergent property that is strictly structural in the macrosociological sense. The analysis of the influences on social life of each of these distributions separately is insufficient because it ignores their interdependence. A third structural property, designed to take these interrelations into account, discloses the degree to which people's differences in any one dimension are related to their differences in other dimensions (or the extent to which a set of social differences are related to one another).

Macrostructural analysis treats the last two types of emergent properties as the major structural conditions that influence the first, intergroup relations. I have referred to these two—population distributions and their relationships—as structural parameters. The term *parameters* is used in statistics for the attributes that describe a population distribution, such as its mean and its standard deviation (as distinguished from *statistics*—the estimates of them based on samples). I confine the term *structural parameters* to those characteristics of a population of principal concern in macrostructural analysis, namely, those that refer to a population's distributions or degrees of differentiation in various respects (rather than to its members' average attributes).[13] There are two types of univariate parameters: the criterion of distinction is whether reference is to the distribution of a population among discrete categories or on a continuum.

. . .

Nominal parameters are population distributions among discrete categories or groups. Ethnic affiliations, industries, and occupations illustrate nominal parameters. The degree of differentiation among nominal positions in a given dimension indicates its *heterogeneity*. The criterion of the degree of heterogeneity is the chance expectation that two randomly

13. In operational terms, these measures of distinctly macrostructural significance are measures of dispersion rather than of central tendency.

chosen persons belong to different groups. The greater the number of categories in a population and the more even people's distribution among them, the greater the heterogeneity. The number of categories is unambiguous for some nominal parameters, such as gender and mother tongue. But it is problematic for others, either because there is no un-equivocal boundary (neighborhood) or because there are broader and narrower subdivisions (division of labor). The labor force, for example, can be divided by major occupational groups, detailed occupations, or increasingly narrower specialties. Finer subdivisions indicate more occu-pational heterogeneity than broader ones. The choice depends on one's substantive problem, but the same subdivisions must, of course, be used in comparisons.

Graduated parameters are population distributions in a continuous rank order. The most important ones for macrostructural analysis are those that refer to resources, like income, education, socioeconomic status, wealth, and power. A population's differentiation in terms of a graduated parameter indicates its *inequality*. The criterion of the degree of inequality is the chance expectation of the absolute difference in given resources between two randomly chosen persons relative to the mean resource difference in the population (which is represented by the mean absolute difference for all possible pairs in the population). The theoreti-cal minimum of inequality is an even distribution of resources, and the theoretical maximum is the concentration of all resources in the hands of one person. In short, the more resources are concentrated in a few hands, the greater the inequality.[14]

The most important emergent structural property is the extent to which various parameters are correlated, the concomitant variations of several differences among people. If differences in race, occupation, edu-cation, and income are substantially correlated, as is the case in American society, group boundaries and status distinctions are consolidated and barriers to social intercourse and to overcoming poor social background by social mobility are strengthened. In contrast, the closer a number of parameters approximate being orthogonal, the more do social differences in various respects intersect and thereby mitigate one another's influences on promoting the opportunities of some and restricting those of others.

14. Some differences in inequality appear as discontinuous hierarchies in ranks, such as grade in the army or other bureaucracies, but I conceptualize these as nominal categories strongly correlated with some graduated ones, such as rank being correlated with scope of authority and income.

Intersecting social differences find expression in weakly related parameters. They represent Simmel's (1923) crosscutting social circles, except that circles imply nominal affiliations whereas intersection includes graduated as well as nominal ones. But Simmel's verbal imagery vividly communicates that multigroup membership implies that people, particularly in modern society, are at the intersection of numerous social affiliations that have largely different though somewhat overlapping memberships. When social differences improve the chances of some and impede those of others, intersection mitigates these opposite effects. To illustrate: the advantages of being a WASP are minimized if most Protestants are black and most whites are not Anglo-Saxon. *Consolidation* and *intersection* are opposite extremes of the strength of the covariation of parameters in a population.

In sum, three structural parameters have been distinguished to characterize generic forms of differentiation in population structures. Nominal parameters refer to the population's distribution among nominal positions; graduated parameters refer to its distribution in a continuous rank order; and the correlations of one parameter to several others, or those of a set of parameters, refer to their concomitant variation. The opposite extremes of differentiation for nominal parameters are heterogeneity and homogeneity; for graduated parameters, inequality and equality; and for correlated parameters, consolidation and intersection.

By speaking of generic forms of differentiation, I mean that these are abstract concepts, pure structural forms abstracted from their empirical content. Heterogeneity, inequality, and intersection are theoretical concepts that do not exist as such; only specific manifestations of them do, just as competition is a form that does not itself exist. Only in combination with a substantive content—economic or political competition or rivalry in love—is competition observable in the empirical world. What I have attempted here is to combine Simmel's insight that sociology must abstract social forms from their empirical contents (Simmel 1923: 4) and Braithwaite's (1953: 76) that theoretical terms must be abstractions, not merely "logical constructions out of observable entities." The propositions employing these abstract terms can be tested by their diverse empirical implications.

THEORETICAL OBJECTIVES

The objective of this book is to develop a macrosociological theoretical analysis of the influences of large population structures on social life. It

investigates structural influences on people's social relations, their occupational chances and mobility, their participation in organizations, the exchange processes in their relations, and some historical roots of the existing social structure. I again emphasize that by confining the theoretical analysis to structural influences on people's lives I do not mean to imply that these are the only influences or that no others are of any importance.

Every endeavor to advance a systematic analysis, in the social sciences as in other disciplines, must confine itself to a limited aspect of the welter of empirical reality. In doing so and analyzing a limited set of influences and processes, one inevitably ignores other effects, or at least takes them as given. One can only hope that these neglected effects do not distort the influences on which attention is centered, for instance, by interacting with them, making them spurious, or suppressing some of them.

To reemphasize that I recognize the existence of important influences on people's lives other than the structural ones here examined, let me call attention to a few. Historical antecedents and traditions affect, of course, not only people's lives but the very structures that are here being analyzed; some of these influences are discussed in the last chapter. I also recognize that cultural values and norms and, particularly, the institutions in which they become embodied greatly influence social conditions, and my focus on structural rather than cultural sociology is intended partly as a counterweight to the prevailing cultural emphasis in American sociology.

Quite independent of the cultural values they reflect, established institutions that perpetuate social systems and practices, like capitalism and monogamy, clearly exert much effect on social conditions. Institutional analysis is another approach that has received renewed attention recently. A country's degree of industrialization and stage of economic development surely affect its social structure and people's lives profoundly; a few of their influences are noted in the last chapter. The psychological makeup of personalities undoubtedly governs the behavior and interpersonal relations of individuals, and so does their biological constitution. Although these topics are not sociology's subject matter, psychological and even biological influences no doubt combine with and modify social ones.

· · ·

The theoretical analysis to be presented here is an expansion of an earlier theory (Blau 1977), as noted at the outset. The earlier analysis attempted to develop a rather formal theory in which a set of theorems were derived from a few assumptions, and the theorems' empirical implications were tested in subsequent research (Blau and Schwartz 1984). The substantive question posed is how the population structure influences intergroup relations. The theorems deal with the influences of social structure on intergroup relations, defined as the rate of dyadic associations between members in different social positions—differing in some group membership or some aspect of hierarchical status.

To convey some initial idea of the theory, which is fully presented in the next chapter, I shall indicate a few of its major propositions in this introductory summary. The two basic assumptions are (1) that the probability of social associations depends on opportunities for contact and (2) that proximity in multidimensional social space increases the probability of social associations.

[margin note: Blau's 2 basic assumptions]

From the first assumption and the definition of heterogeneity, it follows that heterogeneity increases the chances of intergroup association, which is one of the main theorems. Another theorem can be derived from the same assumption and the definition of inequality, namely, that the greater the inequality, the more likely are status-distant associations. This proposition seems counterintuitive, as one would expect greater status differences to discourage, not to encourage, social intercourse. Nevertheless the theorem as stated is not only logically implied by premises but also corroborated by a number of empirical tests.

[margin note: 3 related theorems]

A third theorem follows from the second assumption and the definition of intersecting social differences, which imply that many people who belong to the same group in one dimension belong to different ones in others. If social proximity fosters ingroup relations and if many persons who belong to the same group in one dimension belong to different ones in others, it follows that the very ingroup choices in one dimension involve many persons in intergroup relations in others. In short, intersection promotes intergroup relations, as supported by the empirical tests in chapter 3. These results can explain why prevalent ingroup preferences are not incompatible with many intergroup relations, their frequency depending on the degree of intersection in the social structure.

. . .

The objective of this book is to apply the theoretical scheme used in the theory of intergroup relations to the analysis of macrostructural influences in other areas. Whereas the application of the macrostructural conceptual scheme to intergroup relations yielded a relatively formal theory, however, its application to other subjects did not succeed in formulating the analysis into a formal theory.[15]

After presenting the influences of population structures on inter-group relations in the next two chapters, the fourth one will analyze the implications of the population structure for occupational choices and op-portunities of social mobility. Society's occupational structure, which re-flects its division of labor, is treated as a matrix of life chances, which circumscribes opportunities and limitations. National differences and changes over time are examined. The role of ascribed traits and of quali-fications, notably education, is analyzed, and Boudon's education para-dox is interpreted as an illustration of the structural implications of prevalent changes in individual qualifications. Conjectures are advanced about the effects of structural differences among markets on labor de-mand. Finally, attention is directed to the difference between structural and circulation mobility and the significance of the recent decline in structural mobility.

Chapter 5 examines how the membership and growth of voluntary associations, organizations, and other substructures are influenced by the multidimensional social space that constitutes their structural context. Turning to study firms and corporations, the internal structure of orga-nizations is analyzed, the expanding number of firms in an industry is studied, and the chapter concludes with a discussion of the intersection of corporations and markets.

Macrostructural influences on social relations are ultimately trans-mitted to the daily personal relations of individuals. Multilevel structural analysis traces this transmission. The processes of face-to-face interaction and exchange constitute the end product of the transmissions of these macrostructural influences on interpersonal relations. The sixth chapter starts with a critical analysis of Coleman's transition from micro- to macrolevels, which suggests that the proper analysis of this transition requires it to be reversed. The chapter's central focus is on the theoretical analysis of interpersonal interaction and processes of social exchange in dyadic relations and face-to-face groups, in which the social bonds are established that integrate individuals, through enlarging social circles, in their neighborhoods, communities, and society. The last part of the chapter discusses the distinction between two kinds of power, the inter-

---

15. The analysis of exchange processes in chapter 6 is formulated in fairly rigorous theoretical terms, though not in terms of the same conceptual scheme as the theory of intergroup relations.

personal power of influence in direct interpersonal exchange and the impersonal power to dominate, economically or politically, thousands and even millions of people without having any direct contact with them and often without even knowing who they are.

The final chapter turns to an examination of historical developments to seek answers to the question of what antecedents have affected the population structures, the consequences of which have been studied in all the preceding analysis. It starts with a study of demographic trends, which are the major influences on the population composition in terms of ascriptive attributes. It then analyzes the implications of industrialization and rates of economic growth for the expansion of the United States and the growing opportunities in it during most of this century, ending by seeking to explain the recent sharp downturn in our economy and in people's career opportunities.

In conclusion, some conjectures are advanced about the significance of the recent economic crisis, the danger it entails for increasing class conflict, and the chances of reversing the downturn, stemming the expanding poverty, reducing the increasing inequalities, and restoring to the underprivileged the opportunities for social mobility that once existed but no longer do.

CONCLUSIONS

A conclusion for an introduction seems to be an oxymoron. Although I have retained the subhead used for the last section of all chapters, let me substitute for an attempt to conclude this introductory chapter a few remarks about my metatheoretical assumptions and orientation.

I consider sociology a social science and its objective to be, like that of all sciences, to strive to develop systematic theories that explain empirical reality and that can be tested in empirical research. By systematic theory I mean an explanation of some aspect of reality that involves logically interrelated propositions on different levels of generality. The more general propositions include some abstract concepts that go beyond any empirical observation or variable, whereas the lowest-order propositions, which are implied by others, are empirical predictions that can test and possibly falsify the theory.

But I hasten to add that this is an ideal for which we should strive but which we have not attained and cannot yet attain except in very limited areas in sociology. Much good theoretical analysis has been carried out that is far from this utopian conception of nomothetic-deductive theorizing. I have developed a fairly formal structural theory of inter-group relations (briefly illustrated in this chapter and fully developed in the next), but my attempts to extend it to other subjects presented in this book largely involve less rigorous theoretical analysis that is not expressed in formal terms. This is doubtless owing to my own short-comings, but it reflects limitations of much contemporary sociological theorizing. I hope that we shall persist to strive to develop formal social theories but that we continue in the meantime to be as systematic as possible in our theoretical analysis and not turn in despair to sheer specu-lation, or deconstruction.

Finally, a few words about my conception of and approach to soci-ology. I have already indicated that my preference for structural analysis does not mean that I assume structural influences on social life to be the only ones or that I do not consider other approaches—institutional, cul-tural, rational choice—legitimate. I must admit, however, that I would not have spent a large part of my academic career studying the effects of social structures if I did not consider such effects to be of special importance.

Two

FORMAL THEORY OF
POPULATION STRUCTURE

T HE MULTIDIMENSIONAL STRUCTURE OF A population governs
people's opportunities to make certain friends and even to choose
certain spouses as well as their occupational opportunities and
many other life chances. This chapter analyzes the effects of the population structure on the probabilities of social relations between members of
different groups and persons differing in vertical status, as well as the
probabilities of their mobility and conflict. A theoretical formulation of
intergroup relations between individuals is presented, and it is applied to
mobility and conflict between members of different groups and strata.
The theory analyzes the influences of heterogeneity, inequality, and intersection on the dyadic associations of persons in different horizontal
(nominal) or vertical (graduated) positions, including their conflicts as
well as their mobility between different positions. The term *intergroup
relations* is used broadly to refer to all relations between persons in different social positions. (If only vertical differences are considered, they
are also referred to as status-distant relations.)

Ingroup relations are by far the most prevalent of all relations between people, as much research has demonstrated.[1] People associate in
disproportionate numbers with others like themselves. Intergroup relations do occur, however. Personality differences undoubtedly affect their
likelihood, and so do circumstances in one's immediate environment. The
structural explanation advanced will assume, however, the predominance
of ingroup choices and will indicate how variations in population struc-

---

1. For a short and a full report of an early empirical study, which coined the term
homophily for ingroup tendencies, see Robert K. Merton (1948; Merton, West, and Jahoda
1951); another classical study of the subject is Laumann's (1973).

tures can have the effect of constraining people to engage in intergroup relations even on the extreme (and unrealistic) assumption that everybody prefers ingroup friends.

The criterion of intergroup relations is the rate of dyadic relations of persons in one social position with those in other social positions, for example, the proportion of Catholics whose best friend is a Protestant. (For continuous differences, since rates would be based on arbitrary divisions, the criterion is the mean absolute difference in status, such as the mean income difference of friends.)[2] Thus, intergroup relations do not include one-sided preferences, and are therefore not applicable to (unreciprocated) sociometric choices, and neither do they include other than pair relations, like that of one speaker to a large audience. But the theoretical propositions to be advanced are applicable to all aspects of actual dyadic intergroup relations, ranging from casual acquaintance to marriage and including, for instance, interaction rate, visiting frequency, and duration of relation.

This chapter centers attention on propositions about structural influences on social relations, and it includes related propositions about mobility and conflict. The analysis here is a somewhat reformulated version of the theory originally developed on the basis of the parameter scheme (Blau 1977). Whereas the following chapters (except the next, as noted below) apply the theoretical scheme in general terms, this chapter presents a more formally developed theory. It starts with two major assumptions, derives a set of theorems from them, and traces the major theorems' implications, which are then empirically tested. These tests, including some by other investigators and some new ones as well as a summary of the original ones, are presented in chapter 3.

POPULATION STRUCTURE AND SOCIAL RELATIONS

In his famous essay *Die Kreuzung sozialer Kreise,* Simmel (1923: 305–44) stresses that the crosscutting of social circles is rooted in the multigroup affiliations that are characteristic of modern society. To be sure, people in simple societies also belong to a number of groups, but

---

2. Rates are equivalent to averages, and absolute mean differences are too. Although the theoretical scheme adopted requires that social structures be characterized by forms of differentiation, not by averages, the outcomes they influence are generally mean probabilities.

the membership of most groups is largely if not entirely the same; for example, most residents of a Nuer village belong to the same kinship lineage (Evans-Pritchard 1972: 203–5). In complex societies, by contrast, the memberships of the different groups to which an individual belongs are often, though not always, only in small part overlapping. Moreover, many of the different groups to which a member of a simple society belongs constitute concentric circles—as illustrated by family, extended kin group, minor and major lineage, and broad clan—whereas most groups to which persons in complex societies belong are intersecting circles, such as those based on their race, age, religion, and occupation.

Another implication Simmel draws from multigroup affiliations is the dialectics of freedom and constraint, which is a central theme in an essay by Breiger (1990). Breiger analyzes there the paradox that intersecting multigroup affiliations simultaneously increase freedom and constraint. The source of this paradox is the duality of multigroup affiliations, to which he had earlier called attention, namely, their involving both persons linking groups and persons being linked by groups through common membership (Breiger 1974). Multigroup affiliations provide individuals with multiple social support and thereby free them, at least partly, from oppressive domination by society and its agents as well as by one primary group and its predominant pressures. At the same time, however, multigroup affiliations make a person subject to the constraints of many groups and thereby circumscribe her conduct more fully by the role expectations different groups have of her.

The multidimensional population structure determines people's various life chances, the chances of meeting congenial friends or marrying a desirable spouse, which is the topic of this chapter, as well as the chances of successful careers and social mobility, which will be discussed subsequently. Life chances comprise opportunities and constraints, and whether outcomes are defined as one or the other depends in large part on their objective nature but in part also on people's perspectives and evaluations.

Opportunities are limited, and I cannot obtain my first choice if it has been preempted by others. Not only is this the case in economic life, where not all persons who compete for the best jobs get them and the rest must resign themselves to other work, but it is also true in social relations. A main reason is that there are a number of attributes people want their friends or lovers to have. Our acquaintances who meet our expectations in some respects are unlikely to meet them in all respects. Hence, we typically have close associates who have some attributes that do not meet our expectations in every respect. Of course not. People are not perfect.

Although this conclusion seems obvious, it helps explain how the population structure constrains freedom of choice of associates.[3] To illustrate these constraints with intergroup relations, we make the extreme assumption that all people's first choices are always members of their own group. (The assumption is unrealistic, but it is used as a counterfactual condition to show why people nevertheless sometimes choose intergroup relations.) Human beings have a large number of characteristics, and the assumption is that they prefer ingroup associates in all of their relations (except, in the case of most people, in sexual relations). The smaller the proportionate size of their own group, the smaller is the probability that they will find congenial ingroup associates.

A much stronger constraint, however, is exerted by the fact that people in complex societies belong to many ingroups that are not entirely overlapping. It is easy to satisfy one ingroup choice or a few. With every ingroup choice we satisfy, we thereby restrict our subsequent freedom of choice until we get to a point where we run out of such freedom. At this point, when we find someone who is a member of our own group along a number of lines, our own choices create constraints forcing us to choose an associate who, though an ingroup member in several respects, is not one in still other respects. This anticipates an important principle underlying the reason that people engage in intergroup relations, but we still must determine what structural conditions make such a situation more or less likely. This will be done when the theory is formulated.

. . .

Before presenting the theory on intergroup relations, as well as some closely related theorems, let us recapitulate briefly the conceptual scheme

3. People, of course, make choices, which must be taken into account in studying their social relations, their careers, and their opportunities and chances in other respects. I note this because my emphasis on influences of the external structure has prompted the criticism that I ignore choices of individuals. I not only consider choices important for analyzing social conduct but even go further and assume that individuals have freedom of choice, the only social limits being those imposed by their own previous choices and those of others. Although I do not ignore choices, my objective is not to investigate the internal psychological motives that affect them but to analyze the external structural conditions that govern opportunities but also constrain and limit the choices that are possible in a population.

outlined in chapter 1 and discuss some criticisms made of the theory and the research testing it. The criticisms and my own reconsiderations prompted some modification of the theory presented in the next section and some revisions of the procedures for empirical tests, which, together with summaries of earlier research, will be discussed in chapter 3. But first a short review of the basic concepts.

Population structure refers here to the social differentiation along various lines of the people in a society or its subunits. It has been conceptualized as the distributions of people among social positions in multiple dimensions. Social positions are defined by the social distinctions people make in their social intercourse, notably the distinction they make between ingroup and outgroup—persons in their own position or a close one and those in other or distant positions. People's distributions among different positions limit their options—for instance, their choices of associates (analyzed in this chapter) and their chances of mobility (outlined in this and more fully analyzed in the fourth chapter). These structural limits are a major condition engendering intergroup relations despite the prevailing tendencies to choose ingroup associates.

Structural parameters refer to the degree of differentiation of a population in various respects. Two types of univariate parameters are distinguished. Nominal parameters divide people into nominal positions or groups (people in the same position are called a *group* regardless of how many of them there are), such as ethnic groups or women and men. The differentiation among nominal positions is heterogeneity. Graduated parameters are social differences in a continuous rank order, such as education or income. The differentiation in terms of graduated parameters is inequality. Multivariate parameters, indicated by the correlations of various forms of differentiation, are the most important structural properties. Strongly correlated social differences consolidate group boundaries and social distances, whereas parameters that are nearly orthogonal mitigate the social differences among people.

Of the various comments and criticisms of my theory's original version (1977) that have influenced its reformulation here, I note particularly Jonathan Turner's (1986: 425–34, see also the 1982 edition). I have been greatly influenced by his criticism that the theory should include fewer assumptions and fewer theorems;[4] that it is too narrow and needs

---

4. Some of this specific criticism had already been addressed in the concise version of the theory that we published as part of the empirical research testing it (Blau and Schwartz 1984: 8–16 and passim), but Turner was apparently not aware of it.

Crits of theory

a broader scope; and that it should stipulate some influences on the structural conditions (heterogeneity, inequality, and intersection) that were treated only as exogenous factors. This chapter is responsive to the first comment; this entire book reflects the second; and the last chapter attempts to address the third. (I do not agree with his criticism that my theory is a functional theory, nor with the reformulations of assumptions and theorems he suggests.)

Steven Rytina has been another major source of helpful comments, criticisms, and suggestions, some methodological ones on the published research (Rytina 1987) and extensive ones on the first draft of the present book. I discuss here only one of the former comments, which has important implications for theoretical concepts as well as for research procedures, and merely acknowledge how greatly the latter comments benefited the entire book. The distinction Rytina makes between gross and net salience—the strength of group attachment as indicated by the prevalence of ingroup associates—applies not only to group salience but quite generally to the difference between gross and net effects of one factor on another. But our original tests of the theory did not take this distinction into account.

This failure was not an oversight. We made the deliberate decision to perform the most conservative tests of the major theorems by using simple correlations. Although we knew, of course, that other factors than the population structure influence choices, we expected the structurally generated probabilities to have strong enough effects to be apparent despite various psychological and cultural influences. Moreover, we wanted to protect the tests of the theory from the misuse of the phrase *ceteris paribus.* All sociological theorems are qualified by this phrase, but if the qualification is taken literally it precludes falsification, because it can be used to dismiss any negative finding as resulting from some unknown interfering condition. To forestall such misuse, we (Blau and Schwartz 1984: 21–22) decided to start with simple correlations as a conservative test of the theory's implications, on the assumption that they should be sufficiently immune to unknown disturbances to be observable without controls (unless the theory itself implies another influence, in which case we did control for it).

What Rytina's discussion of gross and net salience called to my attention is that the assumption made earlier is simplistic. A simple correlation between one structural condition and intergroup relations may be spurious as well as one of several influences, and in the former case it furnishes incorrect results unless all (known) influences are controlled. Furthermore, even if the structural condition's influence on social relations is not as strong as the influence of another condition or the combination of several others, it is worth discovering rather than ignoring it by failing to control the other influences. Although race and income as well as a city's racial heterogeneity and income inequality are substantially correlated, we want to find out their independent influences on social life, which requires substituting multiple regressions for simple correlations. In short, all other structural conditions available must be controlled to isolate the effect of one, which will be done in testing empirical implications of the theory in the next chapter.

Actually, both the zero-order and the partial coefficient are of interest, but for different reasons. To infer a causal influence on intergroup relations, the net effect, controlling as many correlated influences as possible, should be determined. But to ascertain how strongly a given structural condition is in reality related to intergroup relations, the gross effect is needed. For example, assume that the racial heterogeneity in a metropolis does not exhibit a simple correlation with interracial friendships. We know, however, that disproportionate numbers of blacks are poor and not well educated and that these differences influence friendships. The simple correlation confounds the influences of all these factors. It does reflect the actual experience of people, the likelihood of black-white associations for whatever reason, but not the distinct influence of race or racial heterogeneity.

If we control for racial income and educational differences (and for other factors, if possible), racial heterogeneity may exhibit the expected positive relationship with interracial friendships. (A similar empirical finding will be noted in the next chapter.) This finding suggests that racial heterogeneity exerts some causal influence on racial intergroup relations. However, the fact remains that friendships between blacks and whites in a metropolis are very rare regardless of that city's racial heterogeneity, though part of this is not the result of racial discrimination itself but, rather, of economic and educational differences between the races. This existing infrequency of black-white friendships is the reality blacks (and whites) face, whatever the underlying causal influences.[5]

5. Actually, racial differences in this case are the ultimate cause, because the differences in education and income result largely from the underprivileged conditions of racial minorities.

Skvoretz (1990: 384–85) discovered a computational error that has substantive implications for our intermarriage measure for continuous dimensions. The data used for this measure are young, recently married couples. The measures are the average absolute difference between spouses in education, occupational status, and earnings divided by the average difference in education, occupational status, and earnings in the population.[6] Except for education, however, the average for young couples is probably lower than that for the entire population of adults, most of whom are older and many of whom have advanced in their careers. This implies that the differences between young couples were divided by too large a denominator and hence are not quite correct.

This computational error would affect the results, however, only if the differences in occupational status and earnings between the young persons in the subsample and the population sample covaried with the other terms.[7] Such a covariance apparently was not the case, as implied by the results, which are as expected and parallel to those of other empirical tests of the same theorem. Since the measures are not absolutely correct, I shall not include the results in the tables as part of the theory's revised tests, but I shall present them in footnotes as information of interest.[8]

INTERGROUP RELATIONS

An underlying assumption of the macrostructural theory presented here is that the population structure, conceptualized as people's distributions in a multidimensional social space, exerts independent effects on social relations by circumscribing the opportunities and limiting the choices in a population. Gouldner (1970: 31–35) calls such assumptions *domain assumptions,* which are often implicit and reflect a theoretical orientation or world view that affects the theoretical terms and assumptions or axioms from which theorems are derived. Although such

6. Personal income (including earnings and any other income) was also measured, but it is virtually identical to earnings; since it does not provide independent tests, it will not be used.

7. I am grateful to Steven Rytina for pointing this out.

8. Other criticisms Skvoretz made refer to procedures in regression analysis and will be discussed when research testing the theoretical implications is analyzed in the next chapter.

Assumption I : Probability of social relations depends on opportunities for contact

broad orientations or views cannot be empirically demonstrated, empirical evidence corroborating the theory indirectly lends some support to the underlying assumptions. In the case at hand, it would support the claim that population structures and distributions, independent of culture, influence the relations between members of different classes and groups of all kinds.

The formal theory in this chapter derives theorems about structural influences on social relations and mobility from the definitions of theoretical terms (specified in chap. 1 and summarized earlier in this chapter) and two major assumptions, which are next presented. All theorems are assumed to be qualified by ceteris paribus, without this being explicitly stated. The theoretical terms are abstract, as are the theorems.

I interpret the term *abstraction* in social theory in Simmel's sense of abstracting social forms from the various empirical contents in which alone they can find expression. Thus, heterogeneity and inequality are abstractions from such observations as a population's ethnic or religious heterogeneity, its inequality in education or income, just as Simmel's term *competition* abstracts the distinctly social element from economic and political and other forms of competition. The initial and major theoretical analysis derives a set of propositions about a population structure's effects on intergroup (including socially distant) relations.[9] Subsequently, corresponding sets of propositions are derived about macrostructural effects on mobility and conflict between members of groups or strata. (A supplementary assumption is required only for the propositions on mobility and is introduced when they are analyzed.)

The first assumption is that the probability of social relations depends on opportunities for contact *(A-1)*. The word *depend* is designed to emphasize that no social relations can occur without some contact opportunities as well as that the likelihood of social relations increases with growing contact opportunities. The assumption is particularly important for the analysis of structural constraints rather than opportunities, because we do not have to be constrained to take advantage of

9. A population's rate of intergroup relations for nominal groups is the proportion of all social ties, however defined, whose two members have different social affiliations (or one minus the fraction of all ingroup relations). "Intergroup" relations when referring to relations of people differing on a continuum (really status-distant relations) are measured by the average absolute difference in status between all pairs of associates, standardized by the corresponding difference in the sample.

opportunities, such as associating with people like ourselves, but we do experience some constraints if the social environment imposes limits over which we have no control. The rates of unemployment, immigration, and mortality affect the probabilities of contact with various persons, as do the population's density, heterogeneity, and inequality.

The second assumption is that proximity in the multidimensional social space increases the probability of social relations *(A-2)*. Social proximity applies not only spatially but to all dimensions of social affiliations. Two persons may, of course, be close in some respect and distant in others. Proximity influences the choices of associates if there is contact opportunity. In terms of the two types of parameters, the assumption may be divided in two: (1) the rates of social associations of persons in the same nominal position are higher than their rates with outsiders; and (2) the average social distance in graduated positions between associates is lower than that in the population at large. This assumption makes explicit the widely observed tendency of people to make ingroup choices.[10]

. . .

The first theorem on size is not based on these assumptions but on a mathematical truism. Yet it is implicated in all other theorems, because all of them deal with size distributions. The theorem stipulates that the probability of intergroup relations declines with proportionate increase in group size *(T-1)*. In a population composed of two groups, the number involved in intergroup relations must be the same in both, so that a group's outgroup rate depends only on its relative size. Since this is deterministically true for any two groups, it implies the probabilistic prediction that a group's relative size and intergroup relations are inversely related. This prediction is usually studied by comparing the same kind of group in different populations—for instance, the proportion of the same religious denomination in the population of different cities. A number of such studies obtained results that agree with the implications of the theorem (see, for example, Bealer, Willits, and Bender

10. I have stipulated the proximity assumption, because I did so in the original version of the theory, and much research has demonstrated the prevalence of ingroup and proximate associations. Strictly speaking, however, this assumption can be dispensed with, for it is implicit in the contact-opportunity assumption (A-1) conceptualized in terms of distances in a multidimensional social space. Since distances in social space refer to differences in positions or attributes, they imply extent of proximity in various respects and hence probability of social relations.

1963; Burma 1963; Blau and Schwartz 1984: 36–38). The smaller a religious group's proportion of the population, the higher its outmarriage rate.[11]

The other theorems are derived from one of the assumptions and an analytical proposition defining a theoretical term or from two synthetic propositions, which may be two previously derived theorems or one plus an assumption. In addition to the influence of subgroup size, the theorems examine the effects of the three major aspects of the population structure—heterogeneity, inequality, and intersection—and of one condition closely related to that structure, social mobility in it. The next four theorems, like the one already examined, deal with these influences on intergroup relations.

As heterogeneity is the probability that any two persons belong to different groups and as social associations are assumed to depend on contact opportunities, the greater the heterogeneity, the greater are the chances that fortuitous encounters involve members of different groups. Most of these encounters are soon forgotten, but without some chance of an initial meeting no new social relation could develop. Besides, some chance encounters lead to repeated casual meetings and some ripen into fairly close and a few even into lasting and intimate relations. Even lifelong friendships and marriages typically start as casual meetings. If it is assumed that social relations depend on contact opportunities (A-1), and if heterogeneity is defined by the probability that any two persons belong to different groups, it follows that heterogeneity increases the rates of intergroup relations *(T-2)*.[12] This theorem is formulated in abstract generic terms, which makes it applicable to heterogeneity and intergroup relations generally, whatever the specific nature or content of the nominal dimensions and positions under consideration.

The same considerations apply to inequality, for which the proposition is counterintuitive. One might have thought that inequality would reduce the likelihood of status-distant associations. After all, greater inequality implies generally greater social distances in status (be it based on

11. Probability theory is apparently implicated in the size theorem, and indirectly in the others that rest on population distributions.

12. I use the same numbers for theorems as those used in the theory's revised formulation presented in the publication testing its implications (Blau and Schwartz 1984). There are two ellipses in numbering, because old theorems 5 and 13 have been eliminated, as have several theorems with higher numbers because they can be considered corollaries, some of which will be discussed. Five theorems have been added, numbered 1*–4* and 13*. The total number of theorems is eighteen, thirteen old and five new.

income, education, or occupational standing), which one might have thought would make status differences more meaningful and increase salient barriers to social intercourse. Indeed, it does to some extent by making choices more sensitive to status differences and thereby indirectly inhibiting social associations (see Rytina et al. 1988: 662–64), but this influence is overwhelmed by the structural constraints on status-distant associations.

Whereas much inequality increases the significance of status proximity in choosing associates, this influence is outweighed by the structural effect of the population's inequality. For the inequality in a population, which is defined in terms of status distance, governs the probable status distance between any two persons, including of course any who happen to meet, which makes chance encounters more likely to involve status-distant persons. If social associations are assumed to depend on contact opportunities (A-1), and if inequality is defined in terms of average status difference, it follows that the probability of status-distant social contacts and associations increases with increasing inequality *(T-3)*.

Before turning to the analysis of the most important macrostructural property—intersecting social differences—let us examine an emergent property that is not a structural parameter but that also is of great importance: mobility. Included in this generic term are geographical migration and residential mobility as well as all forms of social mobility, whether it involves vertical or horizontal moves of any kind. The term encompasses changes in social position not usually thought of as mobility, like getting a new job or becoming unemployed, getting married or divorced, or undergoing a religious conversion. Weak barriers between groups may further both mobility and social association between group members. Although such parallel influences of group and status barrier probably exist, there is good reason to assume that the two social processes—the process of social mobility and the process of social association—also influence one another directly.

While mobile persons have acquired new social positions and social surroundings, they continue to have their old social origin[13] and are influenced by it and the social background associated with it. To become adjusted to their new social situation, newcomers must establish social

13. Social origin refers not only to parental home's socioeconomic status but to parental family's position on any dimension for which mobility is under consideration. Thus, in case of migration it refers to previous hometown.

relations with other people there—in the new city for migrants, in the new job for transfers, in the new church for converts, in the new social class for the vertically mobile. Moreover, the presence of many migrants or socially mobile persons increases chance meetings between old-timers and newcomers and the likelihood of associations between them. The newcomers' social origin and its correlates still affect them, however. Thus, lest the movers lose their long-standing social attachments, most of them tend to maintain social contact with their old friends and kin, at least for a considerable time. Particularly on ceremonial occasions— holidays, marriages, funerals—they tend to return home and refresh their old ties. In short, mobile persons occupy two social positions, which makes their ingroup relations from one perspective intergroup relations from the other.[14]

Since the presence of many mobile persons, who differ by definition from old-timers in social origin and related factors, increases the opportunities for contact between persons with varied social origins, and since such opportunities are assumed to increase the probability of intergroup relations (A-1), it follows that mobility improves the chances of intergroup relations (T-4). This theorem implies that, in groups or strata or places to which many persons have moved, the rates of intergroup relations are high. These high rates may stimulate other social processes that further increase the influence of mobility in a population on intergroup relations. An important reason for this proposition— implicit in Newcomb's (1961) ABX theory (especially pp. 4–23, 160–65), a version of balance theory (Heider 1958)—is that friends of friends often become friends, because their common friend promotes their friendship to restore balance. Accordingly, mobile persons are apt to bring their new and old associates together, increasing the intergroup associations of both.

Large-scale migration or social mobility has multiplicative effects that alter and strengthen this social process. If newcomers represent a substantial proportion of a population, most people in that city or profession or social class have intergroup relations with persons in cities, occupations, or socioeconomic strata other than those where they originated. But the more frequent such intergroup relations are, the weaker

---

14. This is similar to the consequences of intersecting parameters, except that mobility entails a person's two positions in a single dimension, such as socioeconomic origin and current socioeconomic status.

are group pressures that discourage them. The more people have pre-marital sexual relations, the less deviant it is to engage in them, and the more people have interracial relations, the less is the group pressure discouraging interracial associations. People who themselves engage in intergroup relations that were once considered deviant cannot easily look askance at others who engage in the same relations they do. When outgroup prejudice weakens, even those who still have some prejudice become reluctant to express it openly, further weakening ingroup pressures.[15]

. . .

The central theorem about macrostructural effects on intergroup relations is rooted in the multigroup affiliations that exist in all societies but are particularly pronounced in complex, modern ones. The assumption that social proximity furthers intergroup relations implies that social differences inhibit them. If several social differences that independently influence social life are closely related, the barriers to social intercourse are strengthened and the probability of social relations diminishes. Indeed, correlated social differences may stimulate the social processes reinforcing them (as extensive mobility does). For instance, they are likely to strengthen group and class barriers and to intensify group pressures, discouraging sociable relations with other groups and inferior classes.

Consolidated social differences thus may well have multiplicative effects inhibiting intergroup relations. In the opposite case, when several social differences are more or less orthogonal—weakly or not at all related—they (their regression lines) intersect in social space, which means that people's positions in different dimensions are relatively independent. This engenders counterforces that have profound implications for intergroup relations and structural change.

Multiple intersection of social differences in various dimensions exerts compelling structural constraints on engaging in intergroup rela-

---

15. Craig Calhoun has criticized similar remarks in the first draft (in a personal communication) for referring not to structural but to cultural influence. I grant that prejudice is a cultural factor. But the passage centers on group pressures that are experienced in social interaction. People may experience these pressures from the mere observation that few others engage in certain relations or possibly from explicit expressions of social disapproval. My basic point is that cultural prejudice that is not expressed in overt group pressures does not strengthen discrimination, which implies that reference is not to cultural influences.

tions. This proposition does not conflict with freewill, or with the assumption stipulated that proximity influences social relations. Indeed, it rests on this assumption. People are, of course, free to refrain from associating with anybody, including anybody whose position is not proximate to their own. They do not have to associate with persons of a different religion or race, with a different education or income. They are not free, however, to choose the combinations of characteristics in their social environment, nor can they decide which combinations of attributes of persons are frequent and which ones are rare in the population. (They can move elsewhere, but doing so merely alters and does not abolish the structural constraints on them.)

Much intersection does not deprive us of our most important ingroup choices, but it implies that we quickly lose our degrees of freedom, so to speak, after having made them. The multigroup affiliations in complex society have the result that people have many ingroup preferences, which naturally vary in importance to them. Multiple group affiliations also have the result that people greatly differ in the combinations of groups to which they belong. If intersection is pronounced, therefore, choosers have many ingroup preferences and their possible objects of choice—others with whom they have contact—often have different combinations of group affiliations.

Consequently, once members of a population with extensive intersection have made the ingroup choices most crucial to them, they cannot readily find anybody who shares still another of their group affiliations. The conjunction of the structure's intersection and their own first choices forces them, sooner or later, to choose associates some of whose group affiliations they do not share, that is, to establish intergroup relations in some dimensions. If social proximity promotes social relations (A-2), and if multiple social dimensions substantially intersect (making many proximate persons in one dimension distant in others), the implication is that multiple intersection increases the probability of intergroup relations (T-11).

Strictly speaking, however, the proximity assumption is not necessary for deriving the intersection theorem and thus can be dispensed with. The more pronounced the intersection of social differences, the greater the probability that people's ingroup choices involve them in intergroup relations. Indeed, much intersection implies that any choice of associates in one dimension entails opportunities for contact with associates that are not a person's choice in another dimension (according to

[handwritten: Assumption #3: Associates in other groups/ strata facilitate mobility there.]

A-1) and thereby promotes intergroup relations. Whether persons make ingroup or intergroup choices on a given dimension, intersecting social differences inevitably engender some intergroup—as well as some ingroup—relations in other dimensions.

Chart 2.1. Theorems about Intergroup Relations [16]

---

1. Relative group size inhibits intergroup relations.
2. Heterogeneity promotes intergroup relations (A-1).
3. Inequality promotes intergroup relations (A-1).
4. Mobility promotes intergroup relations (A-1).
11. Intersection promotes intergroup relations (A-2)

MOBILITY, CONFLICT, AND CHANGE

Another set of theorems specifies corresponding influences on rates of social mobility. It has already been suggested that intergroup relations and mobility both are likely to depend on relatively weak social barriers and directly influence each other. It is therefore to be expected that the same structural conditions that foster intergroup relations also foster mobility and that intergroup relations not only are influenced by mobility, as previously discussed, but also influence it. Transforming these ideas into theorems deducible from premises, however, requires introducing another assumption. The new assumption is that associates in other groups or strata facilitate mobility there *(A-3)*. It is implicit in this assumption that high rates of intergroup (and status-distant) relations increase the probability of social mobility *(T-6)*. [17] (All mobility theorems are confined to achieved status, as ascribed positions cannot be altered.)

[handwritten: Theorem #6]

Four theorems about influences of the population structure on rates of mobility can be derived from the conjunctions of the last theorem

---

16. The entries in parentheses refer to the assumption that, in conjunction with the definition of the antecedent term, implies the theorem.

17. This discussion of mobility, in contrast to that of occupational mobility in chapter 4, does not refer to choosing a certain position—an occupation or employment in a particular firm—but choosing to join a group of people, e.g., moving to another place or joining a fraternity or converting to a new religion. In terms of the distinction drawn in chapter 1, it refers to opportunities for social relations rather than opportunities for social positions.

and one of those already derived about structural influences on inter-group relations. The reasoning is that if A affects B and B affects C, A is likely to affect C.[18] If heterogeneity increases the rates of intergroup relations (T-2) and if rates of intergroup relations increase the probability of mobility (T-6), it follows that heterogeneity increases the probability of intergroup mobility (T-7). If inequality increases the probability of status-distant relations (T-3) and if status-distant relations increase the probability of social mobility (T-6), then inequality increases the probability of status-distant mobility (T-8).

These two theorems require clarification, particularly the second, which seems absurd. The basic point is that T-6 (intergroup relations promote mobility) rests on the assumption that associates in different groups or strata facilitate mobility there (A-3). By increasing intergroup relations, heterogeneity supplies associates elsewhere in the social space and thus encourages mobility there—moves to join other neighborhoods, different political parties, other civic organizations. Correspondingly, in-equality entails associates who are distant in social space from ego, which makes it easier for one to move long distances, geographically and in hierarchical status. The further away one's friends and relatives live, the greater is the likelihood of moving great distances. Similar considerations apply to socioeconomic mobility. Associates whose occupational status and business connections are superior to one's own are often of help in getting a job. Even weak ties with mere acquaintances of superior so-cioeconomic status facilitate moving to better positions, as Granovetter (1973, 1974) has pointed out.

The formal derivation of the intersection theorem is equivalent to those of T-7 and T-8. If multiple intersection raises the rate of intergroup relations (T-11), and if intergroup relations raise the probability of mo-bility (T-6), the implication is that multiple intersection makes mobility more probable (T-12).[19] To illustrate: the less the various differences in a population are related to one another, the greater the likelihood that my

18. If the two effects A–B and B–C were deterministic, they would definitely imply A–C. But the probabilistic theorems here, and in the social sciences generally, make long chains of deductions impermissible, as has been pointed out (see Costner and Leik 1964; Blalock 1969). The reason is that multiplying probabilities reduces them and that long chains therefore reduce the probability between antecedent and final consequence to insig-nificance if not to the vanishing point. Hence, only two-step deductions are used here, which are expected to yield reliable results, as the probability in each link is assumed to be substantial.

19. T-12 is deduced from T-11 and T-6; A-2 is not directly involved.

ingroup associates in some dimensions belong to different groups or strata in others and consequently facilitate my mobility there. For example, if race in the United States were not so closely related to education, occupation, social standing, and income, it would not be as difficult as it is for blacks to improve their status in some respects.

As the final theorem in this mobility series, a new one is introduced about the implications of group size for social mobility. If a group's relatively large size lowers the probability of intergroup relations (T-1), and if intergroup relations raise the chances of social mobility (T-6), it follows that the smaller the group, the better are the chances of mobility (T-5). All theorems are qualified by ceteris paribus, as noted, but special emphasis is needed in the case of this theorem to note that it refers strictly to the influence of differences in proportionate size as such, which may be counteracted by the nature and attributes of the different groups under consideration. An obvious example is that discrimination against minorities reduces their chances of upward social mobility below that of the majority, which, unless effectively controlled, would appear to negate the theorem's prediction in empirical tests.

This dry derivation of the mobility theorems must be enlivened by a few substantive illustrations. One example of the size theorem involves mobility from and into an elite. The chances to move down from a small elite are much greater than the opportunities of the large remainder of the population to move up into it. As a matter of fact, relative size exerts a parallel but seemingly opposite influence on the proportions in the two strata. The elite's proportion of *nouveaux riches* who have moved up from the hoi polloi is far greater than the fraction of former elite members who have moved down into the rest of the population. Similarly, despite the large numbers moving from cities to suburbs, both the rate of in-migrants to and that of out-migrants from the average large city are lower than the corresponding rates of the average suburb, owing to the sheer difference in size.

The increase in occupational heterogeneity resulting from the move of a population engaged predominantly in agricultural work to one engaged primarily in work in urban factories and offices has led to a great deal of spatial and occupational mobility in the United States and many other countries. Most of the occupational mobility was structural mobility, which is entirely the product of the expansion of smaller and the contraction of larger occupations. Since the occupations that expanded tended to be superior in socioeconomic status to those that contracted, upward mobility was generated. But this is not necessarily the case. The current contraction of industrial and office jobs and expansion of menial service jobs apparently is creating structural downward mobility.

Pronounced intersecting differences in a population imply not only that people's characteristics are less strongly correlated than they are in other populations but also that individuals there are less likely to have the combination of attributes that prevail elsewhere. The diverse social affiliations of many members of a community further imply that they tend to have more diverse friends—a more complex role set, as R. Coser (1975) calls it. A complex role set broadens people's horizons, increases their tolerance, and makes them welcome new experiences and new situations.

Intersecting parameters, accordingly, facilitate and encourage migration and social mobility. If people want to change their jobs, diverse acquaintances improve their chances that one of them will know about a suitable job and may even be in a position to recommend them for it. Moving to a strange city across the country is less likely to be experienced with discomfort by people who expect to find there professional colleagues and members of their former college. Immigrants and migrants to a new city typically settle in their own ethnic neighborhoods, where chances are good they will meet others they know, and even if they do not the common ethnic background will help them become socially adjusted and make friends.

. . .

Not all social relations are cordial or even civil. Many involve overt conflict of various sorts, such as economic, political, or ethnic conflict. To be sure, some important types of conflict do not involve personal contact, as illustrated by ethnic discrimination and economic exploitation. Attention here, however, is confined to those conflicts that do, and it is largely restricted to interpersonal conflict involving direct contact between members of different groups or strata, except that the analysis of intersecting political cleavages refers also to collective conflict.

The term *intergroup conflict,* therefore, applies both to the rate of interpersonal conflict between members with different affiliations in a population and to the collective conflicts in the political arena, which are discussed briefly at the end of this section and some more in chapter 6. Both frequent interpersonal conflict and conflicting cleavages in the political arena are expressions of the divergent or even antagonistic relations of different groups and strata. The reason that collective political relations are introduced in the analysis of intersection and conflict is that crosscutting cleavages have a distinctive significance for political controversies in a democracy.

It bears reiterating that concern is confined, as it has been in the analysis of intergroup relations and mobility, to the structural influences of population distributions on the probability of conflict. To be sure, conflict does not occur unless at least one party has a substantive reason to engage in it—to argue or fight or rape or murder. The same is the case for strong cordial relations. Although quite casual relations may be largely the result of contact opportunities, even lasting acquaintanceships and certainly friendships and marriages depend on various personal conditions affecting choices, not solely on contact opportunities. But just as substantive influences have been ignored in the theorems about intergroup relations, they are ignored in those about conflict. The underlying assumption is that if the population is large enough, purely structural influences on the probabilities of social relations can be detected even though substantive influences are not taken into account.

If the probability of conflict depends on contact opportunities, the first assumption applies to it, whatever the personal reasons and other circumstances affecting its occurrence. The mathematical tautology from which the first theorem has been inferred also applies to conflict. Members of smaller groups are more likely than those of larger ones to be involved—as victims or malefactors—in intergroup conflict $(T\text{-}1^*)$, because the former's probability of intergroup contact is greater $(A\text{-}1)$.

Heterogeneity increases the rates of intergroup conflict $(T\text{-}2^*)$. This theorem is deducible from the assumption that conflicts requiring direct contact, just as any associations that do, depend on contact opportunities $(A\text{-}1)$ and from the definition of heterogeneity in terms of frequency of chance contacts by members of different groups. Inequality increases the probable status distance in conflicts $(T\text{-}3^*)$, which is deducible from the same assumption $(A\text{-}1)$ and the definition of inequality in terms of status distance. Since the presence of many migrants or mobile persons increases contacts of people with different social affiliations, much mobility into a population also increases the probability of intergroup conflict $(T\text{-}4^*)$. This theorem is also derivable from the contact-opportunity assumption $(A\text{-}1)$ and the definition of mobility as involving differences between one's current social position and one's social origin or other earlier social position.

If various forms of heterogeneity make intergroup conflict more likely, and so do various forms of inequality, one might infer that the consolidation of such differences further intensifies conflict between different groups and strata. Experiencing parallel forms of heterogeneity, inequality, or both may well exacerbate people's animosity and hence increase the frequency of conflicts between them. If consolidated social differences enhance the chances of conflict, it follows that intersecting social differences, modifying one another, reduce the likelihood of intergroup conflict (T-13*).

A major theme of the political theory of pluralism also supports this inference. Pluralism generally refers to political institutions that enable diverse groups with conflicting views to influence the government—to change its policies and achieve positions of political power within it. The stability of democracy requires, Lipset (1963: 1) notes, "conflict or cleavage so that there will be a struggle over ruling positions, challenges to parties in power, and shifts of parties in office." Legitimate cleavages, he continues, contribute to the integration of societies and organizations.

For pluralism to sustain peaceful political conflict, it must assure that hostilities do not become so severe that they tear society asunder as each side seeks to vanquish the other. Crosscutting cleavages keep conflicts within bounds. They are the result of multigroup affiliations and intersection in complex societies, which create cross-pressures for the many persons who belong to groups that have opposite views on some issues. A person's ethnic group and colleagues at work, her union and church, his fraternity and professional association often have different political viewpoints and support opposite candidates in elections. Such situations put individuals under cross-pressure, which may lead some not to take sides at all and undermine others' inflexible opposite convictions. The consequent weakening of antagonism serves to sustain democratic processes, for their perpetuation depends on political ideologies and confrontations that are not utterly unyielding and do not seek to destroy the opposition (Lipset 1963: 77–82, and passim; Schattschneider 1975: 60–75). In short, intersecting cleavages mitigate intergroup conflict.[20]

---

[20] Not all differences among people affect political cleavages, only those referring to major social positions for which politics is important. Social class, income, education, ethnic background, and religion undoubtedly do, but weight and golf score probably do not. Correspondingly, not all intersecting differences but only crosscutting cleavages that have political implications diminish political hostilities.

The theorems derived so far can be schematically presented as follows:

Chart 2.2. Schema of Theorems

Structural Antecedent	Consequent Process		
	Intergroup Relations	Social Mobility	Intergroup Conflict
Group size	T-1	T-5	T-1*
Heterogeneity	T-2	T-7	T-2*
Inequality	T-3	T-8	T-3*
Mobility (IR)[21]	T-4	T-6	T-4*
Intersection	T-11	T-12	T-13*

. . .

Three final theorems deal with the changes large-scale mobility effects in the population structure, specifically in the distributions of people manifest in the parameters. To be sure, mobility has already been considered, as the schema shows, both as antecedent and as consequence. What has not been analyzed, however, are its influences on the other antecedents—heterogeneity, inequality, and intersection. Its influence on subgroup size is too obvious for it to be called a theorem: changes in size depend on whether in-moves exceed or fall short of out-moves. Its influence on heterogeneity, though I will designate it as a theorem, is also fairly evident; that on inequality is more complicated; and that on intersection is quite unexpected.

Exogenous conditions are the ultimate sources of macrostructural change, but most changes in population structures are mediated by processes of social mobility. Mobility translates, so to speak, the causal force of new or altered exogenous conditions into changes in the population structure. The central column of the chart indicates structural effects on mobility, but now we turn to mobility's effects on changes in structural parameters, after briefly illustrating their significance. Some forms of heterogeneity and changes in them are important indications of economic development and modifications in the economic infrastructure, including the division of labor, the occupational structure reflecting it, and the distributions of industries and markets.

21. The antecedent is mobility, except in the case of the column where the dependent variable is mobility, in which case it is intergroup relations.

Inequality reflects crucial aspects of the economy too, such as the market concentration of power, but perhaps its greatest significance is its relevance as an expression of society's equity. Inequality of power creates oppression and exploitation, deprivations and injustices that are incompatible with an equitable social system. Intersection, finally, is a major source of the character of modern society, its complex structure, and its recurrent change. It generates the multiple population differences that are at the root of the diversity of associates, the flexibility of people in modern society, and its dynamics.

In formal terms, how does mobility change parameters? An excess of moves from larger to smaller groups raises and an excess from smaller to larger ones lowers heterogeneity *(T-9)*. If disproportionate numbers of the majority group in large cities move to smaller suburbs, the city's ethnic heterogeneity is increased. When increasing numbers leave small enterprises for jobs in large corporations, the heterogeneity of firms is reduced. If the majority of farm workers' offspring move into a variety of smaller occupations, their intergenerational mobility increases occupational heterogeneity. These cases exemplify the influence of mobility among groups on heterogeneity. However, heterogeneity also changes without internal moves among groups as the result of differential expansion of various groups.

Immigration may alter heterogeneity, independent of internal migration among groups, and so may differential fertility. Thus, if large streams of immigrants to a country have different religious or ethnic affiliations, heterogeneity is enhanced in this respect. The great heterogeneity of the United States has resulted from successive waves of immigrants who differed in national or ethnic background from the people who were already here. Differences in fertility rates among ethnic and religious groups also increase heterogeneity (though the often parallel differences in mortality may weaken this effect). A final change in heterogeneity is the result of subdivisions and mergers. Sects separating from a church and political parties that split into opposing factions increase political heterogeneity. Mergers of firms and corporations reduce economic heterogeneity (and with it, competition).

How does vertical mobility affect inequality, whatever its form—inequality in wealth, power, or education? The complete answer is not as simple as that for changes in heterogeneity, but parts of the answer are simple enough. Upward mobility of all persons below the median (in education, income, or whatever) reduces inequality, and the downward mobility of persons who already were below the median raises inequality.

Downward mobility of the top stratum diminishes inequality, and if some of them move still further up—get still higher incomes or become even wealthier—inequality is enhanced. These influences are as one would expect.

What is less simple is how changes of the upper-middle strata influence inequality. In any population distribution based on a continuous gradation, such as income or occupational status, a line can be mathematically determined such that any move toward this line—from below or above—lessens and any move in the opposite direction expands inequality.[22] The greater the existing inequality, the nearer to the top is this line. This statement implies, for instance, that the same income loss of persons in the middle class with identical incomes—say at the 25th percentile from the top—would reduce inequality in a society where it had been very pronounced but increase it in another society that had less inequality. (The example in note 22 indicates this.) The inequality theorem implied by these considerations is as follows: mobility, up or down, toward the boundary between the upper and middle classes reduces inequality *(T-10)*.

To introduce the implications of intersection for mobility, let us briefly explore a consideration entering into the mobility choice. When circumstances make it advantageous or necessary for people to move but they have some choice over where to move, what would influence their choices? The theoretical scheme implies an answer. If people have to move from one location to a different one in one dimension, they are likely to choose one where they have associates in another dimension or, at least, know that there are people with the same affiliation as their own. When immigrants came to this country, they moved to locations and found work where they had kin or friends. If this was impossible, they went to live in neighborhoods and got jobs where they were among others with the same ethnic background, whose common affiliation made them likely future associates.

22. The mathematical derivation of the exact location of the dividing line between top and middle stratum depends on the inequality measure. For the Gini index, the dividing line is at the percentile of the status distribution where the proportion below minus the proportion above equals the Gini index. For example, if the Gini coefficient is .40, 30 percent of the population is in the stratum above and 70 percent in the strata below this line (as .70 − .30 = .40). If the Gini coefficient is .60, which indicates more inequality, 20 percent (.80 − .20 = .60) of the population is in the upper stratum. (For a mathematical derivation, see Blau and Schwartz 1984: 64–66.)

The same tendencies are observable in a great variety of situations. Children who graduate from one school and enroll in another seek to get into classes with some of their former schoolmates; when they are unsuccessful, they tend to look in their new class filled with strangers for some who at least have the same ethnic or religious or class background. A recent recruit to the army or a traveler who is alone in a foreign country tends to greet people he has barely known as if they were long-lost friends. Socioeconomic background and ethnic background are so important a basis for making new friends because they are universal characteristics shared by large numbers that make it possible to find an associate with some common affiliation in virtually every new situation.

These plausible illustrations have unexpected implications, for they seem to conflict with the earlier conclusion that intersection is an important cause of social mobility, which is a major mechanism of structural change. But the pattern of social mobility we are examining now is that people who have to change their position in one dimension are likely to move to a new position where they actually have, or expect to find, proximate associates in other dimensions. Before further examining the conflicting consequences implied, let us formulate the theorem. If social proximity increases the probability of ingroup relations (A-2) and if associates in other groups or strata facilitate mobility there (A-3), it follows that people who have to move to a different social space in one dimension probably select one where they have or can find proximate associates in other dimensions (T-14). A corollary of this theorem is that social mobility increases the consolidation of social differences.

Paradoxically, then, intersecting social differences promote social mobility (T-12) and thereby further structural change, but the form that mobility-induced change takes diminishes intersection. For the tendency of people who have to adjust to a new position in one respect is to find associates who share some of their affiliations in other respects. In formal terms, intersection furthers mobility but mobility enhances consolidation, which is the opposite of intersection. This suggests a counteracting feedback loop that slows structural change and not merely sustains but even restores stability. Many developments in today's rapidly changing and increasingly interdependent world require recurrent adjustments in social structures. Perhaps the consolidating tendencies implicit in the last theorem are self-regulating adjustments, like servomechanisms, to maintain some stability in the face of rapid dislocations. But perhaps they simply express the prevalent resistance to change that protects the status quo and vested interests in periods of great turmoil.

MULTILEVEL STRUCTURAL ANALYSIS

Multilevel structural analysis dissects population structures into the structures of their subunits of successively narrower scope. Early in his analysis of crosscutting social circles, Simmel (1923: 305–44) distinguishes the intersecting circles of predominant importance in modern society (and a foundation of the theory here presented) from the concentric circles found in all societies. Both entail multigroup affiliations but of different kinds. Crosscutting circles refer to affiliations with groups that have partly overlapping memberships, like those of a female physician of Italian descent. Concentric circles refer to affiliations of increasingly inclusive scope, like being a member of a congregation, thereby being a member of its diocese and its religious denomination. This is not meant to imply that the face-to-face groups are absorbed in the larger population. On the contrary, these groups in regular direct contact are the ultimate expressions of the social relations in the population as influenced by its structural opportunities and constraints.

The study of structures on multiple levels analyzes the connections linking the structures of large populations and the networks in which face-to-face relations actually find expression. The more and more encompassing concentric circles are the structural features that incorporate the diverse small groups in face-to-face contact into ever larger groupings and populations, and this process is reinforced in complex societies by the crosscutting circles that link people in multiple ways. To be sure, the common language and culture serve to unite the members of a society, but the multiple levels of substructures that encompass them in widening circles constitute a structural form of incorporating networks of direct interpersonal relations in entire populations.

The opposite perspective traces the impact of the population structure on direct interpersonal relations. Its effect on intergroup relations depends on the extent to which it penetrates into the substructures of face-to-face social relations, because some of it is dissipated before it reaches the narrowest social circles. As a first step in dissecting how far macrostructural differentiation penetrates into substructures, differentiation on two levels is examined. Any form of heterogeneity or inequality in a social structure can be decomposed into that within and that among its subunits, and the same is the case for intersection. To illustrate with polar extremes, the racial heterogeneity in a city can result either from all neighborhoods being equally heterogeneous with no differences among them, or from all neighborhoods being completely homogeneous and the city's heterogeneity resulting from the proportions of neighborhoods where different races live.

Black-white percentages (which are for a dichotomy equivalent to heterogeneity) make the case obvious. A city that is 10 percent black may be made up of 100 (same-size) neighborhoods each with 10 percent blacks or of 10 all-black and 90 all-white neighborhoods. In reality, of course, the differences in segregation vary by degree among cities. (This is apparently analogous to ANOVA [analysis of variance], but the outcome of interest is the opposite. The focus in ANOVA is to find that subunits differ, as shown by a high ratio of "between" to "within" variance, whereas the focus of the theory presented here is to discover penetration, which is shown by a high ratio of within- to among-subunit variance.)

The inequality in a social structure can be similarly decomposed into the proportions of it resulting from inequality within and inequality among its substructures. For example, one can investigate how much of the income differences among nurses with the same training is attributable to salary differences among hospitals rather than earning differences among individual nurses within hospitals. The greater the income inequality of members of the same occupation relative to the mean differences among places of employment, the more does income inequality penetrate down to the level of face-to-face relations and affect these relations. The latter sentence is from the theory's perspective, the former from ANOVA's perspective. But the two statements are evidently in essential agreement, though they use opposite results for illustrative purposes.

· · ·

We have discussed the decomposition of population structures and that within and among subunits, but we have not drawn any inferences from such decomposition for intergroup relations. Although such inferences could be drawn, we will postpone doing this until after our analysis of structures and substructures has been extended from two to multiple levels. Since decomposition of structural differentiation can be carried out for any two levels, whether they are adjacent or not, it is possible to perform decomposition for multiple levels. To do so, we ask whether heterogeneity, inequality, or intersection on successive levels results primarily from the respective form of differentiation within the subunits or from that among them.

Penetrating differentiation refers to the depth of successive levels of substructure to which a macrostructural property—heterogeneity, inequality, or intersection—penetrates. It indicates how far down structural differentiation on one level can go and still be accounted for largely by the differences within rather than the differences among its subunits on a lower level. Thus, the following questions can be asked. How much of the United States' religious heterogeneity results not from that among but from that within regions? How much of it results not from that among but from that within states? How much of it results not from that among but from that within towns? How much of it results not from that among but from that within neighborhoods?[23] Corresponding questions can be raised about inequality. How great is the income inequality (for comparable work) within and not among industries? within the firms and not among them in an industry? within the establishments of a firm compared to that among firms?

The more heterogeneity, inequality, or intersection (for which corresponding considerations apply) penetrates into successive substructures, the more this form of differentiation cuts across the variable used as a criterion for defining levels or concentric circles. For instance, the more income inequality occurs within rather than among successively narrower occupational specialties, the more income and occupation intersect, just as would be observed if occupation as well as income had been analyzed as a parameter. The case of heterogeneity cutting across levels is parallel, and intersection that intersects subunit boundaries also increases intersection. In short, multilevel-penetrating differentiation is formally equivalent to intersection (or increasing intersection).

Hence, corollaries about the influence of penetrating differentiation on intergroup relations follow from the theorem that intersection promotes intergroup relations (T-11). The first three of six corollaries are (1) the more heterogeneity penetrates into low-level substructures, the

23. The total variation in any encompassing unit is the sum of the mean variation within subunits and the variation among them. Hence, the mean heterogeneity (a form of differentiation) in the subunits cannot be more than that in the encompassing unit, and that much only if there are no differences among subunits. The same applies, mutatis mutandis, to inequality and intersection.

more probable are intergroup relations; (2) the more inequality penetrates into low-level substructures, the greater is the likely status distance between associates; (3) the more intersecting differences penetrate into low-level substructures, the more probable are intergroup relations.[24] These corollaries can also be derived directly from the second assumption and the specification of penetration. If heterogeneity, inequality, or intersection within subunits of a larger structure exceeds that among them and if proximity promotes intergroup relations (A-2), it follows that there is a greater probability of intergroup relations.

Population differentiation that penetrates down to low levels of subunits also raises the probabilities of social relations between members of different subunits. Thus, if different religious groups are dispersed in various places rather than each being concentrated within a separate area, religious proximity, according to the second assumption, fosters association between fellow believers residing in different places, raising the rates of inter-subunit associations. The same applies, of course, to all other widely dispersed groups or strata. Hence, the proximity assumption and the intersection theorem imply three additional corollaries: (4) the rates of inter-subunit associations increase with increasing penetration of heterogeneity; (5) they increase with increasing penetration of inequality; and (6) they increase with increasing penetration of intersection.

Penetrating differentiation reveals how well desegregation has been accomplished, not only along racial but also along other lines. But two caveats must be entered. First, penetrating differentiation itself does not indicate how well desegregation furthers integrative relations among diverse groups. To determine this, its influence on intergroup relations must be tested. (A set of such tests will be presented in the next chapter, with some unexpected results.) Second, although the multilevel structural analysis has not dealt with conflict (or mobility), the basic sets of theorems imply that penetrating differentiation increases not only the likelihood of cordial relations but also that of friction and conflict. Propinquity promotes congenial relations and friction, often among the same associates, as illustrated by recurrent disputes in families. Improved integrative relations resulting from desegregation, however, may well be

24. I must acknowledge that in the original formulation of the theory I included a theorem that is the opposite of this corollary, namely, that *consolidation* that penetrates into successive subunits promotes intergroup relations (Blau 1977: 178–79). On reconsideration, I have decided that I simply was wrong.

worth some friction. To paraphrase Eisenhower, the surest way to avoid friction is solitary confinement.

CONCLUSIONS

Concentric as well as crosscutting circles are essential conditions of complex societies, though some concentric circles also prevail in simple societies. Simon (1962) defines complex systems as consisting of interdependent elements that themselves are social systems, which, too, consist of interdependent elements that are social systems, and the same may recur. The population structures of complex societies are concentric circles involving substructures on multiple levels. Their complexity is further increased by crosscutting circles, resulting in a multidimensional space of social positions on multiple levels. One dimension still missing is time, except for the brief discussion that feedback tends to slow structural change (T-14). Some conjectures about historical time will be suggested in the last chapter.

Multigroup affiliations of people are another mark of contemporary society. They are the source of complex role sets, which R. Coser (1975) considers "a seedbed of individual autonomy" and intellectual flexibility. Complex role sets are reflected in people's diversity of associates. The most important implication of multigroup affiliations, in terms of the theory here presented, is that they are the source of intersecting differences in a population and of the consequent relative prevalence of intergroup relations.

The multiple intersection of complex societies, particularly if it is penetrating into lower levels, raises problems for people's choices of ingroup associates, which the proximity assumption (A-2) implies are the preferred choices. For people to confine themselves to ingroup choices implicitly assumes that they are free to refrain from associating with any kind of person. Although human freedom of choice is limited by a variety of external conditions, even leaving these aside our freedom of choice, such as that of refraining from choosing certain associates, is limited by the choices of other people and by our own previous choices. Other people's choices restrict mine and may even preempt them; for instance, if I am a member of a small ethnic group composed largely of male immigrants, I may not be able to find an ingroup bride because all the available women have already been married to others.

Generally, people are free to refrain from associating with all persons who have any characteristic whatsoever. But people's multiple group affiliations imply that each person has many ingroup tendencies. If people prefer to associate only with ingroup members in numerous dimensions, there are many dimensions and a multitude of groups with whose members they seek to avoid associating. Moreover, multiple intersection also makes it likely that one's combination of affiliations differs from those of many if not most others with whom one comes into contact. To be sure, I am still free to satisfy my most important ingroup choices. But the more of them I have satisfied, the more my own past choices restrict my remaining freedom of choice, that is, the more difficult it is to find someone who has all the characteristics I already chose and still others in common with me. Sooner or later I exhaust my freedom of choice and, unless I want to remain an isolate, I must choose associates who, though they do share my most important affiliations, differ from me in some affiliations.

This process of compromise is a fundamental source of intergroup relations in populations. The choices of individuals are limited mostly by their own earlier ones and somewhat by the choices of others. For an entire population, however, these constitute compelling constraints for most members to engage in some intergroup relations despite prevailing ingroup preferences. In a large population with intersecting differences, members differ enough in their strong dislikes that some intergroup relations exist in virtually all dimensions, with rare exceptions.

Multilevel structural analysis indicates my attempt to combine two seemingly contradictory requirements—that structures on different levels have emergent properties and that a theory should use consistent terms in analyzing equivalent objects, for instance, populations of varying scope. The major structural concepts are heterogeneity, inequality, and intersection, which are used in the analysis of structures on all levels. Nevertheless, there are emergent properties as one moves from substructures to encompassing structures. The heterogeneity of the encompassing structure, for instance, has the same definition but not the same value as the heterogeneity of its substructures, because the former includes the variation among as well as within the substructures. The same is the case for inequality and intersection.

Although the common culture and language are undoubtedly major integrative forces that unify the people in a society, social structures engender processes of their own that integrate face-to-face relations and groups through intergroup relations and multiple levels into a coherent society. Heterogeneity, inequality, and particularly intersection promote intergroup relations that link diverse groups. The multiple levels of complex structures, finally, incorporate small groupings of kin and friends and colleagues in ever-widening social circles that ultimately encompass society's entire population.

THREE

TESTING THEORETICAL
IMPLICATIONS

EMPIRICAL TESTS OF THE THEORY formulated in the preceding chapter are presented in this chapter. Most of the research tests the core theorems that were the starting point for constructing the theory—those pertaining to the influences of the population structure on intergroup relations. Attention centers on the influences on intergroup relations of the structural parameters—heterogeneity, inequality, and intersection. Research testing two other sets of propositions is also summarized: empirical studies of crimes against persons testing some of the conflict theorems, and a study of a school system testing corollaries about penetrating differentiation.

As the theory's concepts and propositions refer to population structures and their effects on rates of social relations, tests of its implications must be based on a sample of populations, not of individuals. Only a comparative study of populations can ascertain whether differences in population structures have the consequences for social relations the theory stipulates. After I had developed and published my theory (Blau 1977), I obtained grants from the National Science Foundation to test it in a study of all large Standard Metropolitan Statistic Areas (SMSAs) in the United States.[1] A colleague and I analyzed the pertinent data from 125 SMSAs and reported them (Blau and Schwartz 1984 [hereafter, in this chapter, B&S]). After briefly presenting the research procedures, I summarize the results in the first section of this chapter as well as a few empirical studies by other investigators that tested implications of the theory for conflict.

1. I am grateful to the National Science Foundation for grants SOC782516 and SOC7919935 to support this research.

The initial tests had some shortcomings, as mentioned, and I performed revised tests of the major theorems, which are presented next. Although no new data were collected for this analysis, the procedure was improved. Raw scores were transformed into their natural logarithms, and regression analysis was employed to study how intergroup relations are affected by heterogeneity, inequality, and intersection in various respects when other structural influences are controlled. In the last section, an empirical analysis by Schwartz of penetrating differentiation in a school system is reported, which involves a multilevel structural analysis of school districts, schools, grades, and classrooms.

RESEARCH PROCEDURES AND EARLY TESTS

The initial and the revised tests of the theory's core proposition are based on the same data representing the populations of all American SMSAs with a population of more than 250,000 in 1970. The data base is the 1 percent public use sample of the 1970 U.S. census, confined to data on the population living in the 125 largest SMSAs in 1970. The total number of sampled persons in these SMSAs was nearly 1.25 million, 9,941 in the average SMSA, with a range from about 2,500 to more than 100,000. The data on the sampled persons in every SMSA were aggregated to construct measures of several kinds of heterogeneity, inequality, and intersection.[2]

The dependent variable is a specific form of intergroup relations—intermarriage.[3] Its measure is based on a subsample of recently married couples in every SMSA, which ranges from 30 to more than 1,000. (The criteria for recently married were designed to make it very unlikely that the marriage occurred elsewhere or that the SMSA's population structure had changed much since the marriage.)[4] The measure for intermarriage

---

2. The heterogeneity measure is Gibbs and Martin's (1962) index for industrial diversification ($H = 1 - \Sigma p_i^2$), which is the inverse (complement) of the Herfindahl index of concentration (Σp_i^2). The inequality measure is the Gini coefficient. Intersection is indicated by one minus the mean of the correlations of the form of heterogeneity or inequality corresponding to the form of intermarriage (the dependent variable) and all other forms of heterogeneity and inequality in the data set (deleting any whose deletion improves Cronbach's [1951] alpha [see B&S: 91]).

3. Marriage is the only interpersonal relation on which the U.S. census provided information on both members.

4. The criteria for selecting the subsample—the best available for our purpose—were that the bride was currently married, was under twenty-five, and had been living in the county for at least five years.

for a nominal variable is the proportion of couples whose affiliation is not the same, and for a graduated variable it is the mean difference between spouses. This index was refined to take account of the constraints on intermarriage produced by a variable's (such as occupation's) gender difference (as exemplified by the impact on occupational intermarriage of the disproportionate numbers of nurses who are female and of construction workers who are male).[5]

The major research objectives are to test whether various forms of heterogeneity, inequality, and intersection affect intermarriage in conformity with theoretical expectations. The empirical tests are based on a comparative analysis of 125 populations, those in the 125 largest metropolitan areas in the United States in 1970.[6] (An exception is racial intermarriage, which is based on 124 cases, because Honolulu is an outlier and hence omitted.) Weighted least square (WLS) procedures are employed, primarily to correct for the differences in the case base of the intermarriage measure. For theoretically predicted results, one-tailed tests are used; for other variables when used as controls, two-tailed tests are used.

The data set and the above-described procedures were the same in the original tests of the theory's empirical implication, which are first summarized, and in the revised ones, which will subsequently be discussed. The two main differences between the original and the new procedure, as already indicated, are that the new procedure corrects for nonlinearity by logarithmic transformation and controls for all other structural influences (on which data are available) in the test of any one by using multiple regression.[7]

Before summarizing the original results, I want to point out that testing the theory with data on intermarriage in SMSAs constitutes a severe test of it. The assumption that structural opportunities affect choices of associates, which implies that choices depend partly on chance circumstances, is most likely to be correct for casual acquaintanceships, which

---

5. This adjustment has not been made for racial intermarriage, because it would lower the case base of the measure and racial intermarriages are so rare that the loss in reliability owing to few cases would be greater than the gain achieved by the adjustment.

6. To treat the population structure in 1970 as affecting marriage rates some years earlier implicitly assumes that the changes in various SMSAs were largely parallel. To check on this, we collected data on the populations of these SMSAs for 1960 from published sources (available for most but not all variables). The relationships of various forms of heterogeneity and inequality in 1960 and those in 1970 to intermarriage (in the 1960s) were essentially parallel (see B&S: 44, 48).

7. For a fuller discussion of procedures, see B&S: 16–22.

often result from chance encounters. But theorems based on chance are much less likely to make accurate predictions for such a profound and lasting relation as marriage, which is based on culturally and psychologically conditioned choices that may well be resistant to external constraints. Moreover, while the limitations imposed on marital choices by the population structure are great in a small village, they are much less confining on choices of mates in a large metropolis with hundreds of thousands or millions of diverse people. In short, if the theory proves viable for intermarriage in a metropolis, it is apt to be applicable to less intimate relations in smaller towns.

. . .

Although subunit size is not strictly speaking a structural parameter, size has been included in the theory, as small size has effects on intergroup relations that parallel those of the three population parameters. Indeed, small subunits may be considered an element of heterogeneity, since prevalence of small subunits is one of two factors affecting heterogeneity, the other being subunits that are of uniform size or nearly so. A number of empirical studies observed that the proportionate size of, for example, a religious group in a city is negatively related to the likelihood that its members will marry outsiders. Examples of these studies have been mentioned.

Our research also observed negative relations of the relative size of various population subunits in an SMSA and their outmarriage rate (B&S: 37). Thus, the smaller an SMSA's proportion of persons of native stock, the more they are likely to be married to spouses of foreign stock ($r = -.57$). Similarly, the proportion of an SMSA living in the region of their birth and the proportion married to a spouse born in another region are negatively related ($-.82$). The same is the case for the proportion of professional and technical workers in an SMSA (including only couples where both spouses report an occupation) and the proportion of them whose spouse is in a different major occupational group ($-.33$).

The heterogeneity theorem (T-2) was tested with six forms of heterogeneity and intermarriage[8]--with respect to differences in race, national

---

8. Actually, we presented data on nine relationships of heterogeneity and intermarriage, but three dependent variables are so closely related to one of the six used that they cannot be considered independent tests and are not discussed. The three are ethnic group (a combination of race and national origin) and mother tongue, which are closely related to each other and to national origin, and a white-nonwhite dichotomy, which is very closely related to the eight-category racial variable (not surprisingly, as 99 percent of the 1970 sample were either blacks or whites).

origin,[9] birth region, major industry, major occupation, and detailed occupation.[10]

The zero-order correlations are positive, supporting the theoretical prediction, in four of the six tests (B&S: 44). Heterogeneity and intermarriage are positively related for national origin (.86), birth region (.84), industry (.32), and major occupation (.13). There is no significant relationship between heterogeneity and intermarriage with respect to differences in detailed occupation or in race. Although two of six cases fail to confirm the theoretical prediction, one of those two cases can be accounted for on methodological grounds and the other can be explained by the theory itself.

The reason for the negative result for detailed occupations is essentially methodological. There were 444 detailed occupations in the data set for 1970, which is about thirty times the number of categories of any other nominal variable. What is even more important, the distribution of heterogeneity in detailed occupations is extremely skewed, as reflected in the mean for SMSAs of .988, and its intermarriage distribution is also very skewed (the SMSA mean is .95), which severely restricts the possible correlation of these two variables. Logit transformation of both independent and dependent variables increases the ranges of possible variation from plus to minus infinity. The transformed variables exhibit a significant correlation of .25, in accordance with theoretical expectation.

One might be tempted to attribute the lack of influence of racial heterogeneity on racial intermarriage to the prevailing prejudice against such marriages in our society, but there is no reason to resort to such an ad hoc explanation, because the theory can explain the result in its own structural terms. One of its propositions is that consolidated differences strengthen group barriers, and we know that racial differences in this country are strongly related to differences in socioeconomic status and other factors. If only one of these differences is controlled—the racial difference in socioeconomic status (represented by the ratio of the means of white and nonwhite socioeconomic status [SEI])—racial heterogeneity

9. National origin refers to native stock and one of twelve categories of foreign stock (defined as having at least one foreign-born parent). Only 15 percent of the sample in the average SMSA were of foreign stock.

10. Intermarriage rates for industry, major and detailed occupation, occupational status (SEI), and earnings are only computed for spouses both of whom were in the labor force. (Intermarriage in major occupation and intermarriage in detailed occupation are not multicollinear [$r = -.09$].)

is seen to be significantly, albeit weakly, related to racial intermarriage, supporting the theory (B&S: 46–47).

Data on three forms of inequality and intermarriage are available to test the theorem predicting a positive relationship between them— education, SEI, and income.[11] Inequality in education and mean difference in years of education between spouses are, as the theory predicts, positively correlated (.65). So are inequality and spouses' average distance in occupational status and earnings, but Skvoretz's criticism noted in the preceding chapter makes these data questionable tests of the inequality theorem.[12] (Tests not subject to Skvoretz's criticism are presented below.)

In sum, the original empirical tests support the theoretical expectations of the influence of the population structure on intergroup relations quite well. To be sure, two analyses initially produced results that failed to corroborate the theory, but after some adjustments they also corroborated it. In one case, the reason was methodological, which should have been anticipated by using appropriate procedures, and the revised tests to be presented are designed to accomplish this. It deserves to be noted that the theory received empirical support even with simple correlations; if controlling other influences support it too, it would corroborate the theory. Before turning to the alternative tests based on regression procedures, earlier research on violent crime by others is examined to test some of the theory's implications for conflict.

. . .

A number of criminologists have tested propositions of the theory about conflict in studies of crimes against persons. Thus, Sampson (1984) derives his own inferences about victims from the theory about influences of the population structure on conflict, quite correctly reasoning that the probability of conflict affects not only the chances of committing a crime against another person but particularly the probability of becoming a victim of such a crime. His hypotheses are that a group's relative size in a neighborhood is negatively and a neighborhood's heterogeneity is positively related to the proportion of victims of four crimes (rape, robbery,

11. Data on personal income are also available, but the variables based on them are virtually identical to those on earnings, which are used here. Thus, personal income, which includes unearned income as well as wages or salaries, supplies no independent test and is not discussed. The simple correlation for inequality in personal income and that in earnings is .93 for the 125 SMSAs.

12. The correlations of inequality in status distance and intermarriage are .38 for SEI and .23 for earnings.

assault, and larceny) committed by a member of another group than the victim's own. Two dichotomies of groups were used by Sampson, race (black or white) and age (juvenile or adult). Black victims' reports of white perpetrators as well as white victims' reports of black perpetrators are analyzed as outgroup crimes, and so are the corresponding two complementary age-outgroups.

The results support both hypotheses for all four groups' chances of being victimized by a member of the outgroup. Although the overall probability that victim and assailant will be members of the same group is disproportionately great, the smaller a group's proportion of the population in a neighborhood—whether black or white, juvenile or adult—the more likely it is that its members will be victimized by an outgroup member. Further, the greater the racial or age heterogeneity of a neighborhood, the greater is the probability that victim and criminal will belong to different races or that they will differ substantially in age.

Messner and South's (1986) study of the influences of a city's black minority on interracial and intraracial robbery is also concerned with the significance of relative size on the likelihood of being victimized. The authors infer from the theory that increasing the size of the black minority in a city increases its opportunity for ingroup and reduces its opportunity for intergroup contacts, including the chances that a member of that minority will be a victim of robbery. Since an increase in the proportion of blacks reduces the proportion of whites, such a population change reduces the opportunities of whites for contact with and being robbed by other whites and increases their chances for contact with and being robbed by blacks.

These considerations imply that an increase in the proportion of blacks increases the likelihood that blacks will be robbed by blacks, reduces the likelihood that blacks will be robbed by whites, reduces the likelihood that whites will be robbed by whites, and increases the likelihood that whites will be robbed by blacks. This seemingly crazy-quilt pattern, which is precisely what the findings show, is implied by the effects of changes in the racial size distribution on the likelihood of being victimized. This study also supports the theory that segregation increases the likelihood of intragroup and decreases that of intergroup robberies, for both races. These results "offer strong support for macrostructural opportunity theory" (Messner and South 1986: 987).

To mention briefly a few other crime studies utilizing this theory, South and Messner (1986) find that interracial marriage and crime are positively correlated, as implied by the theory, but different structural conditions seem to influence the two, which was not anticipated by the theory. O'Brien (1987) cites my theory to support his argument that the greater frequency of blacks raping whites than whites raping blacks results from contact opportunities owing to differences in the two groups' sizes, not from blacks' greater desire for white women. South and Felson (1990: 89) also analyze interracial rape and conclude that its best predictors are not attributes of offenders but "the relative size of the black and white populations and their distributions in physical space," in accordance with macrostructural theory.

Differentiation and Intermarriage

The new tests of the theory are based on the same data set as the original ones were, but the procedure for analysis has been changed. Although the original results supported the theory quite well, further corroboration would be offered by results supporting the theory based on somewhat different and improved procedures. The theorems of the influence of heterogeneity (T-2) and inequality (T-3) are tested in this section, and the intersection theorem (T-11) in the next section.

Weighted least squares (WLSs) is again used, as it was in the original tests, to correct for heteroscedasticity. One change from the original procedure is that regression analysis is substituted for zero-order correlations, which makes it possible to control other conditions. All structural parameters that influence the intermarriage under consideration are controlled.[13] Another change in the current tests is that all variables have been transformed into their natural logarithms, which has several advantages. It corrects for nonlinearity to meet the linearity assumption of regression analysis. Besides, it corrects for any skewness to the right. Finally, it substitutes for the variables' absolute values and differences proportionate ones (elasticities), which can be more meaningfully compared for entirely different variables and for SMSAs greatly varying in size. It thereby changes additive to multiplicative relationships. A matrix of simple correlations of the transformed variables is in this chapter's appendix.

The means in raw form of the variables, which are analyzed con-

---

13. All other forms (in addition to the one tested) of heterogeneity and inequality (including those in occupational status and earnings) are controlled if they influence the dependent variable. The criterion for inclusion is a coefficient significant on the .05 level (two-tailed) and meeting the tolerance level of .3. (Skvoretz's criticism discussed in chap. 3 applies only to the intermarriage measures of SEI and earnings, not to their inequality measures, which can therefore be used as possible controls.)

Table 3.1 Mean Heterogeneity, Inequality, and Intermarriage

Variable	Differentiation	Raw Inter-marriage Rate	Constrained Inter-marriage Rate
Heterogeneity			
Race	.20	.01	.01
National origin	.27	.11	.07
Birth region	.38	.25	.18
Industry	.87	.81	.66
Major occupation	.87	.84	.60
Detailed occupation	.988	.97	.95
Inequality			
Education	.16	.13	.12
SEI	.32		
Earnings	.46		

strained to control for gender differences and in logarithmic transformation, are presented in table 3.1. (The means for intermarriage are actually means [for SMSAs] of means [for the young couples in an SMSA].) The average heterogeneity in the 125 SMSAs is low for race (.20), intermediate for national origin (.27) and region of birth (.38), and high for industry (.87), major occupation (.87), and, particularly, detailed occupation (.988).[14] Mean intermarriage rates exhibit about the same order: they are very low for race (.01), fairly low for national origin (.11) and birth region (.25), high for industry (.81) and major occupation (.84), and very high for detailed occupation (.97). Apparently, ascribed status differences inhibit marriage much more than achieved differences. The influence of heterogeneity on intermarriage, to which we presently turn, is not parallel to these differences. (Comprison of columns two and three show effect of gender adjustment.)

But before analyzing the influences of heterogeneity, a regularity in table 3.1 should be noted which reveals the proximity assumption, the prevalence of ingroup choices. Heterogeneity and inequality indicate the

14. These heterogeneity and inequality means in raw form indicate the chance expectation that a random pair differs in nominal position or by a certain amount in graduated status (years of education), and intermarriage means in raw form refer to the percentage of couples not having the same nominal position or the average difference between them in graduated status (years of education).

chance expectation that any two members in the average SMSA differ (in percentages for nominal and in social distance for graduated parameters). The raw rates of intermarriage refer to the proportions of couples in an SMSA who are not members of the same nominal group or to the average difference between them on a graduated parameter, like years of education. In every comparison, the mean in the second column is lower than that in the first. This manifests the prevalence of ingroup marriage: spouses are consistently more proximate than the expectations based on differences in the population, which is, of course, to be expected. Note that such is also the case for industry, major occupation, and detailed occupation, although in these respects the large majority of spouses are intermarried, yet the proportion who are inmarried exceeds chance expectations.

. . .

Seven regressions of different forms of intermarriage on heterogeneity or inequality are presented in table 3.2, in which every column refers to one regression analysis. Each of seven forms of intermarriage is regressed on the corresponding form of heterogeneity or inequality and any other structural parameters (in the data set) that exert an influence. The coefficients of the theoretically implied positive relationships are on the diagonal, surrounded by heavy lines. Unstandardized regression coefficients and their standard errors are shown.

The results for the theoretical tests on the diagonal disclose that the data conform to theoretical expectations in five cases but fail to conform in two. One of the two is the same one that originally failed to support the theoretical prediction until an appropriate control was introduced, namely, racial heterogeneity. The other is different, however. Originally, detailed occupation did not support the heterogeneity theorem until logit transformations were substituted for raw variables. In the new tests, which use logarithmic transformations throughout, detailed occupation corroborates the theory but major occupation does not.

Let us start by examining the regression results for one of the two negative cases. Racial intermarriage is not related to racial heterogeneity, contrary to theoretical expectations. It is positively related to a metropolitan area's heterogeneity in nativity[15] and in birth region, which reflect, respectively, proportionately more persons of foreign stock and

15. The only information on nativity or national origin obtained in the 1970 U.S. census was whether a person was of native stock (both parents were native-born) or of foreign stock (one or both parents were born in one of eleven groups of countries).

Table 3.2. Differentiation and Intermarriage

	Intermarriage in						
	Race	Nativity	Birth Region	Industry	Occup.	Detailed Occup.	Educ.
	b (s.e.)	b (s.e.)	b (s.e.)	b (s.e.)	b (s.e.)	b (s.e.)	b (s.e.)
Racial heterogeneity	0.065* (.158)	0.280 (0.118)					
Nativity heterogeneity	0.774 (0.144)	1.929 (0.107)					
Birth region heterogeneity	0.647 (0.200)		1.597 (0.131)			−0.019 (0.009)	
Industry heterogeneity				2.190 (0.583)			
Occupational heterogeneity					5.802* (6.118)		
Detailed occup. heterogeneity						6.977 (4.102)	
Educational inequality							1.024 (.111)
SEI inequality	−5.784 (2.150)			−0.770 (0.293)	−2.533 (1.181)		−0.519 (0.213)
Earnings inequality		7.913 (1.999)					
Constant	−10.011 (2.673)	6.192 (1.606)	−0.261 (0.153)	−0.985 (0.364)	−2.637 (1.099)	−0.006 (0.043)	−0.841 (0.298)
Adjusted R^2	.367	.720	.543	.173	.022	.033	.405

* Not significant at .05 (one-tailed) level.
Note: Except for predicted results (boxed) only coefficients significant at 0.5 (two tailed) level are presented.

proportionately more migrants from other regions. ~~These findings suggest that whites of foreign stock and migrants from other regions to an SMSA, both of whom are often not fully integrated in the majority population, are more likely than other whites to be interracially married.~~[16] But

16. These positive influences imply that controlling them should strengthen the influence of racial heterogeneity on intermarriage. This is the case. Indeed, in the regression of

a broader inference may be drawn that takes into account that racial heterogeneity too affects racial intermarriage when nativity heterogeneity alone is controlled (as just indicated in note 16), namely, that ethnic diversity, encompassing substantial racial and national differences, increases the probability of racial as well as nativity intermarriage.

The pronounced negative effect of socioeconomic inequality obliterates any significant influence of an SMSA's racial composition on racial intermarriage. It undoubtedly reflects the prevailing poverty among blacks, particularly back in 1970, when blacks were in even worse economic circumstances than they are now (and when nearly all nonwhites were blacks). The great socioeconomic differences between races reinforced the prejudice and group pressure against racial intermarriage.

In our original test of this theorem, which also initially had negative results, we found that just controlling the ratio of the average occupational status of the two races sufficed to reveal a slight, but significant, positive relationship between racial heterogeneity and intermarriage, as predicted. This was a weak test, however. The racial differences in this country are pervasive and were even greater a quarter of a century ago when these data were collected. Controlling for racial differences in occupational status, important as its adverse effect on racial intermarriage is, does not take into account all handicaps suffered by blacks compared to the opportunities enjoyed by whites. Although we do not have the data to take into consideration all of these advantages and disadvantages, we can do better than controlling only one. A much superior measure would be to control all racial differences on which data are available in our data set, and the measure of racial intersection essentially does that. The more race intersects with various other differences, the less are racial differences reinforced by correlated ones to discourage intermarriage.

The various forms of intersection are analyzed in the next section, and the test of whether controlling for intersection reveals an influence of racial heterogeneity on intermarriage is postponed until then. The intersection analysis must control for heterogeneity to ascertain whether intersection and heterogeneity influence intermarriage independently, since the theory predicts positive effects for both. Hence, this analysis will provide an opportunity to ascertain not only whether the intersec-

---

only racial and nativity heterogeneity, the coefficient for racial heterogeneity is significant on the .05 (one-tailed) level ($b = .291$; SE $= .158$; $t = 1.848$). But the strong negative effect of SEI heterogeneity again makes this regression coefficient entirely insignificant, as the table shows.

tion of race with other social differences overcomes some resistance to racial intermarriage but also whether controlling for racial intersection discloses that racial heterogeneity does affect intermarriage. These tests are presented when intersection is analyzed.

Let us look at the influences of heterogeneity on intermarriage that corroborate the theorem (T-2) before turning to another one that fails to do so. Heterogeneity in nativity promotes intermarriage between persons of foreign and native stock, confirming the implication of the heterogeneity theorem. Its intermarriage rate is also increased by racial heterogeneity, possibly indicating (as does the coefficient of nativity in the regression of racial intermarriage) that whites of foreign stock are more likely than those of native stock to marry blacks.[17] These two findings (the only case where two forms of intermarriage are affected by the same two independent variables) strengthen the broader interpretation that a population's ethnic diversity promotes both racial and national-origin intermarriage. A final structural condition that has a substantial positive effect on nativity intermarriage is inequality in earnings. One might speculate that this condition reflects trade-offs of superior income for "inferior" national background, or vice versa.

The effects of heterogeneity in birth region and in industry on the corresponding intermarriage rates strongly corroborate the theorem. No other parameter that influences birth-region intermarriage was discovered, but industry intermarriage is also adversely affected by socioeconomic inequality. The greater the variety of a city's industries, the more likely it is that working spouses are employed in different industries. Great inequality in occupational status, however, inhibits marriages between members of different industries, possibly because it often involves some industries with mostly high-status and some with mostly low-status employees.

Heterogeneity in detailed occupation has merely a slight positive effect on occupational intermarriage, which only becomes apparent when the negative effect of birth region on intermarriage is controlled. Migrants from other regions are somewhat more likely than others to marry spouses in their own occupation, perhaps because doing the same work is one of the meeting grounds for newcomers, and once this is controlled, occupational heterogeneity and intermarriage exhibit a weak positive relationship, thus supporting the theorem, though just barely.

17. The majority of whites and nearly all nonwhites in 1970 were of native stock. Hence, more nativity heterogeneity implies more persons of foreign stock.

The negative result for major occupation is made particularly puzzling by the preceding finding. Why do heterogeneity and intermarriage in major occupations fail to reveal the relationship with refined procedures that they did before with simpler procedures? The simple correlation of raw variables revealed the opposite: an influence of major but not of detailed occupation on intermarriage (B&S: 44; logit transformations yielded a positive correlation for detailed occupations [p. 46]).[18] One might suspect that the skewness to the left, not to the right, of major-occupation heterogeneity is the reason that logarithmic transformation does not correct the skew but makes it worse, yet this result should also be the case for the heterogeneity of detailed occupations, which is even more skewed.[19] If data to control other structural influences were available, the expected result might be observed, but this is hardly a satisfactory answer. The negative finding just must be accepted.

Before leaving the discussion of heterogeneity's influence on intergroup relations and turning to that of the influence of inequality, some inferences can be suggested about the social mechanisms and processes that mediate the structural constraints of heterogeneity on choices of associates. In all respects that we have examined and undoubtedly in virtually all others, people make both some ingroup choices and some intergroup choices. To be sure, in some dimensions, notably ascribed ones, ingroup choices are by far the most prevalent and in others, like occupation, intergroup choices are the most prevalent, although in all dimensions, including those in which ingroup choices are rarest, ingroup choices exceed what is expected by chance alone. Given the proclivity of making ingroup choices, what social conditions and sociopsychological processes govern the decisions to insist on choosing ingroup associates in some respects while compromising by making outgroup choices in others?

The social mechanisms, as previously indicated, are multigroup affiliations and intersecting social differences, which imply that people belong to many groups, as do their potential associates, and chances are that associates who satisfy some of their ingroup choices do not satisfy all of them. But how do people decide which ingroup choices to give up?

18. It is also unexpected that inequality in SEI, which is based on detailed occupations, adversely affects intermarriage only in major and not in detailed occupations, as table 3.2 indicates.

19. I examined whether logit transformation would produce an improvement, but it does not. The regression coefficients (with no other variable in the equation) are for major occupation, 1.053 (.882); for detailed occupation, .437 (.882).

They may well make implicit rankings of the importance to them of various ingroup choices and seek to satisfy the most salient ones and then submit to the growing restraints on their options as their earlier choices restrict more and more their freedom of choice. This sociopsychological process may be what effects the constraints of multigroup affiliation and intersecting parameters.

The research design to test these inferences is to regress ingroup relations in one dimension on ingroup relations in numerous others. The prediction is that, though some may be positively and some unrelated to the dependent variable, ultimately one or more should be discovered that are negatively related to it. Van Buren (1991) conducted such a test. He used ethnic *inmarriage* as the dependent variable[20] and entered other forms of *inmarriage* as independent variables. The results support the inference: ethnic inmarriage in the 125 SMSAs in 1970 was positively correlated with mother-tongue inmarriage, evidently a related attribute, and negatively correlated with inmarriage in two respects—region of birth (on the .05 level [two-tailed]) and industry (on the .01 level). The implication is that many people sacrificed these two ingroup choices in order to realize their more important ethnic ingroup choices. (Ethnic inmarriage was not significantly related to five other kinds of inmarriage.)

. . .

The last column in table 3.2 presents the regression of intermarriage on inequality in education, which supports the inequality theorem that inequality furthers status-distant marriage (T-3). Educational intermarriage is also negatively influenced by SEI inequality, which is unexpected, since an individual's education and occupational status exhibit a strong positive correlation.[21] It may be that there is a trade-off between choosing a mate on one's own educational level, even though she is not on one's

---

20. The regression of ethnic intermarriage is not included in table 3.1 because ethnic background is a combination of race and nationality and thus does not provide an independent test. But in its own right, ethnic background corroborates the theorem. The regression equation of ethnic *intergroup* relations on ethnic heterogeneity and other structural influences (corresponding to those in table 3.2) is (IM stands for intermarriage, H for heterogeneity, INEQ for inequality, SE for standard error, and the subscripts E for ethnic, N for nativity, EAR for earnings, and DEOC for detailed occupation)

$$IM_E = 8.244 + .793H_E + 1.539H_N + 8.815INEQ_{EAR} + 159.126H_{DEOC}$$
$$SE: \quad 1.788 \quad .323 \quad .151 \quad 1.974\,68 \quad 68.527$$

21. Inequality in education and in SEI, however, are not strongly correlated for the 125 SMSAs ($r = .23$).

socioeconomic level, and choosing a mate on one's own socioeconomic level, even though she is not on one's educational level. The negative correlation between educational and SES intermarriage ($-.27$) lends some support to this conjecture. In concluding the discussion of table 3.2, one might note that socioeconomic inequality exerts a fairly pervasive adverse effect on the majority of forms of intermarriage. Class differences typically discourage marriage.

Inequality in occupational status and inequality in earnings are also positively related to status-distant marriage in their respective dimension. These findings do not provide a reliable test of the theorem, since the dependent variable was not correctly computed, as Skvoretz has pointed out. This is the reason that these regressions were not included in table 3.2, but they are worth noting, since there are grounds for assuming that the error does not distort the variables unduly. They are therefore presented as information, though they are not considered entirely valid tests of the theory.[22]

Both SEI intermarriage and earnings intermarriage not only are positively related to their respective form of inequality but both are also negatively related to educational inequality (see note 22). This finding lends some support to the above interpretation that people tend to make a choice between spouses on their own socioeconomic though not on their educational level and those who are on their educational though not on their socioeconomic level. The finding that people often give up some choices to make others also supplies another illustration of the choice mechanism and process reflected in Van Buren's analysis.

A paper by Rytina et al. (1988) uses a saturated model based on the same data set to analyze three implications of the inequality theorem—for educational, SEI, and personal- income[23] inequality. The path model in this paper employs inequality in the subsample and status indifference (the complement of status salience) as intervening variables be-

---

22. The equations are presented below. The abbreviations used (in addition to those defined in note 20) all refer to subscripts: SEI to occupational status, ED to education, and BR to birth region.

$$IM_{SEI} = -.808 + 1.007INEQ_{SEI} - .653INEQ_{ED} - .036H_N$$
$$SE: \quad .299 \quad .202 \quad .102 \quad .014$$
$$IM_{EAR} = -.515 + .557INEQ_{EAR} + .093H_{BR} - .293INEQ_{ED}$$
$$SE: \quad .300 \quad .305 \quad .026 \quad .121$$

23. Of the two virtually identical measures of "income," personal income is used in this paper, whereas earnings have been used in the present monograph. The two differ only in the exclusion of unearned income from earnings.

tween SMSA's population inequality and subsample intermarriage. This provides three tests not subject to Skvoretz's (1990: 384–85) criticism, that the measure of intermarriage in the subsample should have used subsample and not population data in the denominator, which is what is used in the analysis by Rytina et al. Besides, this paper traces the direct effect of (subsample) inequality and its indirect effect mediated by status indifference or salience.

The results of the education and the SEI regression analysis are unequivocal. Subsample inequality in education and in occupational status reduces status indifference, which makes status-distant marriage less likely. In other words, inequality increases the salience of status (the inverse of status indifference), which discourages status-distant marriages. But this indirect effect of inequality inhibiting intermarriage is greatly exceeded by the substantial positive effect of structural inequality on intermarriage, owing to the greater prevailing status distance of all the people one meets fortuitously. Hence, the gross effects of inequality are to increase status distance between spouses, even though they make people more sensitive to status differences. This is the case for education and occupational status, but the results for income do not clearly support the theorem, quite possibly because the income of young couples is not a good indication of their income years earlier when they were courting.

INTERSECTION AND INTERMARRIAGE

The theorem of multiple intersection's influence on intergroup relations is the very core of macrostructural opportunity theory. For its influence on our choices is exercised by the constraints that the joint effects the population structure and our earlier choices exert on our remaining options. The concept of intersection refers to the extent to which social differences in various dimensions are independent or weakly related—the degree to which social differences approximate being orthogonal. The empirical measurement of intersection, therefore, entails multivariate analysis.

Many important social differences do not refer to continuous rank orders but to nominal categories, such as racial, ethnic, and religious groups, which poses a problem for empirical research on intersection. In the late 1970s, when the measures for the data set were constructed, regression analysis was the primary procedure used for multivariate analysis. Refinements that could readily take into account combinations of continuous and categorical variables had not yet been developed or, at best, were not widely known. Log-linear analysis was still in its infancy, and LISREL had not yet been perfected. For combining nominal, ordinal, and continuous variables less conventional procedures were used. The procedure devised to measure and analyze multivariate intersection appears rudimentary if not primitive by today's standards.

We started by using three sets of bivariate relationships. For two nominal variables, Cramer's V was used.[24] For a nominal and a continuous variable, we used eta, the square root of the correlation ratio. For two continuous variables, the Pearson correlation was used. The index of educational intersection, for instance, is one minus the mean of the correlations, however measured, of educational inequality with the other forms of inequality and all forms of heterogeneity. The other intersection measures are based on a corresponding procedure (see B&S: 91, 235). In the original tests of the intersection theorem, heterogeneity was held constant (by regressing intermarriage on both intersection and heterogeneity) to ascertain whether both heterogeneity and intersection independently promote intermarriage, as the theory stipulates. The predicted effects of intersection on intermarriage were observed in all cases (and in all but one without any further controls [see B&S: 92–96]).

Skvoretz makes two suggestions for improving the procedure for analyzing intersection. His first (1990: 380) is that nominal relationship should be measured by the asymmetric tau rather than by a symmetric measure. This is a sensible suggestion, since the asymmetric tau improves measurement accuracy compared with a symmetric nominal measure of association, as Skvoretz indicates. Unfortunately, it has not been included in the final data set, which makes it impossible to take advantage of this good suggestion in this reanalysis. Skvoretz's (1990: 380–82, 387–92) other criticism is that the effect of intersection is not independent of but, rather, is contingent on that of heterogeneity or inequality and that appropriate product terms should therefore be substituted for the intersection terms. He applies this procedure to bivariate intersection measures, with considerable success. The argument that the influence of intersection is multiplicative seems plausible, and the influence of interaction terms is explored in the analysis of multivariate intersection below.

The same procedure used in table 3.2 is used in table 3.3. The only change is that in table 3.3 the intersection measure is added to each analysis as the first regressor. Otherwise, the procedures are the same as before: logarithmic transformations; WLS regressions; tolerance of .3;

24. We actually computed other measures for bivariate nominal variables, but Cramer's V was the one incorporated in the final data set.

Table 3.3. Intersection, Differentiation, and Intermarriage

	Intermarriage in					
	Race	Nativity	Birth Region	Industry	Major Occup.	Educ.
Intersection[a]	8.596 (1.560)	5.403 (2.800)	4.406 (2.604)	1.394 (0.438)	6.823 (2.130)	0.656 (0.283)
Differentiation[a]	0.526 (0.233)	2.045 (0.122)	1.659 (0.135)	2.336 (0.562)	0.213* (4.844)	1.174 (0.128)
Control variables						
Race		0.276 (0.116)				
Nativity						
Birth Region	0.667 (0.220)					
Industry						
Major occup.						
Education	2.749 (1.366)					
SEI	−7.637 (2.108)					−0.499 (0.209)
Earnings		8.523 (2.002)				0.675 (0.281)
Constant	−5.866 (3.420)	7.509 (1.729)	0.394 (0.415)	0.337 (0.142)	2.076 (1.120)	0.273 (0.479)
Adjusted R^2	.369	.726	.550	.193	.064	.435

Note: Except for predicted results in first two (four) rows, coefficients for control variables are presented only if significant at 0.5 level (two tailed).

[a] Reference to same attribute in terms of which intermarriage is defined.

* Not significant at 0.5 level (one-tailed).

since intersection and heterogeneity both predict a positive effect on intermarriage, both are included in all regressions to discern their independent effects; the coefficient of these two test variables is accepted on the .05 level (one-tailed); other variables are shown as influences if they are significant on the .05 level (two-tailed).[25] The product terms suggested by

25. The same variables as before—all available forms of heterogeneity and inequality—are used as controls. The intersection measures are not included as controls, because

Skvoretz are not entered in the original table—and for good reason—but they are subsequently analyzed for all regressions.

. . .

Table 3.3 presents six regressions, one in each column. The boxed data in the first two (double) rows ("double," because standard errors are presented below the coefficients) represent the theoretical tests. Six tests of the intersection theorem (T-11) are presented in the first row, all of which have significant positive coefficients, unequivocally corroborating the theorem. Five tests of the heterogeneity theorem (T-2)—with intersection controlled—are shown in the next row, four of which support and one that fails to support the theoretical expectation. Results of tests of the educational intersection and inequality theorems are supplied in the top rows of the last column, which show that both of them independently promote intermarriage, as theoretically expected. The analyses in table 3.3 are better tests of the heterogeneity and the inequality theorems than those in table 3.2, because the parallel influence of intersection is now controlled.

These results are impressive, even though they do not perfectly corroborate all theoretical expectations. Eleven of twelve empirical predictions of the theory are confirmed (and so is another one—for detailed occupations—shown in table 3.2). As reported above, these theorems had been previously supported by tests using simple correlations in raw form (though in three cases only after minor adjustments had been made). To be sure, we have not yet followed Skvoretz's suggestion to introduce product terms in testing the intersection theorem. This must yet be undertaken, but before doing so let us examine the six regressions in table 3.3.

The intersection of race with other social differences exerts a strong influence on racial intermarriage.[26] Much of the discrimination against blacks is rooted in their poor qualifications and deprived conditions produced by centuries of prejudice, oppression, and exploitation. Intersection indicates that these detrimental conditions exhibit relatively weak relationships with race, which accounts for its positive effect on racial intermarriage.

---

the same bivariate items, although usually in different combinations, are used in constructing all of them. (See B&S: 235.)

26. The coefficient is more than 5.5 its standard error, which indicates a significance level of considerably less than .00005.

Racial heterogeneity, which was not significantly related to intermarriage in table 3.2 and was only barely so when a single difference (the white-black SEI ratio) was controlled, now exhibits a clear positive relation to it. Apparently, to accurately reveal structural influences on racial intermarriage requires controlling at least a substantial number of the many serious handicaps blacks suffer in our society, not just the one of their disadvantaged position. Including racial intersection in the analysis effects such control.

Three other structural conditions influence racial intermarriage. Heterogeneity in birth region promotes it, perhaps because, as earlier suggested, it implies the presence of many migrants from other regions who are less integrated than the natives in a community. Inequality in SEI discourages racial intermarriage, in all likelihood because it reflects great socioeconomic differences between racial minorities and the white majority. However, inequality in education undoubtedly also expresses differences between racial minorities and the majority. Thus, one might expect it to discourage racial intermarriage too, but the data show that it makes such intermarriage more likely, provided that SEI inequality and birth-region heterogeneity are controlled.[27]

A possible interpretation treats occupational status (SEI) and education, which are closely related, as two aspects of class differences. If the socioeconomic-status dimension of class is controlled, what remains of education is no longer the status superiority of being well educated but the greater understanding and tolerance education is expected to promote. In other words, by controlling the dominant superior-status dimension of class one may also remove the status-superiority aspect of education and free the more impartial and liberal orientation education is assumed to foster, which makes interracial marriage more likely. To be sure, this is pure speculation, possibly affected by the educational bias of an academic.

Nativity's intersection promotes intermarriage, independent of the parallel influence of heterogeneity on it. Two other factors that encourage intermarriage of nationalities, as shown in table 3.3 (just as in table 3.2), are racial heterogeneity and earnings inequality. The former implies large proportions of blacks and the latter large proportions of poor, which may make spouses of foreign stock a plausible alternative option for the majority of whites of native stock. Since these influences are parallel to those

---

27. Without these two controls, educational heterogeneity's coefficient would not be significant on the .05 (two-tailed) level.

observed in table 3.2, notwithstanding the additional control of intersection, another, and possibly better, interpretation therein suggested is that ethnic diversity encourages tolerance and lowers the disinclination to marry a person of different national descent.

Intersection of birth region encourages intermarriage, independent of heterogeneity's positive effect on it. Similarly, the intersection of industrial affiliation increases intermarriage, independent of industrial heterogeneity's positive effect on it. No other influence on either birth-region or industrial intermarriage has been discovered. These two sets of findings are simply direct manifestations of the intersection theorem (T-3) and the heterogeneity theorem (T-2). Since heterogeneity increases the probability of meeting, getting to know, becoming intimate with, and even marrying a person different from yourself, the findings show this to be the case for diversity of regional origin and of industrial affiliation. Substantial intersection implies a high probability that one's ingroup choices in one dimension entail intergroup relations in others, and the findings indicate that people's salient ingroup choices in other respects lead to intergroup choices in terms of the undoubtedly not very salient differences in regional origin and industrial affiliation.

The only empirical result that fails to conform to theoretical expectations is that the heterogeneity of major occupational groups does not promote occupational intermarriage. This negative finding has already been observed in table 3.2 and was discussed there. We see now that controlling the intersection of major occupations with other social differences does not alter the negative result. This is the case despite the fact that major-occupation intersection has a substantial positive effect on occupational intermarriage. The weaker the correlation of major occupations with other social differences, the higher the rate of major-occupation intermarriage tends to be. Heterogeneity in major occupations, however, is unrelated to occupational intermarriage, the single case negating the theory's implications.[28]

The intersection of education with other social differences also encourages marriages between spouses who differ in education, and so does educational inequality, whether intersection is controlled or not. The table also shows that inequality in occupational status (SEI) discourages educational intermarriage, as it does when intersection is not in the re-

28. No intersection measure for the 444 detailed occupations was constructed. The high cost of doing so made it impossible within the limitations of our budget.

gression (table 3.2). But inequality in earnings encourages educational intermarriage, just as educational inequality does, though this influence is not observed unless educational intersection is controlled (table 3.2). Thus, whereas there seems to be a trade-off between marrying a spouse in one's own educational stratum and marrying a spouse in one's own occupational stratum, as previously noted, inequality in education and income seems to have parallel positive effects on status-distant marriage. Finally, both intersection and inequality in occupational status (SEI) independently promote intermarriage, and so do intersection and inequality in earnings (not shown in table 3.3), in accordance with the theoretical predictions.[29]

We turn now to an examination of whether the use of product terms for intersection yields improvements, as Skvoretz suggests it should. He uses bivariate intersection measures, but after exploring bivariate measures, I decided that multivariate ones better represent my concept of multiple intersecting differences as well as Simmel's of crosscutting circles. Since Skvoretz's formula assumes bivariate intersection,[30] it must be adjusted for the multivariate measure used here. I modified the procedure by first entering the multiple intersection measure, next the corresponding measure of heterogeneity or inequality, and then the product of the two (H∗Int or Ineq∗Int), and only then the control variables that met the criteria of exerting an influence. This was done for the six regressions in table 3.3. In not a single one did the product term's coefficient meet the criterion (significance on the .05 level [one-tailed]).

The reason for this failure may be that the logarithmic transformations also produce multiplicative effects, as product terms do, and the former may have taken account of most departures from linearity, obviating the need for the latter (that is, leaving insufficient departures for the product term to correct). There may be another reason for the failure to obtain interaction effects, namely, that Skvoretz's procedure was not

---

29. The two regression equations, where INT stands for intersection and the other abbreviations are explained in notes 20 and 22, are

$$IM_{SEI} = .943 + 1.276INT_{SEI} + .968INEQ_{SEI} + .070H_{BR}$$
$$SE: \quad .230 \quad\quad .225 \quad\quad\quad .193 \quad\quad\quad\quad .020$$
$$IM_{EAR} = .601 + 1.095INT_{EAR} + .819INEQ_{EAR} + .102H_{BR} + .039H_{N}$$
$$SE: \quad .312 \quad\quad .475 \quad\quad\quad .318 \quad\quad\quad\quad .024 \quad\quad\quad .015$$

30. Skvoretz's (1990: 382) formula is "$Y = b_1X_1 - b_2X_1X_2$, where Y is the appropriate measure of intergroup relations."

precisely followed, for he suggests, as his formula (in note 30) shows, that the interaction effect not be added to the two main effects but, rather, that it be substituted for one of them. Although it is not conventional to do so, and I consider it quite inappropriate, I have made an attempt to duplicate his procedure exactly with my measure of multiple intersection for the six regressions shown in table 3.3.[31]

In four of the six regressions of intermarriage (in nativity, birth region, industry, and education), the product term's coefficient did not meet the criterion of significance, and it did so only in two (intermarriage in race and in major occupation). Since the tests in table 3.3 produced more consistent results, there is no advantage in substituting the use of product terms. Logarithmic transformations, multivariate intersection, and controlling possible other influences provide adequate procedures for testing the theorems, though the rudimentary measure of multivariate intersection surely could be improved.

In sum, a series of empirical tests essentially support the substantive implications of the theorems on intergroup relations and some of their implications for conflict. The theory implies that heterogeneity, inequality, and intersecting social differences in a population structure, whatever their substantive content, promote intergroup relations. The theoretical implications were tested in research on various empirical forms of such structural influences on intermarriage. Early tests based on simple correlations and later ones, including those here presented, based on natural logarithms and regression analysis corroborated the theory. The intersection theorem, which is the structural theory's core, is supported by the positive relationships of all eight independent forms of intersection and intermarriage analyzed. Five of six empirical tests of the influence of heterogeneity on intermarriage revealed the predicted positive relationships, whether or not intersection and other influences were controlled. The only negative case is that heterogeneity and intermarriage in major occupations are not related. Three forms of inequality increase the status difference between spouses, as theoretically expected.[32]

31. For this purpose, the measure of heterogeneity or inequality was entered; the multiple intersection measure was not; instead, the product term of the heterogeneity or inequality and the intersection measure was entered and only then were other influences meeting the criteria admitted.

32. Two of the three inequality measures have a computational flaw, but it apparently does not distort them much, as implied by the parallel results with a flawless measure and other tests of the inequality theorem.

Penetrating Differentiation

The first tests of corollaries about penetrating differentiation were performed by Schwartz (1990). He tested the corollaries that the penetration of heterogeneity or inequality into successively lower levels of subunits increases the chances of intergroup relations. For this purpose, he studied a school system composed of several levels of substructures. Specifically, he investigated two forms of heterogeneity and three forms of inequality observable in eighteen school districts, 245 schools, and 362 grade levels, and he ascertained the extent to which these differences penetrated down into 1,360 classrooms. He then tested the prediction that such penetration increases intergroup friendships. The subjects were 29,090 girls and boys in the third and sixth grades.

The two forms of heterogeneity Schwartz examined are gender and ethnic affiliation (six categories), and the three rank orders of inequality are parental occupation (six ranks) and scales of academic performance and behavior based on teachers' ratings. Social ties are based on reciprocated choices in answer to the question, "How often do you like to do things in class with [check list of names of every student in the classroom]?" (p. 360).[33] Intergroup social ties are the proportion of reciprocated choices involving two pupils whose sex or ethnic background differs, and the social distance of a mutually chosen pair is the average absolute difference between them in social class (ranked parent's occupation), teachers' rating of school performance, or teacher's rating of school behavior.

The results for four of the five differences among students support the theoretical predictions. Ethnic heterogeneity raises the rate of interethnic friendships substantially more if it penetrates into classrooms than if it is confined to higher levels of the school system. Lack of or weak penetration implies that classrooms, schools, or districts are more segregated than the entire school system is. Similarly, inequalities in socioeconomic background, school performance, and behavior in school increase intergroup friendships much more if these differences penetrate into classrooms than if they exist primarily among classrooms, often the result of tracking, or among schools or districts, perhaps owing to differences in neighborhoods.

33. Since only friendships within classrooms were ascertained, Schwartz could not study the influence of penetration on intergroup relations between different classrooms and grades, but he did analyze the influences on intergroup friends of differences *from* different levels that penetrated into classrooms (in separate regressions).

Greater differences between friends in all four respects are observed if the diversity penetrates into classrooms. This is the case whether the differentiation in ethnic or class background, in school performance or behavior within classrooms is compared with the corresponding—but less pronounced—differentiation among grade levels, schools, or school districts. In each of the twelve (four times three) regressions, the unstandardized regression coefficient for penetrating differentiation, with differentiation on the superordinate level controlled, is significant on the .001 level. The proportion of the variance in intergroup relations accounted for is also significantly greater in all twelve comparisons when penetrating differentiation is added to the analysis than when only higher-level differentiation is the regressor.

The young students under consideration readily associated with others who differed from them in ethnic and class origins and in school performance and behavior, provided that the classroom structure created opportunities for doing so. The implication is that school administrators have considerable control over the opportunities of pupils to associate with others who differ in background and academic conduct. These results nicely support the theoretical proposition that multilevel penetration of structural differentiation enhances intergroup relations. There is one important exception, however.

. . .

The negative case is gender. Cross-sex choices are not influenced by penetrating heterogeneity, contrary to the theoretical prediction. As a matter of fact, even the prediction of the basic heterogeneity theorem fails: sexual heterogeneity has no significant bearing on the rate of cross-sex relations among these preteen youngsters. One reason for this is methodological: there is hardly any variation in gender heterogeneity, the girl-boy ratio being uniformly close to 50 : 50. But this very small variation is surely not the only reason for the negative finding; there is also a substantive one.

The great salience of same-sex bonds in the latency period makes preteen youngsters reluctant to risk ridicule by choosing playmates of the opposite sex.[34] A group's consensus (or near-consensus) on the most important ingroup choices creates strong social pressures that make its members greatly resistant to structural constraints that require violating

34. There were a few sociometric choices of the opposite sex, but only one-eighth of the percentage expected by chance.

the social pressures and courting disapproval, if not ostracism. Klansmen do not have African-American friends (nor do the latter have friends in the Klan), regardless of how much racial heterogeneity there is where they live, just as boys and girls in the latency period largely refrain from having friends of the opposite sex.

Consensus on the single most important ingroup choice, however, is rare and usually confined to relatively small groups. It is most rare if not practically impossible in a population of many thousands or millions for nearly everybody to agree on what the most salient ingroup allegiance is and, in addition, even for those who are in agreement never to be compelled by circumstances to violate it. Widespread as racial prejudice still is and particularly was in the 1960s in the United States, for example, it is not so uniform that it prevents any interracial marriages, let alone interracial friendships.

The finding on cross-sex choices in classrooms of primary schools discloses a limitation of the theory of structural influences on intergroup relations that must be acknowledged. However, the very nature of this limitation largely confines it to relatively small groups and makes it most improbable, though not impossible, in large populations. If there is virtual consensus in a population or group on which one ingroup choice is more important than any other and if there is nearly complete conformity in making this ingroup choice in preference to others, this consensus makes persons independent of the structural constraints on intergroup choices stipulated by the theory in this one dimension. Such consensus is unlikely in a large and complex society or community, however, owing to people's multigroup affiliations and the great differences among them on which of their group affiliations is most important. The larger the population, the smaller the probability of consensus that one particular group affiliation is the most vital.[35]

Hence, the theory is most applicable to large populations and is least applicable to small groups. Moreover, a population's adamant insistence on ingroup choices in one or a few respects, in defiance of structural constraints, restricts individuals' freedom of choice in other dimensions and increases the influence of other structural conditions on their intergroup relations in other dimensions. Nevertheless, a qualification of the theory is necessary to take account of the finding that consensus on the

35. In small groups, however, such complete consensus on the primary common enemy as well as on many other matters is not only often observable but serves to sustain the unity of the group and its solidarity.

ingroup affiliation of primary significance inhibits structural effects. To wit, it is assumed that there is not consensus in the entire population that a specific dimension of ingroup affiliation is more important than any other (A-4).

CONCLUSIONS

This chapter has presented empirical tests of the theory formulated in the preceding chapter about the effects of the population structure on intergroup relations. The theoretical terms used are abstract in Simmel's sense of abstracting social forms from their empirical contents, such as competition being a social process abstracted from its empirical expressions, like economic or political competition. In this sense of abstraction, heterogeneity, inequality, and intersection are abstract theoretical terms, which find expression in empirical forms of these structural concepts, such as ethnic or religious heterogeneity, inequality in wealth or political power, and the degree of intersection of various kinds of empirical social differences. Intergroup relations and intermarriage similarly are forms abstracted from differences in particular social affiliations between associates and spouses, respectively.

Thus, testing the theorems involves obtaining empirical data suitable for constructing operational measures of the theoretical concepts. In conceptualizing the theoretical terms, some consideration has to be given to anticipating their translation into operational measures, lest the concepts are so vaguely defined that they defy attempts to operationalize their empirical manifestations, thus making the theory untestable. I realize that my theory may be accused of having gone too far in the opposite direction and employing theoretical terms too close to their operational definitions, but this is necessary at the early stages of the development of a science, lest theorizing become mere speculation that cannot be tested by and hence grounded in empirical research.

The population structure generates opportunities and constraints that govern people's choices of their associates and their careers. Changes in the occupational structure, as we shall see in chapter 4, expand opportunities for some careers and restrict opportunities for others, providing sometimes many opportunities for upward mobility and exerting at other times many constraints to move downward. There is much opportunity for ingroup choices of associates, but the differentiation, multigroup affiliations, and intersecting differences in complex social structures also exert constraints to choose intergroup associates, as shown in chapter 2.

The theory of the structural conditions that govern choices of associates could be couched in somewhat formal terms, and research testing the major theorems has been presented in this chapter.

I first collaborated with a colleague to conduct an empirical study testing the theory's major implications (B&S). Although quite simple procedures were employed in these initial tests—for example, mostly zero-order correlations to test theoretical propositions—the research essentially supported the major theorems. Some criminologists used the theory's propositions about the effect of size distributions on conflict to interpret research findings on victimization in crimes against persons, and a few of these studies have been noted.

Procedures were revised for the new tests reported in this chapter. The major revisions were to transform all variables logarithmically and to use regression analysis in which other structural influences were controlled when testing a theorem positing the influence of one structural parameter on intermarriage. Regressions were performed on the influences exerted on intermarriage by six forms of heterogeneity, three forms of inequality,[36] and eight forms of intersection. All but one of these seventeen regression analyses corroborate the theory. (The exception is major occupation group, for which heterogeneity was not found to promote intermarriage.)

Finally, Schwartz tested corollaries about the penetration of heterogeneity and inequality into substructures. The research is based on more than twenty-nine thousand third-graders and six-graders in a school system. The hypothesis, in Schwartz's (1990: 362) own words, "states that the effect of differentiation on intergroup relations is greater if it penetrates into the subunits of the social structure." This theoretically derived hypothesis is supported by four of the five differences among the pupils examined. The more the entire system's (or one of its subunit's) differentiation among pupils in class and ethnic background and in school performance and behavior penetrates into classrooms and thus is reflected there, the more likely it is that friends differ in these four respects. These findings support the hypothesis, but there is one negative case, namely, gender. Indeed, cross-sex choices, which are very rare, fail to be affected not only by penetrating heterogeneity but even by heterogeneity

---

36. Two of the inequality measures—SEI and earnings inequality—were flawed by a computational error, but there are indications that this error did not affect the validity of the results. One of these two—the one on SEI inequality—is replicated in another paper (Rytina et al. 1988) with an SEI measure not containing this computational error.

itself (whether the heterogeneity in school districts or that on any other
level is examined), which is a negative case of the heterogeneity theorem (T-2).

Both the positive and the negative results of this study have important implications, one for policy and one for theory. The finding that a
community's or school district's class and ethnic diversities discourage
intergroup friendships mostly if these diversities are not mirrored within
classrooms has clear implications for educational administration. If integrative relations between persons with different affiliations and backgrounds are important in our multicultural society, as I think they
certainly are, school boards and administrators have the responsibility to
make provisions to facilitate diversity within schools and classrooms.

Facilitating diversity may require drawing district lines that do not
impose segregated schools on the community, busing pupils to improve
diversity where segregation in housing makes this necessary to develop
integrated schools, and devising other procedures to help local officials
create class and race mixtures in classrooms. Superintendents and prin-
cipals have the responsibility to make classroom assignments that reflect
the diversities of their communities, to bring youngsters from different
backgrounds together, and thereby to promote at early ages positive experiences of relations with diverse playmates and friends.

The finding that cross-sex friendships of preteen pupils, which are
very rare, are not affected by heterogeneity requires a qualification of the
macrostructural theory. The great salience of same-sex bonds in the latency period apparently made gender ingroup choices for the most part
independent of structural conditions. Consensus (or near-consensus) on
the dominant salience of a specific group affiliation makes people's social
relations largely impervious to structural constraints. Skinheads do not
have black or Jewish friends, whatever the population composition where
they live.

Such rigid insistence on some ingroup choices restricts freedom of
choice in other respects and makes other intergroup choices more likely.
Furthermore, perfect consensus on the single most important group affiliation can exist only in relatively small subunits and is hardly, if at all,
feasible in populations of millions. Yet a qualification of the theory is
needed in view of the observed lack of cross-sex choices of preteen youngsters. It is stipulated by the assumption introduced above (A-4): the
theory assumes that there is no perfect consensus in the population that
a particular ingroup choice is of primary importance.

Appendix

Correlations of Intermarriage, Heterogeneity, Inequality, and Intersection

Variable Labels and Descriptions:

RAC _ IML	Race (detailed), Intermarriage, Logged
NAT _ CIML	Nativity, Constrained Intermarriage, Logged
BIR _ CIML	Birth Region, Constrained Intermarriage, Logged
IND _ CIML	Industry (major), Constrained Intermarriage, Logged
OCC1CIML	Occupation (major), Constrained Intermarriage, Logged
OCC2CIML	Occupation (detailed), Constrained Intermarriage, Logged
EDU _ CIML	Education, Constrained Intermarriage, Logged
EAR _ CIML	Earnings, Constrained Intermarriage, Logged
SES _ CIML	Socioeconomic Index, Constrained Intermarriage, Logged
RAC1HETL	Race (white-nonwhite), Heterogeneity, Logged
RAC2HETL	Race (detailed), Heterogeneity, Logged
NAT _ HETL	Nativity, Heterogeneity, Logged
BIR _ HETL	Birth Region, Heterogeneity, Logged
IND _ HETL	Industry (major), Heterogeneity, Logged
OCC1HETL	Occupation (major), Heterogeneity, Logged
OCC2HETL	Occupation (detailed), Heterogeneity, Logged
EDU _ INQL	Education, Inequality, Logged
EAR _ INQL	Earnings, Inequality, Logged
SES _ INQL	Socioeconomic Index, Inequality, Logged
RAC _ INTL	Race, 5-variable Intersection, Logged
NAT _ INTL	Nativity, 7-variable Intersection, Logged
BIR _ INTL	Birth Region, 6-variable Intersection, Logged
IND _ INTL	Industry, 6-variable Intersection, Logged
OCC _ INTL	Occupation, 5-variable Intersection, Logged
EDU _ INTL	Education, 6-variable Intersection, Logged
EAR _ INTL	Earnings, 5-variable Intersection, Logged
SES _ INTL	Socioeconomic Index, 6-variable Intersection, Logged

Correlations of Intermarriage, Heterogeneity, Inequality and Intersection

Correlation Coefficients

	RAC_IML	NAT_CIML	ETH_CIML	BIR_CIML	IND_CIML	OCC_CIML	OCC2CIML	EDU_CIML	EAR_CIML	SES_CIML
RAC_IML	1.0000	.3457**	.4096**	.0979	.2051*	-.1026	.1665	-.0685	-.1941*	-.0507
NAT_CIML	.3457**	1.0000	.9767**	.0473	.0866	.0137	.0290	-.0458	.2143*	-.0652
ETH_CIML	.4096**	.9767**	1.0000	.0523	.1219	.0348	.0538	-.0126	.2125**	-.1015
BIR_CIML	.0979	.0473	.0523	1.0000	-.0390	.0888	-.2109*	.0683	.1597	.0742
IND_CIML	.2051*	.0866	.1219	-.0390	1.0000	.2116*	.4453**	.1088	.1266	.0230
OCC_CIML	-.1026	.0137	.0348	.0888	.2116*	1.0000	.1454	.0883	.0556	-.0230
OCC2CIML	.1665	.0290	.0538	-.2109*	.4453**	.1454	1.0000	-.0201	.0796	.0547
EDU_CIML	-.0685	-.0458	-.0126	.0683	.1088	.0883	-.0201	1.0000	.0225	-.0682
EAR_CIML	.1941*	.2143*	.2125*	.1597	.1266	.0556	.0796	.0225	1.0000	.2424**
SES_CIML	-.0507	-.0652	-.1015	.0742	.0230	-.0230	.0537	-.0682	.2424**	1.0000
RAC1HETL	.0203	-.1906*	-.1689	.2528**	.1221	.1312	.0649	.3125**	-.0366	-.2869**
RAC2HETL	.0388	-.1811*	-.1600	.2401**	.1247	.1296	.0639	.3038**	-.0304	-.2882**
NAT_HETL	.3555**	.7724**	.7534**	.0329	-.1335	-.1085	-.1131	-.0841	.1812*	-.0404
ETH_HETL	.2893**	.5157**	.5230**	.0993	.0400	-.0121	-.0265	.2955**	.0597	-.2179*
BIR_HETL	.2047*	.1997*	.1983*	.6584**	-.0866	.0026	-.2611**	.0321	.3071**	-.0223
IND1HETL	.1541	.0175	.0451	.1465	.3344**	.1391	.0013	.1516	.1386	-.0766
OCC1HETL	.0337	-.1438	-.1394	.2411**	-.0478	-.0711	-.1515	.1197	.0397	.0276
OCC2HETL	.0913	.0544	.0703	-.0010	.1397	.1192	.0556	-.0659	.0133	-.0508

EDU_INQL	−.0696	−.2155*	−.2144*	−.1662	.1013	.0120	.0839	.5284**	−.1807*	−.2409**
EAR_INQL	.0501	.1042	.1219	.1844*	.0620	.1205	−.0804	.1154	.2408**	−.1243
SES_INQL	−.1643	−.2748**	−.3079**	−.1027	−.2303**	−.2599**	−.0323	.0183	−.0556	.2649**
RAC_INTL	.0666	.2571**	.2336**	−.1055	−.0816	−.0530	.0083	−.2656**	.0978	.2798**
NAT_INTL	−.1300	−.2945**	−.2630**	−.0119	.2563**	.3168**	.2658**	−.1064	−.1385	−.0089
BIR_INTL	.1149	.1558	.1718	−.1661	.2138*	.1741	.1804*	−.1416	.0088	.1387
IND_INTL	.1274	.2095*	.2283*	.1722	.2254**	.4385**	.1695	.0323	−.0580	−.0376
OCC_INTL	.1627	.1993*	.2208*	.2341**	.2728**	.3560**	.1332	−.1279	.0727	−.1043
EDU_INTL	−.1463	−.2916**	−.2783**	.0612	.0943	.1386	.1154	−.2026*	.0106	.1314
EAR_INTL	.0586	.0429	.0620	.0586	.0806	.2745**	.0634	−.0944	.1093	.0353
SES_INTL	.0361	−.0241	−.0252	−.0771	.0377	.0668	.1163	−.3938**	.0347	.2683**
Mean	−5.68	−3.67	−3.6	−2.22	−0.45	−0.66	−0.06	−2.11	−0.52	−0.72
Std. dev.	1.48	1.94	1.9	1.39	0.26	1.01	0.08	0.21	0.2	0.16
Minimum	−6.91	−6.91	−6.91	−6.91	−1.6	−6.91	−0.59	−3	−1.1	−1.15
Maximum	−1.2	−1.3	−1.33	−0.45	0	0	0	−1.47	0.71	−0.33
N	125	125	125	125	125	125	125	125	125	125

* Signif. LE .05
** Signif. LE .01 (2-tailed)

Correlation Coefficients

	RAC1HETL	RAC2HETL	NAT_HETL	ETH_HETL	BIR_HETL	IND1HETL	OCC1HETL	OCC2HETL	EDU_INQL	EAR_INQL	SES_INQL
RAC_IML	.0203	.0388	.3555**	.2893**	.2047*	.1541	.0337	.0913	-.0696	.0501	-.1643
NAT_CIML	-.1906*	-.1811*	.7724**	.5157**	.1997*	.0175	-.1438	.0544	-.2155*	.1042	-.2748*
ETH_CIML	-.1689	-.1600	.7534**	.5230**	.1983*	.0451	-.1394	.0703	-.2144*	.1219	-.3079*
BIR_CIML	.2528**	.2401**	.0329	.0993	.6584**	.1465	.2411**	-.0010	-.1662	.1844*	-.1027
IND_CIML	.1221	.1247	-.1335	.0400	-.0866	.3344**	-.0478	.1397	.1013	.0620	-.2303*
OCC_CIML	.1312	.1296	-.1085	-.0121	.0026	.1391	-.0711	.1192	.0120	.1205	-.2599*
OCC2CIML	.0649	.0639	-.1131	-.0265	-.2611**	.0013	-.1515	.0556	.0839	-.0804	-.0323
EDU_CIML	.3125**	.3038**	-.0841	.2955**	.0321	.1516	.1197	-.0659	.5284**	.1154	.0183
EAR_CIML	-.0366	-.0304	.1812*	.0597	.3071**	.1386	.0397	.0133	-.1807*	.2408**	-.0556
SES_CIML	-.2869**	-.2882**	-.0404	-.2179*	-.0223	-.0766	.0276	-.0508	-.2409**	-.1243	.2649*
RAC1HETL	1.0000	.9988**	-.3757**	.3769**	.2706**	.2265*	.1728	.0323	.4623**	.1521	-.1399
RAC2HETL	.9988**	1.0000	-.3652**	.3791**	.2745**	.2316**	.1734	.0353	.4595**	.1512	-.1387
NAT_HETL	-.3757**	-.3652**	1.0000	.5536**	.1221	-.1923*	-.2066*	.0017	-.3380**	-.1192	-.1634
ETH_HETL	.3769**	.3791**	.5536**	1.0000	.1059	.0496	-.0594	-.0381	.2336**	-.0123	-.1776*
BIR_HETL	.2706**	.2745**	.1221	.1059	1.0000	.1855*	.3103**	.0324	-.1707	.3674**	-.1542
IND1HETL	.2265*	.2316**	-.1923*	.0496	.1855*	1.0000	.4217**	.0763	.3160**	.4310**	-.1520
OCC1HETL	.1728	.1734	-.2066*	-.0594	.3103**	.4217**	1.0000	-.0198	.2572**	.4163**	.4101**
OCC2HETL	.0323	.0353	.0017	-.0381	.0324	.0763	-.0198	1.0000	-.1467	-.0774	-.3701*
EDU_INQL	.4623**	.4595**	-.3380**	.2336**	-.1707	.3160**	.2572**	-.1467	1.0000	.0806	.2312*

EAR_INQL	.1521	.1512	-.1192	-.0123	.3674**	.4310**	.4163	-.0774	.0806	1.0000	-.1973*
SES_INQL	-.1399	-.1387	-.1634	-.1776*	-.1542	-.1520	.4101**	-.3701**	.2312**	-.1973*	1.0000
RAC_INTL	-.7944**	-.7930**	.3610**	-.3941**	-.1461	-.2895**	-.2689**	.1037	-.5024**	-.2390**	-.0101
NAT_INTL	.1815*	.1699	-.4098**	-.2172*	-.2109*	-.0526	-.1690	.3715**	-.2121*	-.0655	-.2706**
BIR_INTL	-.3968**	-.3998**	.2302**	-.0529	-.3272**	.0212	-.2324**	.3164**	-.4296**	-.2773**	-.2110*
IND_INTL	.1052	.0984	.0758	.0708	-.0607	.0320	-.3194**	.4485**	-.2037*	-.0699	-.5755**
OCC_INTL	.1479	.1493	.0638	.0420	.1198	.1504	-.2710**	.3491**	-.2651**	-.0249	-.5030**
EDU_INTL	-.0991	-.1090	-.2180*	-.3117**	-.1492	-.1433	-.2053*	.2242*	-.4069**	-.3419**	-.0808
EAR_INTL	.0100	.0114	.0469	-.0687	-.0803	-.0889	-.2142*	.2232*	-.2726**	-.1037	-.1259
SES_INTL	-.4813**	-.4819**	.1200	-.3791**	-.2267*	-.3274**	-.2872**	.3608**	-.6611**	-.3886**	-.0965
Mean	-1.91	-1.9	-1.55	-0.91	-1.10	-0.14	-0.14	-0.01	-1.8	-0.77	-1.12
Std. dev.	0.81	0.82	0.79	0.36	0.54	0.03	0.01	0	0.12	0.05	0.05
Minimum	-4.35	-4.34	-3.67	-2.56	-2.74	-0.27	-0.18	-0.02	-2.07	-0.97	-1.32
Maximum	-0.74	-0.3	-0.38	-0.24	-0.22	-0.10	-0.11	-0.01	-1.51	-0.64	-0.92
N	125	125	125	125	125	125	125	125	125	125	125

* Signif. LE .05
** Signif. LE .01 (2-tailed)

Correlation Coefficients

	RAC_INTL	NAT_INTL	BIR_INTL	IND_INTL	OCC_INTL	EDU_INTL	EAR_INTL	SES_INTL
RAC_IML	.0666	-.1300	.1149	.1274	.1627	-.1463	.0586	.0361
NAT_CIML	.2571**	-.2945**	.1558	.2095*	.1993*	-.2916**	.0429	-.0241
ETH_CIML	.2336**	-.2630**	.1718	.2283*	.2208*	-.2783**	.0620	-.0252
BIR_CIML	-.1055	-.0119	-.1661	.1722	.2341**	.0612	.0586	-.0771
IND_CIML	-.0816	.2563**	.2138*	.2254*	.2728**	.0943	.0806	.0377
OCC_CIML	-.0530	.3168**	.1741	.4385**	.3560**	.1386	.2745**	.0668
OCC2CIML	.0083	.2658**	.1804*	.1695	.1332	.1154	.0634	.1163
EDU_CIML	-.2656**	-.1064	-.1416	.0323	-.1279	-.2026*	-.0944	-.3938**
EAR_CIML	.0978	-.1385	.0088	-.0580	.0727	.0106	.1093	.0347
SES_CIML	.2798**	-.0089	.1387	-.0376	-.1043	.1314	.0353	.2683**
RAC1HETL	-.7944**	.1815*	-.3968**	.1052	.1479	-.0991	.0100	-.4813**
RAC2HETL	-.7930**	.1699	-.3998**	.0984	.1493	-.1090	.0114	-.4819**
NAT_HETL	.3610**	-.4098**	.2302**	.0758	.0638	-.2180*	.0469	.1200
ETH_HETL	-.3941**	-.2172*	-.0529	.0708	.0420	-.3117**	-.0687	-.3791**
BIR_HETL	-.1461	-.2109*	-.3272**	-.0607	.1198	-.1492	-.0803	-.2267*
IND1HETL	-.2895**	-.0526	.0212	.0320	.1504	-.1433	-.0889	-.3274**
OCC1HETL	-.2689**	-.1690	-.2324**	-.3194**	-.2710**	-.2053*	-.2142*	-.2872**
OCC2HETL	.1037	.3715**	.3164**	.4485**	.3491**	.2242*	.2232*	.3608**
EDU_INQL	-.5024**	-.2121*	-.4296**	-.2037*	-.2651**	-.4069**	-.2726**	-.6611**

	RAC_INTL	NAT_INTL	BIR_INTL	IND_INTL	OCC_INTL	EDU_INTL	EAR_INTL	SES_INTL
EAR_INQL	-.2390**	-.0655	-.2773**	-.0699	-.0249	-.3419**	-.1037	-.3886**
SES_INQL	-.0101	-.2706**	-.2110*	-.5755**	-.5030**	-.0808	-.1259	-.0965
RAC_INTL	1.0000	-.1301	.4236**	.1206	.0690	.1033	.1921*	.5753**
NAT_INTL	-.1301	1.0000	.3662**	.5803**	.5066**	.6387**	.3971**	.5139**
BIR_INTL	.4236**	.3662**	1.0000	.5130**	.5273**	.5885**	.4670**	.7203**
IND_INTL	.1206	.5803**	.5130**	1.0000	.7612**	.4618**	.5307**	.4711**
OCC_INTL	.0690	.5066**	.5273**	.7612**	1.0000	.5790**	.6648**	.4589**
EDU_INTL	.1033	.6387**	.5885**	.4618**	.5790**	1.0000	.5456**	.7517**
EAR_INTL	.1921*	.3971**	.4670**	.5307**	.6648**	.5456**	1.0000	.5462**
SES_INTL	.5753**	.5139**	.7203**	.4711**	.4589**	.7517**	.5462**	1.0000
Mean	-0.21	-0.13	-0.14	-0.33	-0.39	-0.48	.30	-0.39
Std. dev.	0.08	0.04	0.03	0.04	0.03	0.05	.03	0.05
Minimum	-0.45	-0.29	-0.23	-0.46	-0.49	-0.66	-.40	-0.55
Maximum	-0.08	-0.08	-0.08	-0.27	-0.33	-0.38	-.25	-0.30
N	125	125	125	125	125	125	125	125

* Signif. LE .05
** Signif. LE .01 (2-tailed)

FOUR

OCCUPATIONAL CHANCES

A SOCIETY'S DIVISION OF LABOR is its social structure, which governs the population's occupational chances. The occupational distribution of a society's members indicates their probabilities of ending up in various lines of work. This distribution does not remain constant, however. It changes in response to variations in the economy's demand for different services, as well as to variations in other conditions, such as number of years of schooling, age at retirement, and the proportion of women in the labor force. These changes make it impossible to predict occupational chances on the basis of the occupational structure at any given time. Nevertheless, gross comparisons between highly and less developed countries and different historical periods that are far apart can be made, because the changes occur more or less gradually.

By governing the probabilities that a population's members pursue various occupations, the occupational structure creates career opportunities but simultaneously imposes limits on career choices that constrain many people to make a living in jobs in which they have little if any interest. Which occupations are looked upon as opportunities and which ones as misfortunes entered under constraint depends in good part on the social origins of persons. The same occupation may be looked upon as a great opportunity by some persons and as a misfortune by others, depending partly on whether it represents an improvement given their socioeconomic background or the opposite, and partly on personal and other considerations. The implication is that the direction of intergenerational mobility substantially affects which careers are looked upon as opportunities.

The first section of this chapter, after briefly illustrating the significance of national differences in occupational structure for career opportunities, analyzes a recent suggestion for studying mobility chances and how it can be used to improve the analysis of occupational mobility. The second section raises the question of who benefits from the existing occupational opportunities and seeks to answer it by analyzing the influences of individual differences on careers, with emphasis on education's role as a mediator between background handicaps or advantages and occupational success. This leads to a discussion of Boudon's (1974) paradox of the opposite influences of an individual's education and the population's educational level, another indication of the contrasting influences exerted by an attribute characterizing individuals and the same attribute when it characterizes the population structure.

Internal structural differences among economic sectors, industries, and firms affect labor demand and employment conditions, as has been emphasized in the recent literature on labor markets. The third section presents a critical review of some literature and research on this subject and the controversies they have aroused. The final section analyzes social mobility, with special emphasis on the contrast between structural mobility and circulation mobility and the changes in them in the United States and other countries during this century.

Three major issues are discussed in this chapter. First, the analysis of structural mobility must take into account internal moves within the occupational structure, not merely changes of it, as is usually done. Second, the two major forms of social mobility in a population—structural and circulation mobility—can be expressed in terms of structural parameters, but quite different procedures are used in the two cases. Third, emergent population characteristics influence both opportunities, as exemplified by the occupational structure, and the chances of achieving them, as exemplified by differences in background and education.

OCCUPATIONAL STRUCTURE

The division of labor is a fundamental characteristic of a society and a major component of its economy and its social structure. Both the economy's productivity and development and the population's careers and life chances depend on it. This is reflected in the fact that one of the major classics of economics and one of the major classics of sociology start by analyzing the division of labor and its significance—*The Wealth of Nations* (Smith 1776) and *De la division du travail social* (Durkheim 1893).

The distribution of the labor force among occupational positions reflects the division of labor. The more specific the subdivision of work one wants to consider, the narrower must be the occupational classes, which can range from broad occupational groups to detailed occupations and even to narrower specialities. If most workers are engaged in the same type of work, say, farming, or the same specific task, say, picking cotton, the division of labor is less pronounced than if workers are more evenly distributed among different positions. Narrower definitions of social positions define people's work and the division of labor more precisely, but research, especially mobility research, tends to use broad occupational categories. (Alternatively, it may transform detailed occupations into a measure of occupational status, such as Duncan's [1961] socioeconomic index [SEI], but this refers to a form of hierarchical status and no longer to the division of labor.) A possible indication of the probability in a society of entering various occupations is the proportion of the labor force in various occupations.

The occupational structure can be considered the social matrix of the occupational chances the population's labor force has experienced. It indicates the probabilities that members of the labor force have of achieving various occupational positions. However, the occupational structure does not remain constant but continually changes as the result of industrial and economic developments. Hence, the existing occupational distribution does not accurately reflect the changed opportunities of new entrants to the labor force. Nevertheless, these changes are not so great that they entirely obscure the large dissimilarities among societies that vary substantially in industrialization.

National differences in the division of labor of countries that are far apart in economic development are so great that their differences in occupational structure and chances outweigh the changes in them that occur in a few decades. For instance, the chances of becoming a professional are better in the United States than in the People's Republic of China, and the constraint of having to end up in farm work is far greater in China than in America, because the proportion of Chinese peasants is twenty times that of American farm workers,[1] and the proportion of professionals here substantially exceeds that there.[2]

---

1. In 1989, the proportion of Chinese farm workers was 58.7 percent (State Statistical Bureau, China, 1990: 115) and that of American farm workers was 2.8 percent of the labor force (computed from U.S. Bureau of the Census 1991a: 397). The rapid changes in the Chinese economy may very soon make, if they have not already done so, the figure for China obsolete. Yet the difference reported is so large that these changes would not entirely erase it.

2. The categories included under *professional* are too dissimilar to make percentage comparison meaningful, though they indicate that the difference between the two countries is far less for professionals than for farm workers.

Changes in the occupational structure engender changes in people's life chances and in the probabilities of intergenerational mobility, which may be in either direction, depending on the change in occupational distribution. Thus, there was much upward mobility in the United States during most of this century. These extensive opportunities for upward social mobility were in large part the result of changes in industrial composition and the division of labor, primarily the large-scale moves of millions of people from farm to industrial work, reinforced by differential fertility and immigration. In recent years, however, the trend has been reversed: upward mobility is declining, downward mobility is increasing, and so are poverty and unemployment, undoubtedly in part the result of shifts from industrial to service jobs.

The difference between the occupational distribution of the current labor force and that of their parents indicates structural mobility. Specifically, the sum of the same-sign differences in a mobility matrix between the corresponding marginals (the row and column subtotals) discloses the extent of upward or downward structural mobility. This is the case not only for a mobility matrix of respondents and their parents but also for a matrix of the labor force at two time periods. For example, the extensive upward mobility observed in the United States during much of this century has been largely the result of the great changes in the occupational structure. Between 1900 and 1970, the four lowest-ranking (of eleven) major occupational groups (private household workers, nonfarm laborers, farm laborers, and farmers) were the only ones whose proportions declined,[3] whereas all other seven occupational groups increased proportionately, white-collar occupations more than manual ones.

But what does this number represent? Does it refer to the degree of mobility experienced by the sample, whatever *degree of mobility* may mean? It clearly does not indicate the number or proportion of the sample (or population) who have experienced mobility. A difference between professionals and farm-labor parents of 5 percent surely does not mean

3. The ranking is based on Duncan's SEI (1961: 155, table VII-4). The decrease in the proportion of farmers contributed most to the decline of the four lowest categories; their proportion diminished from more than one-half in 1900 to less than 10 percent in 1970. (The population percentages are computed from the data in U.S. Bureau of the Census 1975: 139.) Whereas the low ranking of farmers is sometimes questioned, Ganzeboom, Treiman, and Ultee (1991: 283) imply that farmers' socioeconomic status (Duncan's SEI) is low and state that "sons of farmers who leave farming tend to be concentrated in low status (and low prestige) unskilled and semiskilled jobs." This implies a generally low status of farm workers, since moves from rural to urban jobs tend to raise socioeconomic status.

that 5 percent of the children of farm laborers have become professionals. Very few, if any, of them have made such a dramatic jump. Many probably became unskilled and some skilled factory workers, and some children of industrial workers became salespersons, and a few of the children of salespersons may have moved up to professional jobs. But the numbers of all these persons who experienced short-distance moves, which are most prevalent, do not appear in the measure of structural mobility computed from the broad categories in the mobility matrices used.

The gross effects of structural mobility derivable from a mobility matrix, pronounced as they were earlier in this century, do not exhaust the full impact the dramatic changes in the division of labor had on social mobility. For these changes also had indirect effects (and I do not refer to circulation mobility, which will be discussed later). Most mobility entails short-distance moves. Moves from lower to higher positions stimulate additional moves, so that the total mobility generated is greater than the difference between the distribution of social origins and that of occupational destinations, which is how structural mobility is usually defined. An analysis of short-term change in occupational structure and mobility can make this apparent.

. . .

Harrison (1988) studied short-term changes in the division of labor and the multiplicative effect of short-distance mobility on rates of mobility. For this purpose, he adapted White's (1970) model of vacancy chains in organizations to an analysis of demand in a national labor market. White's study of mobility of the clergy in Protestant denominations reconceptualizes individuals' upward mobility as downward moves of vacancies. For an Episcopal rector to move from a smaller to a larger church, there has to be a vacancy, possibly because the previous incumbent was promoted to coadjutor bishop. Thus, any promotion not only fills a vacancy but also creates a new one for someone else to fill. White conceptualizes this process as downward moves of vacancies.

Long chains of downward movements of vacancies create multiple opportunities for promotions. Since most promotions in formal organizations are short-distance moves, they create multiple opportunities for upward mobility. This important insight of White's cannot be fully appreciated, as the dependence of promotions on vacancies is only natural in formal hierarchies, until it is applied to the open labor market of a national economy. Harrison was the first, to my knowledge, to attempt to do so. (It has been previously applied to internal labor markets, for instance, by Stewman and Konda 1983.)

While stressing his great debt to White's model, Harrison points out that the vacancy-chain concept cannot be directly applied to national labor markets, because these do not have the hierarchies of official positions that characterize formal organizations. Harrison (1988: 7) stresses that "national occupational structures are neither tight nor decomposable into individually demarcated and identifiable fixed jobs." The absence of a close fit between jobs and incumbents has the result that layoffs often leave no vacancies to be filled while expansions elsewhere create different new vacancies. This condition precludes the analysis of occupational mobility in terms of the pull of specific vacancies. Since he considers White's assumptions not justified for national economies, Harrison (1988: 9) replaces them with two new ones for the study of opportunities in large open labor markets: (1) occupational structures "can be decomposed into occupational strata . . . [that require] occupational labor forces of exogenously predetermined sizes" and (2) economic processes "exogenously generate net aggregate demand for additional labor within each occupational stratum."

In short, net aggregate demand for various occupational services is substituted for vacant positions as the driving force of career moves and occupational opportunity in general. Harrison estimated the expanding (or contracting) demand for a category of occupational services on the basis of three components. The first is the difference in the size of an occupational group in a short time interval (less than ten years). This difference represents new jobs created minus jobs terminated or abolished in an occupational stratum, because information on these separate factors is not known, but the difference between them in every stratum is. Second, added to the difference is the number of retirements (and departures for any other reason),[4] which also create demand for replacements.

The third component is the demand created by openings that result from moves of persons who are already in the labor force, since such moves, like promotions, leave unfilled positions, thus creating new opportunities in the process of taking advantage of existing ones. The idea derives from White's analysis of vacancy chains. Upward mobility, just as promotions, may set off chain reactions of upward mobility from

---

4. Harrison (1988: 10) adds explicitly to his formula only retirements, possibly because he implicitly assumes that other departures are included in this term.

successively lower levels, thereby multiplying opportunities for short-distance mobility. White (1970: 25–26, 217–23) shows that the number of additional moves resulting from a promotion can be derived from the multiplier effect used in Keynesian economics, which Harrison adopts as the third component of expanding demand.[5]

In sum, the opportunities to enter an occupation (or the need to leave it) during a limited period depend not only on new positions, resulting from its expansion or contraction and from retirements and other departures in that period, but also on the multiplier effect. The latter is engendered by the mobility of insiders from lower to higher positions, which leaves unfilled positions that provide opportunities to move up from lower levels. How much this process of advancements of existing members of the labor force expands opportunities depends on the level on which new members enter the labor force and on the level on which new positions emerge owing either to departures of old members or to increasing demand.

The higher the level of entry into the labor force (in White's terms, the level at which vacancies leave the system), the weaker is the multiplier effect. In contrast, the higher the level on which new positions emerge, whether as the result of expansion or of retirements and other departures, the stronger is the multiplier. High positions occupied by outside entrants to the labor force, such as newly trained surgeons, do not produce, as insider advancements do, unfilled positions that provide further opportunities for mobility from lower levels. But many entrants to the labor force on bottom levels, as exemplified by the large waves of immigrant workers around 1900, preempt the least advantageous jobs and increase the demand for occupational services on levels above them. If occupations on high levels expand (and are not occupied by outsiders), advancements to them mostly come from levels just below and thus are likely to start chain reactions of advancements entailing high rates of short-distance upward mobility.

The parameter scheme is well suited to the analysis of occupational structures and mobility. I postpone the full analysis of it until we have examined the various aspects of this topic in conventional terms. This is why I have not mentioned parameters in the preceding discussion, but

5. Harrison's (1988: 15) equation (without subscripts) is, $M = D(I - Q)^{-1}$, where M is occupational opportunities; D is the occupation's size difference between the end and the beginning of the period, plus retirements; and $(I - Q)^{-1}$ is the multiplier effect represented by the inverse matrix.

now its applicability should at least be indicated. The division of labor may well be the most important nominal parameter in industrial society. It is the form of heterogeneity that reflects the country's industrialization and economic development.

Positions in the occupational structure exert a pervasive influence on contemporary life. Specific occupations can be ranked by a measure of occupational status—the most widely used is Duncan's (1961) SEI—on the basis of which one can ascertain the population's inequality in occupational status. Thus, measures can be derived from the occupational structure for comparative studies of the extent of the division of labor (a form of heterogeneity) and the degree of occupational inequality (a pervasive aspect of inequality) in different countries or their subunits.[6]

Occupational differences are typically correlated with various other differences, partly because they tend to require different amounts of training and vary in financial and other rewards. Indeed, the SEI measures occupational status on the basis of such differences—the prevailing education and income in an occupation. In the terms used here, this measure of occupational status is an indication of the degree of consolidation of a nominal and two graduated parameters. Even when such a measure is not used, occupations are usually ranked in empirical studies (an early American ranking is that of Edwards 1943). The typical mobility matrix cross-classifies the respondents' occupations with their parents' in the same rank order to analyze upward and downward mobility. The diagonal represents the consolidation of respondents' ranked occupational position and that of their social origins.

Since differences in occupation and socioeconomic origin are related to many other differences, such as ethnic, religious, and national background, it would be of interest to ascertain how strongly occupational status and social origin are consolidated with these other differences in various countries. (Comparative research on the origin-destination relationship, which is rare, is noted below.) The hypothesis suggested by the theory is that the more occupational—or origin—differences are consolidated with other differences, the greater is their impact on people's lives. It would also be of interest to explore which factors are most strongly

6. High rates of upward mobility, which are sometimes considered an indication of relative equality of opportunity, must not be confused with degree of inequality of resources or status, however measured. They may reduce inequality, but only if they are not counteracted by higher rates of advancement of higher than lower strata or rates of downward mobility or an influx of poor immigrants. One of these is often the case.

related to differences in occupation and social origin in various countries and the implications of these national variations. Weak correlations of occupation with the other factors represent intersecting differences, which are expected to counteract or minimize the effects of specific differences. As a matter of fact, intersection is useful to conceptualize one particular aspect of social mobility in a population—circulation mobility—but its analysis requires fuller explication, which will be provided presently.

Who Benefits from Career Opportunities?

The occupational structure, which reflects the demand for different occupational services, governs the total population's chances or probabilities of attaining various occupational positions. But these chance expectations only affect the population at large—how many people are in demand for various positions—and they do not determine who will fill some positions rather than others. Which persons benefit from the advantageous opportunities society's division of labor supplies and which ones are constrained to making a living in disadvantageous positions depends on individual differences in attributes furthering or impeding various careers. The qualifications required or preferred for the most desirable occupations promote career chances, and so do personal qualities that make favorable impressions. Objective deficiencies in skills and knowledge impede career opportunities, as do personal traits that are generally disliked, particularly membership in minority groups that suffer widespread discrimination. In general, differences among the individuals in the labor force govern who benefits from the best opportunities and who must settle for undesirable jobs.

Differences in family background are of special significance for career opportunities. First, they endow the child with a number of ascribed attributes—race, religion, gender, ethnic affiliation, nationality, region, and others. Since numerous ascribed minorities are widely discriminated against, majority groups automatically enjoy career advantages in employment,[7] notwithstanding the assumption in meritocratic society that

---

7. In economic terms, discrimination supplies members of majority groups with a rent, the amount of income beyond the minimum required to obtain the services rendered. (This application of the term *rent* is derived from Sorensen 1992.)

market decisions, including those in labor markets, are based on strictly rational, universalistic criteria. (Universalism is not universal, even in economic decisions in capitalist societies.)

The socioeconomic status of the families in which children are raised has a profound impact on their development and their likelihood of benefiting from opportunities in the labor market. This is the second general reason for the great importance of family origins for careers. The economic and social composition of the neighborhood where the family lives for the most part determines who the children's friends will be, and those friends have an enormous effect on children's early activities and interests. Children's mental development depends substantially on the style of life and atmosphere in their families, including conversations at meals, the friends who visit, the relative importance of books and television, and the extent to which parents share their serious interests with their offspring. Some of these factors are only indirectly affected by the financial resources of the family, but some are affected quite directly, such as children's exposure to concerts and travel. Differences in such conditions nurture in the adolescent more or less cultural capital, in Bourdieu's (1984) terms, and an interest to expand it further.

Education, particularly if its quality as well as quantity (years of schooling) is taken into account, probably exerts the strongest influence on occupational chances in developed countries. In the United States, empirical studies indicate that the influence of years of education on occupational status is stronger than any other influence discovered. If qualitative differences and vocational training were also considered, the influence of schooling on careers would undoubtedly be seen to be still more pronounced. Family origins influence educational attainment, both because the social interaction in the family no doubt affects children's interests in learning and because the family's economic conditions directly influence the offspring's chances of obtaining a superior education. Accordingly, education may be considered a significant mediator between family origins and occupational achievements.

One may divide the study of people's working lives into two main stages, a preparatory stage during which one examines the conditions that affect educational attainment and a second stage during which one examines the conditions affecting occupational achievement. The major influence on education is family origin, but it is complemented and mediated by numerous other factors. These include the ascribed positions that the family produces in its offspring, such as race, religion, and nationality; the family's economic conditions, which help or limit the education attainable, as well as its willingness to make economic sacrifices for the children's education; the influence of peers and friends; the accessibility of good schools and universities; and the students' own commitment to education. The education acquired becomes the major influence on careers, but it also is complemented by others, such as continuing influences of family background, shifts of employment that advance careers, and decisions and moves in one's current employment that result in promotions.

. . .

But where are the structural parameters in the study of the differences between individuals that govern who benefits from structural opportunities? Their effects were not visible, just as they are not visible in any survey of a sample of individuals in a single population. Structural parameters are attributes of populations, and their influences cannot be detected in a study of a single population, just as one cannot empirically ascertain the influences of individual characteristics by studying one person but only by comparing many persons. A person's origins influence his education, for example, and an individual's race influences her occupation, which are links of individual attributes studied in sampling surveys. In contrast, a society's degree of racial heterogeneity or of intersection of racial with other social differences influences the opportunities or probabilities of all its members. This effect on chances is the same for all members of a society[8] and thus cannot be detected except by comparing *societies* that differ in racial heterogeneity or intersection.[9]

The differences among individuals analyzed to suggest who benefits from structural opportunities were just that—*individual* differences. The distribution of these individual differences describes a structural parameter. For example, the distribution of people among occupations describes

8. This is the case of heterogeneity and intersection, which are symmetrical, but not for inequality, which is asymmetrical. Income inequality in social origin or socioeconomic status implies that some persons have better opportunities than others, but to detect the extent of such differences does require comparisons of populations.

9. The invisibility of effects of population conditions in the study of one population is analogous to that of what Burt (1992: 181 and passim), in an original network analysis, calls structural holes. Structural holes refer to the *absence* of relations between a person's associates, which affect her opportunities without being visible to her or her even knowing of their existence.

occupational heterogeneity or the division of labor in a society (or community or organization). The vacancies occurring in this distribution of the occupational structure have been estimated by Harrison in order to analyze the way the changing occupational structure creates occupational opportunities.

The social differences among individuals in a population sample are the variables that are analyzed in regular survey research. Individuals' distribution in race may be one variable, their distribution in income another. In macrostructural analysis, however, such distributions in a population are not variables but measures of the attributes of one case on a variable, such as *this* population's racial heterogeneity or income inequality. Macrostructural analysis of empirical relationships requires data on racial heterogeneity and income inequality and other parameters from numerous populations (or time periods) to determine, for instance, how racial heterogeneity is related to income inequality.

Chapter 1 emphasized that population structures have emergent properties, but this does not mean that the roots from which these properties emerge do not exist among the individual members of the population that they characterize. Of course they do; where else would they come from? They are emergent only by being conceptualized not as variables distinguishing individuals but as an attribute of the social structure; not as ethnic differences among individuals but as the population's ethnic heterogeneity; not as educational differences but as degree of educational inequality in a community. Emergent properties of populations would not exist without the different attributes of individuals, but they have distinct effects from individuals' own attributes, effects that are the same for the entire population but different from the emergent properties of other populations. They could not exist were it not for the attributes of individuals, but they refer to new social conditions resulting from combinations of individual attributes that are characteristic of the population structure and affect all its members.

A third and particularly important structural attribute—in addition to heterogeneity and inequality—refers to the concomitant variations of several dimensions, whether they are strongly correlated (consolidation) or weakly correlated (intersection). The degree to which several differences among individuals are related clearly refers to a population, not to any individual, and can be empirically studied only by comparing populations. Social differences discourage intermarriage, and correlated ones that consolidate group barriers discourage it even more. To illustrate the practical as well as theoretical significance of studying such structural influences by comparing populations, a brief review of data fully analyzed in the preceding chapter is presented.

Ingroup marriages prevail, and social differences discourage intermarriage, especially when it comes to highly salient attributes like race. Indeed, racial intermarriage is very rare in the United States, and when metropolitan areas are compared intermarriage is not significantly correlated to the racial heterogeneity or intersection there, contrary to the theory's implications. Without further analysis one might attribute this simply to the pronounced prevailing racial prejudice and consider it a finding disconfirming the theory. However, it is known that racial differences are related to numerous other differences: on the average, blacks have less education, less desirable occupations, inferior incomes, and lower socioeconomic status than whites. When these other differences are controlled, one finds that racial intersection promotes racial intermarriage, and so does, independently, racial heterogeneity, as theoretically expected (see first column in table 3.3).

. . .

Boudon's education paradox reveals dramatically how the combination of individual attributes in a population may counteract the effects of these attributes. It also discloses that this can happen for certain conditions even if the individual attributes do not refer to the dispersion of attributes among persons, as structural parameters do, but to their prevalence as summarized by their mean. Boudon starts with a puzzle originally pointed out by Anderson (1961). Although educational attainment and occupational achievement, which are highly correlated, are both strongly influenced by social origin, the influence of social origin on education and that of origin on occupational success (as indicated by the two correlations) are not substantially related.[10] Boudon infers from this result that educational improvements may not give rise to occupational advancement, and in the process of analyzing the reason for this he poses a structural paradox.

10. This puzzle involves a correlation between two correlations (that between origin's and destination's education and that between origin's and destination's occupation), and though it is surprising it is not statistically implausible that a correlation between two correlations is weaker than either of the two (see Blau and Duncan 1967: 195–96). But the fact that it is statistically possible does not answer the surprising substantive result that educational and occupational mobility are only weakly related.

Since educational qualifications contribute to occupational achievement in industrial societies, individuals have incentives to improve their career chances by acquiring as much education as possible. Aggregate occupational opportunities, however, as distinguished from the comparative occupational chances of individuals, depend largely on the occupational services in demand in the labor market. The pursuit of superior education by many persons to improve their occupational chances raises the level of education in the population. But a higher prevailing level of education in a country has little effect on occupational opportunities, which are exogenously determined by economic demand.[11] Consequently, fewer positions are available for qualified candidates; there is more competition for available opportunities; and returns to education decline. Since the best educated candidates continue to have the best chance to obtain any given position, it continues to be rational to pursue superior education, which creates the paradox.

The rational choice of individuals to increase their years of education, which is an effective means to improve their occupational chances, has the aggregate result that levels of education in the population rise. This growing supply of educated labor, without a corresponding increase in occupational opportunities, which are determined primarily by economic demand, not by labor supply (notwithstanding the special case mentioned in the preceding note), reduces the occupational returns to education. It is also likely to raise the amount of education employers demand for any given job, since there are now better qualified candidates for most positions.

In Boudon's (1974: 198) words: "Every individual has a definite advantage in trying to obtain as much education as possible. . . . But as soon as all individuals want more education, the expectations associated with most educational levels tend to degenerate, and this has the effect of inciting people to demand still more education in the next period." The rational decision of individuals to acquire substantial education in order to achieve rewarding occupational positions has the paradoxical result in a population that the same education now achieves less rewarding

---

11. Boudon does not deal at all with the possibility that changes in available levels of training and skills may sometimes indeed create new occupational opportunities. There are undoubtedly occasions when technological advancements are retarded by lack of qualified personnel, and in such situations the supply of workers with superior training would give firms incentives to hire better qualified persons than had been previously available, improving their profits and simultaneously raising returns to superior education.

positions than it did before and that, to achieve as rewarding a position as one's parent had, more education is required now than was before.

Boudon's paradox raises a question about the theoretical scheme presented. I have emphasized that emergent structural properties refer to differences among people and not to average characteristics, not to people's average income but to their differences in it reflected in income inequality, not to society's prevailing religion but to its religious diversity or heterogeneity. Boudon's analysis indicates, however, that rising levels of education—which are equivalent to increases in mean education—effect changes in career chances. Does this result imply that mean characteristics of populations should also be considered emergent structural properties that circumscribe opportunities and constraints?

Some mean characteristics of populations probably should be considered *emergent* properties, such as gross national product per capita as indication of economic development, mean income as indication of average standard of living, and mean education as reflecting the nature of labor supply, as Boudon shows. Yet I consider it preferable to restrict the term *structural* property to those conditions in a population that refer to differentiation among its members—the variations and concomitant variations in different respects among them. The very gist of structure is differentiation—to be composed of different subunits and elements. The dictionary gives a quite similar definition of the word *structure:* "Something made up of more or less interdependent elements or parts."

Although Boudon's analysis refers to changed levels or means of education, these are not the structural conditions that determine and limit occupational opportunities.[12] Rather, they describe the qualifications of individuals that govern their chances to benefit from the structural opportunities. Changes in the occupational structure are what governs occupational opportunities, as illustrated by the expansion of positions for professionals, technicians, managers, and officials and the contraction of positions for farm workers and unskilled laborers earlier this century. These changes in the occupational structure did indeed improve opportunities for upward mobility, just as the more recent decline in industrial and increase in unskilled service jobs lowered the opportunities for upward mobility and increased the likelihood of downward mobility and poverty.

Opportunities exist for the entire population, but the qualifications

12. This idea was first suggested by Judith R. Blau (personal communication).

that govern the chances of being able to take advantage of the available opportunities are one's own relative to those of others interested in the same occupations. If the average level of education for certain types of jobs rises and one's own also rises but not as much, one's relative qualifications have declined; only if my education rises faster than the average do my qualifications improve. It is the significance of *relative* qualifications that accounts for Boudon's paradox, and its significance also accounts for the policy implication of Boudon's analysis that equality of opportunity cannot substantially reduce economic inequalities.

ECONOMIC SECTORS AND LABOR DEMAND

The first national studies of social mobility in the United States (Blau and Duncan 1967; Featherman and Hauser 1978) examined essentially how individual attributes affect occupational achievement. They analyzed how careers are influenced by family origins—the indication of intergenerational mobility—and by such other individual characteristics as education, race, region, nativity, and family size. This research has been criticized on the basis of the conception of dual economy and labor market (Averitt 1968; Doeringer and Piore 1971; Piore 1975). Starting in economics and influencing the sociology of work, this literature focuses on the contrast between two economic sectors and labor markets—the core and the periphery.

The largest and richest firms dominate the core. Its primary labor market provides good employment conditions for workers from majority groups: relatively high and rising wages, some employment security, job ladders for promotions, and often labor unions to protect these working conditions. The firms in the periphery are typically smaller, and many are marginal. Its secondary labor market exhibits the opposite employment conditions: low wages, high turnover and unstable employment, dead-end jobs without advancement, and no unions.

Sociologists who have adopted this view of dual labor markets have criticized mobility research in terms of individual status attainment for centering attention on the influences on careers of attributes of individuals who supply labor and ignoring those of the structural conditions of labor demand (for instance, Beck, Horan, and Tolbert 1978; Kalleberg and Berg 1987: 10–11). They allege that the most important influences on opportunities are not the individual differences among those seeking work but the contrasting structural conditions in labor markets. Minorities, women, and others who are being discriminated against must work in the secondary labor market, and their structural location, not primarily individual differences in abilities, is the cause of their inferior opportunities compared to those of the majority groups who work in the core.

I have become increasingly interested in the effects of social structure on life chances, as indicated by the preceding discussion in which I stressed that the occupational structure governs opportunities and distinguished structural opportunities from individual qualities that influence whose careers are most likely to benefit from these opportunities. The occupational structure not only differs among societies and over time but also exhibits internal differences within a society. One such difference I analyzed is that among metropolitan areas. Others are undoubtedly those in the economy among industries, their markets, economic sectors, and labor markets. Although there is nothing wrong with studying the effects of differences among individuals on their careers, the structural variations that affect labor demand admittedly should be taken into account in the analysis of occupational chances. However, the dichotomy of a core and a periphery, insightful as it is, oversimplifies the complexity of the economy and has been criticized on several grounds.

One basic criticism is that economic sectors and labor markets are distinct and must not be confounded. There is empirical support for this criticism from a factor analysis of industries that included both items referring to economic sectors, such as concentration, and others reflecting labor markets, such as average wages (Wallace and Kalleberg 1981: 98–99, 102–3). The two sets of variables loaded on different factors, which indicates that economic sectors and labor markets are distinct dimensions. A second criticism is that neither economic sectors nor labor markets are a dichotomy, since each dimension varies considerably on the very criteria used to distinguish the two. This criticism is also supported by factor analyses which indicate that even with relatively few items both labor markets and economic sectors yield more than one factor (Hodson and Kaufman 1981: 883–85; Wallace and Kalleberg 1981: 99–104). A third issue raised is that differences among firms must not be ignored (Baron and Bielby 1980).

The most serious criticism of research on the dual labor market is that it often entails circular reasoning: some criteria used to define labor markets imply the very employment conditions for workers that they are assumed to produce. For example, Tolbert, Horan, and Beck (1980) present an empirical study to show the adverse effect of employment in the periphery, compared to that in the core, on earnings and the composition of the work force (low educational and occupational skills, many blacks and women). Hodson and Kaufman (1981) note in their critical comment that several items used to distinguish periphery from core labor markets refer implicitly, and sometimes even explicitly, to these effects on workers, the most conspicuous being median income (which is, of course, equivalent to earnings).

This circularity reflects a fundamental conceptual problem. To distinguish more from less advantageous labor markets, one can hardly help referring to the nature of jobs and employment conditions and hence implicitly to the outcomes for workers they are assumed to predict. For instance, low wages, unstable employment, and rare advancements are plausible ways to describe a secondary labor market, but these are essentially equivalent to low earnings, insecure employment, and dead-end jobs, which are the outcomes the inferior labor market presumably influences. But redundant definitions make it impossible to test whether the labor market exerts such influences. This raises serious problems about carefully designing the research to assure that the criteria for market conditions are entirely independent of the criteria of outcomes to ascertain empirically whether the former influence the latter.

. . .

Not all studies of labor markets suffer from these shortcomings. Some empirical investigations employ careful research designs that do not confound the criteria for the independent and those for the dependent variables. Conceptual refinements of labor markets have also been proposed. Starting with an illustration of the latter, Althauser and Kalleberg (1981) distinguish four types of primary from secondary labor markets. The two major ones are firm internal labor markets (FILMs) and occupational internal markets (OILMs). Internal labor markets (Doeringer and Piore 1971) have job ladders that provide career lines for employees. FILMs are confined to a single firm. OILMs are associations of members of a profession or craft that control, and often restrict, entry and that set advancement standards; the American Medical Association and the teamsters' union are examples. Two intermediate types are firm labor markets, which have no job ladders but do have stable employment, and occupational labor markets, associations of workers whose members have no specialized training. All these differ from secondary job markets, where jobs are temporary, advancements are exceptional, and turnover is high.

An interesting empirical study of industrial labor markets is that by

Wallace and Kalleberg (1981), whose research design carefully avoids circular arguments. After presenting the factor analysis already mentioned to show that economic structure and labor market must be distinguished and that neither is a dichotomy, they analyze how an industry's economic structure influences its labor market. Although the variables used to characterize labor markets include mean earnings and job stability (and five others, including race and sex composition), they fully realize that these are outcomes for workers and cannot be used to determine the influences of conditions in labor markets on such outcomes. This is made apparent by their refraining from analyzing any influences of labor markets on workers or the composition of the work force.

The study's objective is not to analyze the consequences of labor markets but, rather, to analyze their antecedents—how the economic structure of industries and the firms in them affects various conditions of labor markets. For this purpose, each of the seven variables by which labor markets are characterized are regressed on the six by which economic structures are (Wallace and Kalleberg 1981: 109). The strongest influence is exerted by the power structure in industrial markets, as indicated by concentration,[13] which greatly influences earnings, job stability, and percentage of union members.[14] The various aspects of the economic structure of the markets in industries influence not only wages, job security, and union membership but also the race and sex composition of the work force.

Another empirical study (Schlussel 1986) asks whether employment in core industries affects individual earnings even when a large number of individual differences that influence them are controlled. Indeed, an industry's economic structure, whether represented by the core-periphery dichotomy or a measure of economic segmentation by degree, influences earnings. The aspects of core industries that exert most of this influence were concentration and, to a lesser extent, capital intensity and sales. For instance, in one analysis (table 3.1), which controls twelve individual characteristics, including occupational status, experience, hours worked,

13. The variable *concentration* is a score based on three items—the four-firm concentration ratio and two measures of proportion of sales by large firms.

14. It would be of interest to ascertain whether union membership affects earnings and job stability and how it does, for example, whether it mediates the influence of concentration in industries on earnings.

and gender, economic structure exerts a small but highly significant ($p = .001$; $n = 968$) effect on earnings. To be sure, it accounts for only 10 percent of the variance explained (.06 of the total R^2 of .65).[15] Yet the research demonstrates that these variations *among* industries influence earnings when such important individual influences on them are controlled.[16]

These two empirical studies analyze how the power structure and related conditions in product markets affect earning (in both cases) and also some other aspects of the labor force reflected by labor markets (in one). This makes it possible to raise the question, in terms of the theoretical scheme on which attention centers here, how the consolidation or intersection of the various differences in economic structures influences their labor markets and workers.[17] The theory implies that high correlations consolidate the differences among economic structures and enhance their effect on labor markets and the work force. In contrast, intersecting differences in the power structure of economic sectors, as reflected in weak correlations of their various conditions, are expected to diminish differences among economic sectors and workers' welfare.

To be sure, one would not anticipate that many conditions contributing to the power structure of markets are negatively related. Some may be, however, and others may exhibit relatively weak correlation. For example, there can be more or fewer strong firms in a market, and more of them may well be negatively related to the concentration ratio; at least, more of them would exhibit a rather weak positive correlation to it. Weak compared to strong correlations of various conditions in economic structures are indicative of relatively more intersection. The more

15. Schlussel was disappointed that the core-periphery difference explains so little of the variation in earnings. Since she has controlled most individual differences that affect earnings, it is not trivial that the core-periphery difference can explain still another 10 percent of the variance in earnings accounted for.

16. It should be noted that in terms of recent developments in statistics the procedure used in this dissertation is flawed, because the variable or variables representing the core industries are probably related to the disturbance terms of the individual variables, which has not been taken into account.

17. One might suspect that multicollinearity of various aspects of power structure in markets precludes such an analysis, but Wallace and Kalleberg's (1981: 100) regressors reveal little multicollinearity. (The reason is undoubtedly that highly correlated items, such as the average firm's assets and profits, were combined into scores to construct the variables.)

various conditions that contribute to the concentration of power intersect, whether indicated by a negative correlation or comparatively weaker positive ones, the more such intersection reduces the influences of specific conditions.

SOCIAL MOBILITY

There has been extensive upward mobility in the United States, as well as in other industrializing countries, during most of this century. This was largely structural mobility, which is the social mobility generated by the expansion of high-ranking and the contraction of low-ranking occupations. This change in the distribution of the labor force was produced by industrialization, reinforced, particularly in this country, by the great expansion of the population of a young nation and the large stream of immigrants it entailed. The expansion of the population enlarged demands for services on all levels, but most of the large number of poor immigrants had few if any industrial skills and had to take low-status jobs. The increase in low-paid workers would have increased economic inequality, but income inequality did not increase in this century until the 1970s. The reason is that the expanded demand for labor in higher- as well as lower-status occupations created opportunities for mobility for the offspring of immigrants, producing the upward mobility mentioned and thereby counteracting the growing inequality. Given that structural mobility has been the predominant form of mobility, Hauser et al. (1975: 295–96) suggested that researchers should stop focusing on circulation mobility and instead center attention on structural mobility and the changes in the occupational structure that produce it.[18]

Most early studies of social mobility were carried out for industrialized countries, and they revealed little variation among countries when broad occupational categories were used. This gave rise to the industrialization hypothesis, which claims that industrialization determines rates of social mobility in modern societies independent of other differences among them (Lipset and Zetterberg 1956; Lipset and Bendix 1959).

18. In a joint paper (Blau and Ruan 1990: 7), we have criticized Hauser and his colleagues for making this suggestion. Although I acknowledge the predominant impact of structural mobility, circulation mobility must not be ignored, because it is significant in its own right. It is an important indication of lack of rigidity in the class structure, and changes since the 1970s have made it of increasing practical significance for policy, as we shall presently see.

However, subsequent research using narrower occupational categories and improved procedures revealed that structural mobility may be affected by industrialization but circulation mobility is not.[19] The new hypothesis advanced by Featherman, Jones, and Hauser (1975)—later termed the FJH hypothesis—is that circulation mobility, not total mobility, is largely invariant among all societies with a market economy, as well as across time.

The implication of the FJH hypothesis is that the class structure of all industrial societies is equally rigid, regardless of their stage of economic development and the nature of their political system. It further implies that it is impossible for any society to reduce the rigidity of the class structure and the prevailing inheritance of socioeconomic positions. This is a dire prospect for people who believe that it is possible to reduce existing injustices and inequalities of opportunity. Fortunately, empirical evidence fails to support the FJH hypothesis. First, results from some case studies questioned it, and then comparative research obtained results that supply strong, though not conclusive, evidence negating it.

"Socioeconomic status has become less important for men's and women's mobility since 1972 . . . [reflecting a] crucial change in inequality of opportunity," reports Hout (1988: 1389) from his American mobility study. In a comparison of mobility in a sample of the third-largest city in the People's Republic of China and a national sample of the largely urban United States, Blau and Ruan (1990: 24) infer that "the influence on careers of both aspects of class background—parental education and occupation—is far less in China than the United States."

To be sure, case studies, particularly ones that compare a single city with a national sample, do not constitute reliable evidence. But the FJH hypothesis is also questioned by the results of a secondary comparative analysis based on 126 mobility studies from thirty-two different countries, with an average of 4 surveys, conducted at different times, per country. The major conclusion (Ganzeboom, Luijkx, and Treiman 1989: 47) is that the results "provide strong evidence against the claim that fluidity levels are identical across countries and over time."

. . .

Implicit in mobility research is the assumption that occupations can be hierarchically ranked, which is typically done more or less impressionis-

---

19. Circulation mobility refers to that part of social mobility that is not the result of differences in the two occupational distributions in the marginals of the matrix.

tically. It can be done explicitly based on data, however. Duncan (1961) derived an index of occupational status for all detailed occupations (SEI) based on the prevailing education and income in each occupation. Mobility is studied with this socioeconomic index by regressing a son's occupation on his father's[20] and on other attributes influencing it, which simultaneously provides information on other factors affecting occupational chances and controls them, thereby insulating the intergenerational mobility process. Since the status differences of hundreds of detailed occupations are much smaller than those of about a dozen occupational groups, regressions using SEI essentially avoid the differences between the numbers in large categories in a mobility matrix which have little if any meaning. On the other hand, regressions using SEI fail to make the important distinction between structural and circulation mobility.

Both the roughly ranked categories of mobility tables and the SEI define occupational status in absolute terms—a limited number of ranked classes and a number reflecting education and income. But the SEI continuum of occupational status can be easily transformed into relative status (as can the categories of a matrix). Rytina (1989) does so by arraying Duncan's SEI scores in a rank order and substituting for their values the number representing every occupation's rank in this rank order. Substantively, this means that relative standing replaces absolute status, which has interesting implications for mobility. All upward movements that surpass others automatically lower the relative standing of these others, and the same in reverse is the case for downward movements. Thus, to use income as an illustration, the rising incomes of others do not lower my constant income (ignoring possible effects of inflation), but they do lower my relative economic standing.

Rytina's index of relative status reveals more occupational inheritance than the absolute measure of SEI, primarily because the mean change in status affects absolute occupational status but not relative occupational standing. If the average occupational status has risen from one generation to the next, children whose occupational status is the

20. It should be noted that early mobility studies were confined to son's and father's occupation, but less sexist measures can be used, such as including all members of the labor force and measuring social origins by some combination of the occupation of both parents (or all breadwinners in the household). For an early comparison of American women's and men's mobility, see Tyree and Treas (1974).

same as their parents', and even those whose status surpasses their parents' but by less than the average increase, have dropped in relative standing from that of their family of origin. Since structural mobility reflects a change in mean occupational status, replacing an absolute by a relative measure of occupational standing in effect abstracts from structural mobility in the analysis of origin-destination moves and reflects the ways most people experience differences and changes in occupational status.

Another advantage of defining status in relative terms is that it can explain Boudon's paradox. If everybody's education increases by the same amount, nobody's relative educational standing rises. Although it is still rational for individuals to maximize their education, as the best educated do have superior occupational chances, the larger the number of persons who raise their education, the less competitive advantage any one person gains from doing so. The rising level of education in the population entails an excessive supply of educated labor and accounts for the decline in returns to education. Similar social processes occur when average incomes increase: standards of living increase and purchasing power tends to decrease, so that increases beyond the average must occur if one's relative socioeconomic standing is to rise. Increasing average incomes may also stimulate powerful chief executives of giant corporations, who essentially set their own incomes, to make more and more millions of dollars a year trying to stay at the top of the heap, which seems to be happening in this country.

The difficulty of staying in the top stratum in terms of relative standing can be seen by visualizing the status structure as a pyramid. The reason that the income structure, like most distributions by size, has a pyramidal shape is that very high incomes, just like very large cities or very old people, are much rarer than low incomes, or small towns or newborns.[21] This pyramidal shape implies that the chance of upward mobility to the top in relative standing is far inferior to the risk of downward mobility from the top.

As a simplified illustration, take a population of 100 million with a top stratum of 1 percent. (Percentages refer to relative standing.) If 100,000 of the 99 million below the top rise up to the top 1 percent, the same number must drop out of the top stratum, because the upper

21. The very lowest incomes are less frequent than those that are not quite that low.

1 percent obviously cannot increase to 1.1 percent, as it otherwise would. This means that the chances to rise to the top stratum are about .001 (100,000 divided by 99 million), but the risk of dropping from the top is .1 (100,000 divided by 1 million). Thus, the risk of moving down from the top is 99 times the chance of moving up into it, corresponding to the ratio of the numbers of people below and at the top.

. . .

These considerations have some bearing on circulation mobility. Mobility research in Western societies has been from the beginning particularly interested in fluidity or circulation mobility, even at a time when most mobility was structural mobility, and for good reason. Fluidity is an indication of an important quality of democratic society—how much equality of opportunity there is, opportunity relatively unconstrained by either family background or changes in the division of labor that necessitate mobility, up or down, by changing the demand for various services. In sum, circulation mobility complements two other conditions reflected in a mobility matrix: immobility, entailing no change from social origin to destination (shown in the diagonal), and structural mobility, generated by differences between the distributions of family origins and occupational destinations (shown by differences in the marginals).

Both structural mobility and circulation mobility are emergent properties of a population, and both are reflected in parameters. Structural mobility refers to the relationship of two parameters, heterogeneity of occupational origins and heterogeneity of occupational destinations. However, the word *relationship* is not used in this sentence in the conventional sense of how closely variations in one factor are related to variations in another. The nexus indicating structural mobility is not the correlation between parent's and child's occupation (which would indicate occupational inheritance) but the sum of the same-sign differences between the array of parent's and that of child's occupational group (the index of dissimilarity).

The case of circulation mobility or fluidity is more complicated. Circulation mobility is reflected by the entries in a mobility matrix that neither are in the diagonal nor can be accounted for by the differences in the distributions of the subtotals in the marginals. This implies that a random distribution of entries outside the diagonal would represent perfect fluidity. But a random distribution indicates no association between social origins and occupational destinations, which, in turn, implies in terms of the parameter scheme that origin and destination are completely intersecting.[22]

Perfect intersection reflects perfect circulation mobility, but the problem is not how to represent pure fluidity but how to distinguish circulation from structural mobility in data in which both are combined in the same figures. A precise procedure for determining circulation mobility requires devising hypothetical models of it and performing empirical tests to ascertain which model fits the empirical observations best.[23] The discussion here is confined to the conceptual problem of distinguishing intersection from both immobility and structural mobility, without attempting to address questions of statistical procedures.

Three forms of "mobility" can be distinguished in the nexus between origin's and destination's socioeconomic status: immobility, structural mobility, and circulation mobility. Immobility is represented by the diagonal of a matrix, or by the slope when occupational destinations are regressed on social origins. Structural mobility is indicated by the differences between the distributions of occupational status and origins in a matrix, or by the intercept of the regression slope provided that it is linear and exactly forty-five degrees (parallel to the immobility diagonal). The reason for the proviso is that nonlinearity and a different angle generally indicate some structural mobility that affects various segments of the population differently, which must be taken into account lest structural mobility be partly ignored.

Circulation mobility is the random distribution around the matrix diagonal, or the random deviations around the regression line, provided that the systematic part of the model is correctly specified to account for all structural mobility (as well as immobility). Correct specification is particularly important, because in addition to the usual reasons for doing so the estimate of random departures from the model depends on it.

The substantive objective of accurate specification is to exclude from the estimate of randomness all structural mobility, for a nonmonotonic regression line indicates structural mobility that benefits or harms some

22. Strictly speaking, a random distribution yields some entries in the diagonal, which reveals immobility. But perfect fluidity or opportunity would also, by chance alone, have some people end up in the same occupational stratum as that of their parents.

23. Earlier procedures for distinguishing circulation from structural mobility in a matrix were shown to be faulty, but improved ones, based largely on log-linear analysis (see Goodman 1984), have been developed.

but not all segments of the population. Threshold dummies and interaction effects as well as transformations must be used in the model to correct for all detectable forms of nonlinearity. Even linear slopes that differ from one (and thus are not parallel to the hypothetical immobility line) typically reveal structural mobility, and they indicate that mobility chances differ for different strata. If structural mobility, including its aspects that affect only parts of the population, as well as immobility, has been correctly estimated, the residual reflects the random component (disturbance term) of the population and thus is an indication of circulation mobility. Accordingly, $1 - R^2$ is indicative of the degree of fluidity in society's occupational structure.

This procedure could be used in a multilevel or contextual study of conditions that affect the degree of fluidity in a society's socioeconomic structure. In the first stage, measures of intersection would be derived, as just outlined, for every population separately, probably using somewhat different models, because the extent of structural mobility and immobility undoubtedly differs. The measure of circulation derived would be the dependent variable to study antecedent conditions that affect circulation mobility.

It would be of great interest to ascertain, for instance, at which stages economic development tends to promote a fluid occupational structure and at which stages it fails to do so or even impedes it. Do great differences in national debt affect fluidity? What is the influence of a nation's political system on circulation mobility? Is there less rigidity in the occupational structure of democratic countries than in that of dictatorships, as we would like to think? A two-stage cross-national study could answer such questions in its second stage after obtaining measures of the intersection of origins and destinations in its first.

CONCLUSIONS

There has been a dramatic change in structural mobility in the United States in the last two decades, which gives circulation mobility renewed importance. The decline in unskilled and farm workers and the expansion of factory, office, and professional work in the century's first three-quarters have turned into a decline in relatively well paid jobs in industry and administration and an expansion of low-paid unskilled service jobs and unemployment in the last quarter. As a result, rising living standards have given way to expanding poverty and increasing economic inequality, and opportunity to climb out of the most underprivileged strata has greatly diminished. These changes, accompanying the change from a growth to a deficit economy, have been called the great U-turn (Harrison and Bluestone 1988), which is more fully discussed in chapter 7.

After a synopsis of the topics of this chapter, the conclusion turns to the implications of these changes for circulation mobility. The occupational structure, expressing the division of labor in broad terms, is the matrix of a population's material life chances. This can be illustrated by national differences in the division of labor and by changes in it that have occurred in the United States and other developed countries in this century. These changes have affected occupational opportunities. Thus, the decline in the lowest-ranking and the increase in all higher-ranking occupational groups in the American labor force between 1900 and 1970 generated much opportunity for upward mobility. Since 1970, however, industrial jobs have declined and low-paid service jobs have multiplied, which has decreased upward mobility and increased poverty, unemployment, and economic inequality.

Structural mobility refers to the extent of social mobility resulting from changes in the occupational structure. However, the broad categories of occupational groups employed in the matrix of mobility studies yield figures for structural mobility that have little if any meaning. They do not indicate the degree of mobility, which is not a meaningful concept, and they certainly do not refer to the percentage of members of the labor force who have experienced intergenerational mobility. The reason is that the numbers used to indicate structural mobility refer to differences in occupations that are often far apart, but most occupational mobility is short-distance, which implies that more persons than these numbers indicate have experienced mobility. A procedure derived by Harrison (1988) that employs a multiplier suggested by White (1970) is discussed to indicate how to estimate the proportion of a sample that has experienced mobility.

The occupational structure governs the opportunities available in the population, but who benefits from them depends on individual differences in qualifications and handicaps. Education improves career chances, whereas being black or female, owing to discrimination, impedes them. Family origins are of special significance for careers, because they influence so many conditions affecting them, such as offspring's ascribed positions, the cultural capital they acquire in the family, and the economic advantages—or lack of them—the family provides. An important mediator between social origins and occupational outcomes is education. Boudon's paradox is a special case of the opposite effects on careers that population characteristics and individual differences often have. An individual usually gains a career advantage from superior education, providing an incentive for pursuing it; but as many individuals improve their education, the population's educational level rises, which reduces the competitive advantage one gains from having improved one's education.[24]

This entire monograph centers attention on structural influences on life chances. Earlier research on social mobility using the status attainment model (Blau and Duncan 1967) to study how various individual characteristics affect occupational chances has been criticized for ignoring the influence of labor markets on careers, notably by the literature on dual labor markets. This chapter includes a short discussion of early research in this tradition, criticisms of it, and improvements in recent research on the topic, which has analyzed the dependence of labor markets on conditions in their economic sectors and the contrasting effects of core and peripheral industries on earnings.

The reputation of the United States as the land of golden opportunity has been rooted in its tremendous industrial expansion and economic growth, and the structural mobility to which they gave rise. These industrial and economic developments provided opportunities for large numbers in the lower strata, including many children of poor immigrants, to move up into the middle class. The recent decline in structural opportunity creates the challenge of how to restore opportunities to the "truly disadvantaged," in Wilson's (1987) apt phrase. The only way to do this, it seems, would be to expand circulation mobility. In contrast to structural mobility, however, circulation mobility is zero-sum, as relative standing is. If the upper occupational strata do not expand and absorb members of the lower strata, the upward mobility of some depends on the downward mobility of others, which is what circulation mobility entails.[25]

Perfect equality of opportunity is probably impossible to achieve, but the extreme inequalities of life chances between children of the rich and children of the poor in the United States can be much diminished, as they

24. Macrostructural parameters refer to differentiation of opportunities in a population, and their having opposite effects on outcomes from those of corresponding individual attributes involves different intervening processes from Boudon's contrast between the effects of mean level of education and those of an individual's relative educational standing.

25. Some opportunity for upward mobility is furnished by class differences in fertility, but these differences are declining.

already have been in most Western countries. At least, most advanced countries have national health insurance for everybody and most have made higher education, including attendance at the best universities, independent of large family resources. Income taxes could be made steeply progressive, instead of more regressive, as they became in the "reforms" of the 1980s; inheritance taxes could be raised to minimize the great economic advantages the children of the affluent already enjoy; public funds could be allocated to provide good precollege education for all; and adequate unemployment insurance could be supplied. Many other changes could help lessen inequalities of opportunity to restore mobility chances by increasing circulation mobility. In a democracy, changes of this sort would have to be accomplished by legislation and, ultimately, by political actions—by electing officials who favor these changes.

Such means for improving circulation mobility to replace the structural mobility that is disappearing would evidently be in the interest of the less privileged but contrary to the interest of the more privileged, including not only the rich but also large segments of the middle class. People who are threatened with the loss of important privileges, particularly for their children, have an interest in opposing the changes that would implement these threats. Hence, there undoubtedly would be much opposition to the political changes needed to increase circulation mobility. Are such changes feasible? Are there alternative methods for restoring mobility opportunities to the children of the underprivileged? In chapter 7, some conjectures about these issues will be offered.

FIVE

STRUCTURAL CONTEXT
AND ORGANIZATIONS

THE MULTIDIMENSIONAL SPACE OF THE population structure is the social context that influences its substructures. The influences on opportunities for, and constraints on, life chances and intergroup relations have been analyzed in the preceding chapters. So has the significance of multistructural analysis for clarifying how these influences are transmitted, and to what extent they are transmitted, to the networks of face-to-face relations. The rates of social relations between persons affiliated with different groups have been referred to as intergroup relations, and the groups whose members' rates of interpersonal relations have been examined were largely major subdivisions of the population that are not formally organized, such as race or national origin, industry or occupation.

What we have analyzed, therefore, is how people's affiliation with groups influences their social relations and opportunities, with special emphasis on the significance of the structural context on these intergroup relations. We have not yet examined how the larger structural context affects the formation and development not only of informal groups but also of voluntary associations and other formal organizations. This is the objective of the present chapter. The questions raised are how the larger social context influences the membership of voluntary associations and formal organizations, their expansion, and their interrelations. Of special importance in modern society are economic organizations, and the second part of the chapter is devoted to studies of American major firms and corporations, their interrelations, their internal structures, and their complex intersection with markets and industries that have developed in recent decades.

The first section presents a study of the influence of the multidimensional social context on voluntary associations and extends the study to other associations and organizations. Next we turn to the ways groups and voluntary associations are linked by their members and how they simultaneously link their members to the larger social structure, and we examine the role of class differences in organizational participation for political influence. The last two sections of the chapter deal with formal organizations, particularly economic organizations, including the dominant ones in the modern economy: large corporations. One section analyzes the internal structure of organizations, the changing number of firms in an industry, and their joint political actions to protect their interests, ending with a classical warning that business interests conflict with the public interest. The last section discusses the largest corporations composed of multiple firms in different industries and the consequent crosscutting links of corporations and markets.

POPULATION STRUCTURE AND ORGANIZATIONAL DEVELOPMENT

In a large democracy, like the United States, intermediate organizations are of great importance to bridge the gap between individual citizens and the country's government, as Tocqueville (1980) has emphasized. He stressed particularly the role of voluntary associations as such links. The question raised in this section is how the structural context of the larger society influences the composition, growth, and change of intermediate organizations, primarily the voluntary associations Tocqueville emphasized but also other organizations. This discussion is based on a study of voluntary associations by McPherson and Ranger-Moore (1991), in which they analyze these organizations in terms of the conceptual framework of a population's multidimensional space of social positions.[1]

The very nature of a voluntary organization provides a focus that attracts individuals who have something in common (Feld 1981). Whatever the type of organization—whether a fraternal order or a literary club, a union or a professional society—persons join one because they have common interests or affiliations, which implies in terms of my

---

1. They compliment me in this paper by referring to this multidimensional property space as "Blau space."

scheme that they are proximate in the multidimensional property space. People who have some common interest or affiliation that is important enough for them to join an organization are likely to share other attributes correlated with the first, which makes them alike in several respects. Only veterans can join the American Legion, and only physicians the American Medical Association, and being either a veteran or a physician implies various other interests and attributes that the organization's members also share. Homophily prevails, in Merton's apt phrase.

Many intermediate organizations have multiple levels. State organizations have local branches, on one hand, and are combined into national organizations, on the other. To join a branch provides channels of communication upward to the national level, channels that give individual citizens on local levels some potential national influence. Inasmuch as local branches reflect the population structures of their local communities, they make the national membership representative not merely of the population structure as a whole but also of the substructures in various locations. Thus, multilevel organizations intersect with the substructures of society on multiple levels, which complements the intersection of people's different social affiliations and further increases society's complexity.

Most voluntary organizations, like most other organizations, seek to grow. Even exclusive clubs that restrict membership to a small elite typically seek to recruit as many members of that elite as they can. The growth of a voluntary association is in considerable part the result of informal recruitment by existing members (unless a fast-expanding social movement succeeds in creating a bandwagon effect). As people tend to associate with others like themselves, chances are that the new recruits will be like them too, so that growth increases the voluntary organization's homophily. In the words of McPherson and Ranger-Moore (1991: 22), "The recruitment of new members to organizations tends to be conservative because the group replicates itself through homophilous connections."

The social proximity of members implies that voluntary organizations occupy "distinctive niches" (p. 22) in the multidimensional space. Since the axes in the social space are dimensions of social differences, an organization's niche is in the region in space where the most common characteristics of the membership are found. There are two major conditions that limit recruitment, particularly homophilous recruitment. One is the region's "carrying capacity" (pp. 24–25), how much organizational participation the people in the region can and will supply, which depends on population density as well as class, age, and other demographic factors that influence organizational participation. The other is how many other organizations compete with the one under consideration for members with the same affiliations, that is, how many compete in the same niche. These two conditions are likely to modify homophilous recruitment and thereby alter the composition of the organization.

The members of a voluntary organization are typically not perfectly alike, even in major respects, but, rather, have a range of attributes, for instance, an age range and an educational range. Hence, the organization's niche occupies an area in the property space, and the carrying capacity may be greater, or the competition may be less, at one edge of the organization's niche than at the opposite edge. The easier recruitment at the former edge undoubtedly makes it more successful, which would tilt the composition of the organization, perhaps by increasing the number of older members or less educated ones. If this change is great enough to alter the voluntary association's membership considerably, it may prompt the resignation of members now in the minority, intensifying the original change in the composition of the membership. For example, if it is easier to recruit to a political organization on the left or the right, that organization may get too radical or too reactionary for the moderates, leading to resignations that change the organization's composition and orientation even more.

· · ·

This scheme is applicable not only to voluntary associations but also to the supporters of many other organizations. Members of different religious congregations, including those that belong to the same denomination, often differ in ethnic, national, and class background, as illustrated by Italian and Irish Catholic churches. Yet even entire religious denominations may differ radically in racial or class composition, as the black and white Baptist denominations illustrate. In multiparty systems and in local elections, supporters of different candidates differ in socioeconomic status, ethnic affiliation, and religion, and even in two-party systems, there are considerable average differences between the two parties. The customers of different retail stores differ in ethnic and class background, even among stores that sell similar price lines.

An important reason for these differences is that considerable influence on people's choices of what associations to join is exerted informally by their associates, and associates typically have many of the same or similar social affiliations. This is implicit in the proximity assumption. These influences of the homophily in informal recruitment are reinforced by the formal appeals organizations make to attract support, because different organizations direct their advertising and propaganda to different segments of the population. The similar interests common background engenders are still another reinforcing influence. In short, homophilous informal recruitment, reinforced by homogeneous formal appeals and the common interests of persons with the same background, promotes homogeneity in organizations.

Indeed, these considerations apply to any set of persons—even when there are no ties between most of them—who are attracted to the same occasion or condition,[2] not only to the membership of an association or organization. People who watch the same television program and those who have seen the same film typically have some background characteristics in common. The same is true for those who attend the same sports events and those who vote for the same candidate, those who go to the same bar or shop at the same store. Moreover, most people who start attending certain places, occasions, or events do so as friends of others who have attended them in the past. In sum, persons in the same niche in social space have many common interests and friends with corresponding interests, and both their sharing some interests and their having friends with similar interests prompt them to join the same groupings and organizations, which contributes to the homophily of these associations' recruitment and composition.

. . .

Paradoxically, homophilous recruitment processes may alter the composition of voluntary organizations in various respects. One reason is that the members of an organization are not identical, but only similar, to one another, with a restricted range of differences. The association's location in social space often makes it easier, owing to variations in carrying capacity and its exploitation by competition, to recruit new members like the existing ones at one rather than the other end of this range, as already noted. But this is not the only reason for the paradox that homophilous recruitment may alter a group's composition. The main reason is the intersection of social differences, particularly if they penetrate into regions

2. In network terms, such common choices make individuals structurally equivalent.

and niches, because intersection implies that people alike in some respects differ in others.

Members of voluntary organizations who have common interests or affiliations that provide strong social bonds are not threatened by other members' having some diverse views and affiliations. The dedicated chess player does not care if the others in the club are Protestants or Catholics, young or old, Democrats or Republicans, as long as they are challenging opponents in games of chess. It is only when the focal interest of the association is not so great or when the diversity in other respects infringes on the basic common interest that such disagreements cause serious friction. On the other hand, just as a complex role set of diverse associates promotes intellectual flexibility, a diverse group of associates with strong interests in common invigorates an organization and makes it more resilient, as Nielsen (1985: 145) infers in his theory of ethnic solidarity.

The conceptual image of a multidimensional space of social positions invites constructing visual images of patterns of social relations and differences. McPherson and Ranger-Moore (1991: 22, emphasis in original) suggest that if homophily reduces the theoretically possible social relations between persons to a much smaller number of actually observable relations it indicates that "the connections that do *not* exist determine how the system behaves." This is somewhat similar to the idea in a recent network analysis of markets that "structural holes are responsible for player differences *between* markets" (Burt 1992: 2, emphasis in original). McPherson and Ranger-Moore (1991: 24) also state that "when dimensions are correlated, individuals are crowded into limited areas of space, while other areas are vacant." My image of intersection, which is the inverse of correlation and implies that individuals are dispersed and not crowded near regression lines, is randomness or entropy.

Changes in the multidimensional space of the population structure alter the opportunities of organizations. The large streams of immigrants to the United States about a century ago provided firms, particularly in New York, with a large supply of inexpensive labor. The extensive entry of women into the labor force has also expanded the labor supply. Immigration has enlarged religious congregations as well and has led to the establishment of new ones—Catholic churches early in this century, Muslim mosques in the last few decades. Recent increases in economic inequality have increased the sales of luxury cars and yachts and the demand for soup kitchens and shelters for the homeless. Affirmative action in education has somewhat improved the opportunities of minorities.

Pronounced changes in fertility and hence in age distributions have repercussions for supply and demand in the labor market, which have opposite effects on the opportunities of employing organizations and on young people seeking work.

Sometimes these fluctuations are alternating, which can be illustrated by an imaginary application of the cobweb theorem of economics[3] to an occupational group in the labor market. When disproportionate numbers of students graduate from business schools with MBA degrees, the job market is flooded with candidates for the available positions in business administration, which depresses opportunities for those starting careers in business. Once young people become aware of this situation, many of them decide not to attend business school. Some years later, consequently, there may well not be enough qualified MBAs to meet the demand for them, which will improve their opportunities, raise their salaries, and speed their promotions. As business administration again acquires the reputation as a promising field for successful careers, more students are likely to choose it, quite possibly producing more candidates for positions than there is demand for them. This oversupply depresses opportunities for careers in the field, which may start the cycle anew. (For an imaginative elaboration of this thesis, see Easterlin 1978, 1980).

INTERRELATIONS OF GROUPS AND SUBSTRUCTURES

To study the relations among subunits of a population, some initial distinctions must be made. One distinction is whether a person can belong to several organizations of a given type or only to one. Voluntary associations, fraternal orders, and clubs are organizations to any number of which people can belong. In contrast, people belong only to one religious denomination, they are members of or vote for only one political party, and most are full-time employees of only one firm, though they can change their affiliation from one to any other of these organizations. Another distinction is that between being a member of an organization, like a church, a firm, or a sorority, and having an ascribed or achieved position in terms of the parameter scheme, such as being of a certain race and gender, or having a certain occupation and income. In this case, the assumption is that the entire population (or its relevant part, like its labor

---

3. A description of the cobweb theorem is found in most economic texts; a good brief one is in Boulding (1955: 164-65).

force) is classified in some position (or a residual category) on every parameter.

When multiple memberships in organizations or groups are possible, these more or less organized groups are linked by the members who belong to two or more of them, and the groups simultaneously link the members who belong to the same one, as Breiger (1974) pointed out in an insightful paper. He shows that a square matrix of individuals, with interpersonal ties in the cells, and a square matrix of groups, with common members in the cells, can both be derived from a rectangular matrix of persons by groups. His analysis, like mine, derives from and quantifies Simmel's concept of the intersection of groups and individuals, but it is not easy to translate one into the other. The reason for this difficulty is not merely that he analyzes microstructures and I analyze macrostructures.

One difference between Breiger's analysis and mine is that I distinguish at the outset ingroup from intergroup relations whereas this distinction is not meaningful for his analysis. Another difference is that he takes the nature of a group as given whereas I treat each group or substructure as a nominal social position shared by persons on a dimension of differences among positions, such as occupation, gender, religion, or national origin. Finally, he is not concerned with differences among individuals except in their group membership, whereas I consider the strength of the correlation of various individual differences of prime importance. His approach is best suited to the interrelations of small groups, such as interlocks of corporate boards, whereas mine is more appropriate for macrosociological analysis.

Yet Breiger's analysis also has macrosociological implications. His conclusion that the multitude of small organized groups are integrated by their members as well as integrate individual members in a common enterprise contributes to a better understanding of the significance Tocqueville attributes to intermediate organizations for sustaining large-scale democracy. It indicates the social processes underlying the ways intermediate organizations not only enhance the political power of individuals acting alone but also achieve more power themselves, because their members' joint memberships unite organizations with one another. The many members shared by civil liberties and civil rights organizations strengthen both types of organizations in the fight for freedom and against repression.

The intervention of intermediate organizations increases the political influence of individuals, but it does not do so equitably, for there are great class differences. Much research has shown that membership in voluntary associations as well as active participation in them is substantially more prevalent in the middle class than in the working class. Empirical studies have also found that most voluntary associations, though by no means all, are class homogeneous. An analysis by McPherson (1981) shows that the combination of these two factors greatly magnifies class differences. Middle-class persons not only belong to more organizations and are more active in them than members of the working class, but the former's greater influence is further reinforced by the greater activity of their fellow organization members. This makes it easier for the middle class than the working class to mobilize many people and various organizations for joint political action. These differences contribute to the greater power of the middle class than the working class.

. . .

One distinction drawn above is that between formally established organizations that people join and the substructures or common nominal positions generated by the population structure's subdivision by parameters, such as ethnic affiliation, birth region, and occupation. This is an important analytical distinction, though the lines are not always sharply drawn. Various religious affiliations are positions on a nominal parameter, but religious denominations are also organizations to which people belong. Specific occupations are nominal positions of the occupational distribution, but many are organized into unions or professional associations that members join. Nevertheless, the nominal position and the formal organization do not completely coincide, and the analytic distinction between them is important.

We turn now to the relations among the substructures of groups of people who share social positions on a nominal dimension of structural differentiation.[4] People have an affiliation with a social position on every parameter, as noted above. This is not literally the case, of course. Infants have no occupation or income. It is advantageous in such cases, however, to use the entire relevant subpopulation,[5] or possi-

---

4. I refer to nominal positions because these create groups of people with identical affiliations. Graduated parameters also create ranges of people with similar positions, such as education or SEI, to which I refer as strata.

5. Examples of relevant subpopulations are the civilian labor force for occupation, SEI, and earnings and people who have completed their schooling for years of education.

bly residual categories. People's common memberships in various voluntary associations or groups, as Simmel and Breiger point out, constitute
links that integrate them. However, the strong linking of people's social
affiliations in various dimensions surely does not integrate the various
substructures of society but, on the contrary, engenders social barriers
between them.

Whereas common memberships link and integrate various voluntary
associations, this is not the case when various parameters of social differences are closely linked or related. Strongly related dimensions of
social differences entail much consolidation, and consolidated social differences, far from integrating various groups and substructures through
the relations of their members, impede intergroup relations. Parallel differences among people multiply their social distance and inhibit intergroup relations, as the preceding chapter showed.

However, the distinction made in the last paragraph is misleading,
because the term *link* is used for two entirely different concepts: how
socially integrated various groups of people are, in one case, and how
strongly correlated various social differences among people are, in the
other. There is no ambiguity in the social influences discussed, only in
my use of the term *link* both for linked (or related) properties or affiliations of people and for linked (or related) groups. Common memberships
of groups, voluntary associations, or other organizations create uniting
bonds, but consolidated social differences in affiliations impede social relations between different individuals. Intersection promotes social bonds
in both cases, whether reference is to the intersection of members and
their groups, which integrate both the groups and their members, or to
the intersecting social differences in various dimensions, which promote
intergroup relations that integrate diverse communities.

In sum, Breiger's analysis and mine seem to come to opposite conclusions but actually do not. I stress the advantage of weakly linked social
affiliations in various dimensions, whereas he implies that it is advantageous for groups to be linked by persons who are members of both (or
all). This only sounds contradictory, because *link* does not refer to the
same concept in the two cases.

In Breiger's analysis *link* refers to the bonds of different groups that
are strengthened by common members—corresponding to my concept of
intergroup relations—which promotes their social integration. But in my
analysis it refers to the strong linkage or correlation of people's social
affiliations in various dimensions, which creates barriers between persons

who exhibit parallel differences in various respects, thereby weakening intergroup relations and impeding the social integration of diverse groups in society.

FORMAL ORGANIZATIONS

Although most of this section and the next deal with economic organizations, owing to their special significance in our society, their discussion is introduced by a theoretical analysis of the internal structure of formal organizations, assumed to be applicable to all organizations composed of employees.[6] The theory centers attention on the internal structure of organizations, conceptualized as the distribution of their employees among official positions along various lines. Whereas I had not yet thought of the macrostructural theory here presented when the theory of the formal structure of organization was developed (Blau 1970), the parameter scheme can be applied to it.

The first principle of the theory is that the size of an organization promotes differentiation in its structure at decelerating rates in various dimensions. Originally based on empirical data on one type of organization, this generalization was subsequently replicated with data on hundreds of organizations of five other types. The larger an organization, the greater its differentiation along all lines observed. Large size tends to be accompanied by a more pronounced division of labor, more local branches, more major divisions, more hierarchical levels, more sections per division, and wider spans of control of supervisors of subsections, but all these forms of differentiation occur at decelerating rates. Some of these influences are obvious—for instance, that numerous levels in the hierarchy depend on large numbers of employees. But others are not—for example, that the number of sections per division is greater in larger than smaller organizations.

The theory seeks to explain this pattern, particularly the decelerating rate of differentiation. Much differentiation in various dimensions implies a complex social structure. Great complexity makes administration a bigger and more difficult job that requires more personnel. Indeed, the more differentiated an organization is in various respects, the greater is its ad-

---

6. The research from which the theory here briefly summarized was inferred included studies of government organizations, like public employment agencies, economic organizations, such as manufacturing concerns, and nonprofit organizations, for example, universities and colleges.

ministrative intensity, the proportion of personnel engaged in administering the organization. Since nearly all organizations are under some budgetary pressure, they tend to seek to reduce administrative overhead, or at least to increase it less than proportionately when they expand.

There is an economy of scale in organization. The larger an organization's size, the lower its administrative overhead. A complex structure differentiated in various respects, on the other hand, increases problems of administration and enlarges the proportion of personnel in administration. Since complexity increases with size, as we have seen, an organization's size has two opposite effects on administrative overhead. Its direct effect, when various aspects of differentiation are controlled, is to reduce it, but its indirect effect, mediated by the greater complexity (differentiation) of larger organizations, is to increase it. However, the direct effect exceeds the indirect one, so that the overall effect of size is to reduce administrative overhead.

The inference of these findings is that the administrative cost engendered by structural complexity acts like a brake to decrease the rate of differentiation of organizations the larger and more differentiated they already are, lest the cost of administrative overhead become prohibitive. This feedback effect of the administrative problems and cost of expanding complexity can account for the decelerating rate of increase of various forms of differentiation with organizational growth.

Parameters are applicable, as noted, to the study of organizations. The progressing division of labor in organizations, just as that in society at large, intensifies heterogeneity in the larger structure by increasing the homogeneity of its substructures. Increasing specialization of medical specialties, for instance, intensifies the division of labor in hospitals but reduces that within distinct occupations, as brain and orthopedic surgeons and other surgical specialties replace the former specialty of general surgeon. This is also the case for other forms of organizational differentiation. Thus, the various parts that are all produced in a small shop are manufactured in different divisions of a large factory.

Differentiation in various dimensions of organizations is a form of intersection, but organizational intersection is not the same as intersection of people. A distinction was made earlier in this chapter between affiliations with substructures and membership in organizations or their subunits, such as a labor union local or a branch of the ACLU. Intersecting affiliation with substructures implies that the various affiliations (and corresponding attributes, like religion or race) are weakly related. Differentiation of an organization in various dimensions, however, does not imply anything about the independence of people's characteristics. It provides people who differ in some respects with common membership in others, which increases opportunities for crosscutting ties and helps integrate employees in the organizations. In short, it increases the interdependence of various segments of the organization.

. . .

Private firms are particularly important organizations in a capitalist society. Organizational ecology is a relatively recent theoretical scheme advanced by Hannan and Freeman (1989) for analyzing the development of populations of organizations in an area, such as the restaurants or the publishing firms in a given city. The objective is to study over extended periods the growth and decline of the entire population of organizations of a certain kind, not of individual organizations. Their approach is evolutionary, considering changes in organizations to be largely the result of selection through the entry of new and the exit of old ones rather than the adaptation of existing ones to changing conditions.

The primary concern of organizational ecology is growth, which refers not to the change in size of a particular organization or to the average size of the entire population of organizations but to the number of organizations of the type under study.[7] A central concept is *density,* which refers to the number of firms of a type. The density, and hence the growth, of a population of organizations depends on the carrying capacity of the environment. But the theoretical analysis is concerned primarily with two other conditions on which density and growth, in turn, depend: an organization's legitimacy and competition from others. The first few firms of a new type have little legitimacy, but as their number increases they become institutionalized as legitimate. Hence, legitimacy is expected to occur at a rapid rate with increasing density, and further growth hardly affects it. Competition, on the other hand, puts a brake on growth, which implies that its adverse effect on growth increases at an increasing rate. Hence, Hannan and Freeman (1989: 134, emphasis in original) conclude that "the effect of density on the founding rate is *non-monotonic.*"

Specifically, they expected growing density to have a positive effect initially and a negative effect subsequently on founding rates. This proved to be the case in their study of labor unions (p. 213); it was not the case in their analysis of semiconductor firms (p. 230) but was for their sub-

---

7. Whether this growth in number occurs at the cost of average sales or assets is not considered.

sidiaries (p. 235); and it was the case in their study of newspaper pub-
lishers (p. 241), as indicated by a positive coefficient for density and a
negative one for its square in the regressions of foundations on these two
and several control variables. The same argument that initial growth
benefits (owing to legitimation) but further growth impedes (owing to
competition) organizations implies that mortality rates first decline and
later rise with growing density, which the results from studies of all three
types confirm.

These empirical results support the implication of Hannan and Freeman's theory that the effect of growth in the number of firms of a given
kind on both entries of new and exits of old firms reveals initially accelerating and then decelerating curves when entries or exits are regressed
on density while controlling other influences. However, their theory
claims that the earlier influence of increasing numbers is the result of
legitimation and the subsequent opposite effect is that of competition,
but their data support neither concept; they merely reveal the influence
of increasing number of firms. To use the polynomial of the number of
cases and its square as substitutes for two theoretical concepts—legitimation and competition—depending on the slope of the regression line
is not proper theoretical procedure. Two theoretical terms have to be
defined and distinguished, not represented by the same operational variable depending on its observed change in slope, before theoretical statements about them can be considered to be empirically tested.

· · ·

Nearly all, if not all, major firms are corporations, which means that they
are incorporated as legal entities that are independent of their owners.
The owners are not employers or partners who are personally responsible
for the debts of their firms but investors who have no personal obligations for the corporation's liabilities beyond the investments they have
made. The limited liability of investors and the standing of corporations
as legal persons, which in the United States rest on court interpretations
of the Fourteenth Amendment to the Constitution,[8] have given corporations and their wealthy investors tremendous economic advantages.

Coleman (1982), who is certainly not a radical social scientist—
indeed, he has been criticized for his conservative views—has called

---

8. It is a sad irony that the Constitutional amendment passed to give freedom to the
most underprivileged segment of the population has been used primarily to fortify the economic power of the most privileged.

attention to the concentration of power in large corporations and the resulting asymmetry in power between corporations and persons. The dominant and continually growing power of the major corporations increasingly infringes on the freedom and power of persons, on whose liberty and sovereignty American democracy presumably rests. The most dramatic instances are direct conflicts in court cases, when corporations are sued for compensation by employees whose health has been seriously impaired at work or by survivors of those who died from harm suffered at work. All the advantages in these cases, of which Coleman cites a number, are with the corporation owing to its large resources.

The overwhelming power of large corporations is based on their economic resources, but it is reinforced by their political influence and the interlocking connections through which they dominate economic markets. Networks of interpersonal relations of their representatives serve to build coalitions that extend their political and economic influence. Interestingly, indirect ties mediated by common ties to a third organization's representative—what Burt (1982) calls "structural equivalence"—apparently play a prominent role in these networks. Research on coalitions that exert political influence and on interconnections that promote economic domination is now briefly examined.

A study by Mizruchi (1989) asks what factors influence the likelihood that elite corporations engage in common political action. To answer this question, he analyzes the campaign contributions to the political action committees (PACs) of the same congressional candidates in the 1980 election by any two of the fifty-seven largest manufacturing firms representing the twenty different manufacturing industries. The fact that firms are in the same primary industry has the strongest effect on political contributions to the same candidate. Apparently the common interest in markets for their product overrides the conflicting interests of competitors in the same industry, perhaps because the largest corporations are price leaders not greatly worried about competition. The constraint of being similarly dependent on oligarchic suppliers and customers also has a substantial influence on political contributions to the same candidate.

An important type of interpersonal networks linking firms entails interlocking directorates, which refer to the same persons being directors of the board of trustees of several corporations. Directorate interlocks, particularly when banks are involved, are assumed to reduce conflict between corporations, which suggests that interlocks promote common interests (Mintz and Schwartz 1985). Mizruchi finds that direct interlocks between manufacturing corporations are not significantly related to parallel political support but that indirect interlocks via banks are. In other words, if two corporations have directorate ties with the same large bank, the likelihood is increased that they will support the same political candidate. This result suggests that large financial institutions are able to use their great economic power to exert not only direct but also indirect political influence by constraining decisions of other corporations that may be dependent on them.[9] This is consistent, as Mizruchi points out, with Mintz and Schwartz's (1985) conclusion.

Mizruchi's (1992: 247) recent book, in which he reanalyzes and expands his earlier work, concludes that "there is an inner circle within the corporate community that is politically unified, as Useem suggests." Useem (1984: 61) stresses that the top executives of the largest corporations form an inner circle "with multiple corporate connections [and] are expected not only to share a vision distinct from that of other business leaders, but also to take a far more active role in promoting their politics."

[margin note: Support for corp. class & unity]

Interlocking directorates are, of course, a form of intersection of corporation boards by common directors, and these conclusions indicate that they serve to integrate corporations and promote their common interest, which often is not that of the public. Mizruchi's (1992: 128–29) findings that the largest corporations are most likely to support the same political candidates and to belong to the policymaking Business Roundtable support Useem's thesis of the political unity of the core business elite. Mizruchi concludes that the dominant power in the American economy is apparently no longer exercised by elite families or very rich individuals but, rather, by interorganizational networks of persons in senior executive positions in major corporations, which supports Useem's conclusion of a dominant inner circle.

[margin note: Dominant inner corp. circle has power]

. . .

All of us act much of the time in our own self-interest, particularly in economic transactions. Yet there are social limits to our self-interest, even within the strictly economic sphere and certainly outside it. We are socially embedded (Granovetter 1985) in interpersonal networks and

9. Particularly in his subsequent book, Mizruchi (1992: 124–26) stresses an alternative interpretation of this finding: two organizations (or individuals) that have the same, positive or negative, relation to another or others (in network terms, that are structurally equivalent) are most likely to have common interests and engage in joint action. Both interpretations may well be correct.

concentric circles of increasingly encompassing collectivities to which we have some obligations that limit our self-interest. An organization's senior executives who act in its behalf also have obligations that limit their self-interest, but in their case the primary obligation is to their corporation and its stockholders, in whose interest they are expected to set aside their personal interests and often do. If conscientious corporation executives act in the interest of the organization even at the cost of their own interest, they are likely to do so also in disregard of the interests of others, including the public's.

The interests of business corporations, as represented by their executives, often conflict with the public interest, and so do the interests of individual business owners, though if there are many owners in competition the public interest may be protected. I conclude this topic by citing at length a classical author who wrote about the conflicting interests of business owners and the public more than a century ago, before the modern corporation had fully evolved. He first divides a country's productive population into three parts, depending on whether a person's income derives from the rent of land, work for wages, or profits of stocks. He then continues:

> The interest of the first [land proprietors] . . . is strictly and inseparably connected with the interest of society. . . .
>
> The interest of the second order, that of those who live by wages, is as strictly connected with the interest of society as that of the first. . . .
>
> The interest of dealers, however, in any particular branch of trade or manufactures, is always in some respects different from, or even opposite to, that of the public. To widen the market and to narrow the competition, is always the interest of the dealers. To widen the market may frequently be agreeable enough to the interest of the public; but to narrow the competition must always be against it, and can serve only to enable the dealers, by raising their profits above what they naturally would be, to levy, for their own benefit, an absurd tax upon the rest of their fellow-citizens. The proposal of any new law or regulation of commerce which comes from this order, ought always to be listened to with great precaution, and ought never to be adopted till after having been long and carefully examined, not only with the most scrupulous, but with the most suspicious attention. It comes from an order of men, whose interest is never the same as that of the public, who have generally an interest to deceive and even to oppress the public, and who accordingly have, upon many occasions, both deceived and oppressed it.

This quotation is not from *Das Kapital* by Karl Marx. It is from an earlier source, *The Wealth of Nations,* by Adam Smith (1776: 249–50).

Notwithstanding this warning that the commonweal must be protected against the proposals of owners whose interest inherently conflicts with the public interest, Adam Smith was, of course, a founder and advocate of laissez-faire capitalism. How has it come about that the capitalist system he described, in which many firms produce for profit in competitive markets, has undergone such fundamental changes since he wrote, particularly since the unprecedented huge conglomerate mergers in the 1960s? To answer this question, recent changes in corporations must be examined, changes that, as J. R. Blau (1993: 125–44) points out, gave rise to giant corporations that have internalized finance markets, inasmuch as they buy and sell companies.

FIRMS AND MARKETS

Large corporations in the United States have undergone a fundamental transformation since the middle of this century. This transformation has been preceded and anticipated by some changes in large corporations in the preceding decades. The declining markets of the Depression in the 1930s posed economic threats to business, which prompted many corporations to try to expand their markets. They accomplished this by diversifying products, typically to some related to their existing products, and instituting a divisional structure appropriate for diverse products. This was a transition stage that laid the groundwork for a new form of corporate control that found initial expression in the conglomerates of the 1950s and 1960s.

Ironically, this recent change in corporate structure and control, which greatly expanded the size of the largest corporations, may have been stimulated by antitrust legislation, according to Fligstein (1990).[10] After World War II, an antitrust campaign developed in Truman's administration, and there was much criticism of big business and, especially, the market concentration of large firms. The result was the passage of the Celler-Kefauver Act in 1950. This legislation prohibited vertical and horizontal integration, on the assumption that these mergers are the ones most apt to suppress competition and promote oligopoly in an industry.

10. My description of the "finance conception of control" and its development is greatly indebted to Fligstein's excellent analysis.

The fact that mergers of firms in the same or in related markets were illegal encouraged corporations interested in expanding to diversify into unrelated products by acquiring or investing in firms in unrelated markets. This was facilitated by, and in turn greatly strengthened, the financial control of corporations by the chief executive officer (CEO).

The diversification that had already developed and the focus of antitrust action on industrial concentration were, according to Fligstein (1990: 191), the two major factors responsible for the emergence of the strictly financial control of corporations by their top executives. This form of executive control became dominant in the conglomerates of the 1960s, but its main features have been preserved in the essentially financial control by chief executive officers of large corporations that continues to prevail. It typically involves leveraged buyouts of companies producing unrelated products for different markets, which often expand the buying corporation's liabilities far beyond its assets. This engenders concentration on short-term returns to meet the financial obligations incurred.

The Celler-Kefauver Act succeeded in preventing the growth of market concentration, but the total concentration of wealth in giant conglomerates increased greatly at the same time. A report by the Federal Trade Commission cited by Fligstein (1990: 203) states that "between 1959 and 1969 the concentration of all manufacturing assets in the 500 largest firms rose 11 percent and was almost entirely due to the merger movement. Between 1965 and 1968 one-fifth of the companies that were larger than $10 million in assets were swallowed up by mergers. From 1967 to 1969 roughly $19 billion in assets were purchased." He also presents a table (p. 195) that indicates that the number of mergers per year increased from the early 1950s to the late 1970s from 30 to 128 and the proportion involving unrelated products increased from 13 to 33 percent.

Although the heyday of conglomerates is past, its legacy is the control of division managers by top management in strictly financial terms, which has spread to many if not most large corporations. The merger of numerous unrelated products is at its very core, for such mergers necessitate financial control, which alone makes it possible to exercise control over the production and marketing of a great variety of unrelated products. Diversification into unrelated product lines has the result that CEOs cannot be experts in the production and marketing of all diverse products of their corporations' subsidiaries. Competent CEOs would be expected to appoint division heads who know more about the diverse products of the different divisions than they can possibly know about all of them. The only way they can evaluate and control them is in purely financial terms, which means CEOs' decisions are based on the same financial criteria on which private investors in the stock market base decisions on which shares to buy, sell, or hold.

Financial control by top management of division heads continues to prevail widely, but it has greatly changed since it developed with the conglomerates of the 1960s, often based on leveraged buyouts. These buyouts enabled some relatively small firms to become giant corporations, though many fell by the wayside. It was only later, in the 1980s, that junk bonds sprouted to finance these buyouts, but their time also seems to have come to an end. Whereas the early period was one of buyouts and mergers, subsequently divestitures have increased more rapidly than mergers, frequently necessitated by the huge debts entailed by buying firms on credit. The economic scene that apparently has emerged involves a number of giant corporations each of which owns a variety of corporations in diverse industries and markets.

. . .

These changes in the economy have been increasingly criticized on several grounds. Chandler (1990) represents the view of business management. He is critical of achieving growth by acquiring subsidiaries in unrelated industries for two main reasons. The corporate management cannot possibly have adequate knowledge and experience of all the different technological processes involved in the manufacture of unrelated products, and the large number of divisions precludes effective centralized direction. Top management, therefore, has to decentralize operating control and exercise overall control by relying entirely on financial considerations. The separation of top from operating management has created serious managerial weakness, which Chandler (1990: 139) considers responsible for "the sale of operating units in unheard numbers." The ratio of divestitures to mergers was 1 : 11 in 1965 but 1 : 2 in 1977. The result has been a restructuring of large corporations, which have become congeries of firms in unrelated industries, firms that are bought, sold, and split up in a continuing process of restructuring.

Fligstein (1990: 298) directs attention in his concluding chapter to the adverse consequences financial corporate control is likely to have for long-range planning and investments. He notes that financial corporate control may well foster a CEO's "obsession with short-run profits and fluctuations of the stock price and lack of attention to replacing capital stock and investing in future products." Such practices are not in an enterprise's long-term interest. Indeed, Fligstein (1990: 313, 314) explicitly stresses the danger these tendencies pose for the national economy: "The large firm is in crisis because it cannot meet the competitive challenge of firms in other countries. . . . American firms have already exited from a number of important markets, leaving them to foreign competitors."

In sum, I consider the financial form of corporate control to make a corporation, as it buys and sells firms, more akin to a market, like a stock market, than to a traditional business enterprise. Just as investors in the stock exchange are not concerned with particular products but make their decisions to buy or sell on the basis of financial considerations alone, the decisions of finance-control corporations are essentially independent of particular products and based on—often short-run—financial returns.

A corporation is not really an impersonal market, however. It certainly is not a neutral third party monitoring the trading of firms where buyers and sellers nearly always can be found. Its acting like a stock market is a strategy for profiting from buying and selling firms, often at huge debts, carried out at the expense of the public—the employees and stockholders of the firms traded, the taxpayers who, in effect, finance most of the debts, and ultimately the country's economic welfare. The United States has been in a prolonged recession, its firms can no longer compete in major markets, and economic inequality has increased with the growing concentration of wealth and expanding poverty.

. . .

Quite a different perspective on these changes concerning the largest corporations is provided by Eccles and White (1986). Figures they cite indicate that the large majority of the largest American manufacturing concerns—the Fortune 500—had a multiple-division structure, largely in diverse industries, in 1976. They raise the question of what accounts for the prevailing decentralization of top executive authority in these organizations. Their answer is that, more than merely reflecting the problems of executive control owing to diversification, it represents an effective way of coping with these problems. They suggest that top executives in these corporations exercise control through portfolio management and thereby govern the interface of their firms with various markets. A cross-classification of firms by the corporation that owns each one of them and the market in which the firm operates provides an image of the intersection of corporations and markets.

The exercise of authority by the top executives over division managers is experienced by the managers as domination, according to Eccles and White. Decentralization to multidivision firms replaces domination by "exploitation" (p. 204), in the sense that managers of subsidiaries are constrained by the market to make those operating decisions that are in accord with top management's interest. In short, top management substitutes market constraints for directives to control top managers of divisions. Firms owned by a corporation are called by Eccles and White (1986: 204) *profit centers*. The manager of a profit center must obtain and sustain profitable niches in the marketplace. The chief executive controls the corporation's market interface.

The CEO exercises this control by portfolio management. Whereas it is possible for CEOs to decentralize operating decisions to middle management, it is not feasible for them to decentralize decisions about resource allocation. For it is through resource allocation, including portfolio management by buying and selling firms or shares of them, that top management exercises control over the entire enterprise. The profit centers of a corporation can be classified in two dimensions—the relative market share its firm owns and the market's growth rate. Eccles and White assume that these two factors are the main guidelines in portfolio management, which they consider (p. 211) "a natural consequence of the widespread implementation of multi-profit-center structures within firms."

Of special interest for the parameter scheme is that recent developments have created intersection of dominant corporations and markets through the firms in diverse industries the largest corporations own. This is another case in which the intersection of organized structures and that of people's affiliations in various dimensions are formally parallel but substantively quite different. Intersecting, in contrast to correlated, social differences in a population imply that people's differences in various respects do not reinforce but tend to counteract one another. The intersection of corporations and markets indicates crosscutting links of corporations and markets: firms in the same market belong to different corporations, and firms in different markets belong to the same corporation. This crosscutting integrates markets through corporations (the formal parallel) and gives the latter tremendous power over markets (the substantive difference), contrary to the ideal of free competition and the public's interest.

CONCLUSIONS

The first section of this chapter dealt with the parameter scheme of multidimensional social space. McPherson and Ranger-Moore's (1991) analysis of the influences of the broader social context on memberships in voluntary associations and other organizations, and my extension of it, stress that the prevalence of homophilous recruitment through informal relations tends to make members more alike than society at large. Hence, voluntary associations tend to occupy a niche of similar persons in the social structure, which manifests their homogeneity.

Such homophily is the case not only for association memberships but also for people attending the same place, event, or occasion—the patrons of a bar, the fans of a rock band, the people who came to Woodstock. However, homophilous recruitment engenders some heterogeneity, because an association's members are not perfectly homogeneous but have a range of similarities—in age or education, for instance—and those at one extreme may be more likely to join the association than their opposites. Moreover, intersecting differences make people who are alike in some respects unlike in others.

Although the macrostructural theoretical scheme was not extensively used in this chapter, an important refinement of the central concept of intersection was introduced. The intersection of social differences has different implications when referring, as it did when first introduced, to affiliation with a substructure of the population, such as ethnic group, religion, occupation, or social class, and when referring to crosscutting memberships in groups, organizations, or subunits of organizations. The original form of intersection implies that two or more lines of social differences are not mostly parallel but intersect one another, in the sense that they are not strongly correlated but are more or less orthogonal. In contrast, the new form reflects not the strength of the correlation of social differences among people but the degree to which common memberships in various subunits supply integrating bonds.

This conclusion will focus on the latter form of intersection, which was analyzed in various passages of the chapter. Breiger concludes from his analysis of attendance at group meetings that common memberships of different groups not only integrate individuals in group activities but also integrate the various groups with one another and thereby promote joint endeavors. Similarly, the internal differentiation of formal organizations vertically, horizontally, and spatially engenders diverse crosscutting connections that contribute to communication and coordination.

Mizruchi infers from his study of the political influence of large corporations that the dominant power in our economy is exercised largely by interorganizational networks of senior executives in major corporations. Interlocking directorates of corporations are crosscutting them and thereby exert a unifying dominant influence, which serves the interest of the business community, particularly its major corporations, but may well conflict with the public's. The largest corporations in recent years have been buying up firms in diverse markets, which constitutes another manifestation of the intersection of corporations and markets by means of the firms the corporations own in different industries. This intersection increases the interdependence of markets and gives corporations power over markets by determining in which ones to invest and from which ones to withdraw investments, enhancing the dominance of corporations but not being in the interest of the public. Adam Smith warned two centuries ago that the commonweal must be protected against profit-making enterprises, whose interests are contrary to the public's.

All these cases involve crosscutting social relations that intersect different social organizations or their subunits. They thereby integrate tne diverse organizations or segments of organizations and help to coordinate common endeavors. Intersecting differences of people's social affiliations and positions in various dimensions also promote intergroup relations. Thus, both forms of intersection further social integration but in entirely different ways. Crosscutting connections integrate subunits of various kinds by serving as channels of communication and coordination (which may—but need not—benefit the public good). In contrast, intersecting differences impede ingroup choices and thereby promote intergroup relations, which are essential for the integration of a diverse community.

Six

SOCIAL EXCHANGE

POPULATION STRUCTURES ARE NOT PRODUCED by the social interactions in millions of little groups, as the conception of the microfoundation of macrosociology implies, although the past activities in face-to-face relations and groups do influence the future population structure. For instance, the differences in the birthrates in families belonging to different ethnic and religious groups alter the emerging population composition. The reason that the study of social processes in face-to-face groups is important, however, is not so much because they indirectly influence the future population structure but because they are the ultimate dynamic expression of macrostructural influences on people's present social lives and role relations. The processes in interpersonal relations and networks shape our social experiences and roles. These social interactions are circumscribed by macrostructural conditions, which do not rob individuals of choice but do limit the alternatives available to them.[1] The macrostructural approach to social theory is neither the only form of macrosociology nor the only form of structural sociology.[2] Max Weber and Talcott Parsons are surely macrosociological theorists, but, at least from my perspective, their approach is primarily cultural, not structural. On the other hand, the study of social ties of individuals, from Moreno's sociometry to the various current forms of network analysis, is structural but micro, not macro.

---

1. Stinchcombe (1975: 12, emphasis in original) interprets Merton's theory as focusing on "*the choice between socially structured alternatives.*"

2. Calhoun and Scott (1990: 13–14 and passim) have criticized me for sometimes ignoring that these are two analytically distinct dichotomies. I was not aware of doing so; if I did, I was wrong.

I have used the terms *macro* and *micro,* but I hasten to add that I consider this juxtaposition, particularly the notion of a single micro-macro link, highly misleading. It invites a simplistic conception of sociology as being the study of only two levels of phenomena and the connection between the two, micro and macro. Besides, most microstudies of social networks—with rare exceptions, such as those of Emerson (1972, 1976) and Cook (1982)—tend to ignore the processes of social interaction and exchange that shape face-to-face social ties and their network structures.

Moreover, studies of the micro-macro link typically treat macrophenomena as an overarching unitary canopy, ignoring that the distinctive characteristic of complex structures (Simon 1962) is their being composed of multiple levels of structure. Multilevel structural analysis is a procedure for analyzing the multiple steps entailed by the macromicro connection, and penetrating differentiation specifies the macrostructural conditions that influence interpersonal relations and networks and explains why they do. Most analyses of the micro-macro link, finally, are essentially microsociological, considering macrostructures merely epiphenomena based on microfoundations. This makes the wrong causal assumption, at least from the perspective of macrosociology.

The topic of this chapter is the analysis of processes of social exchange, which, of course, is based to a considerable extent on my earlier theoretical analysis of the subject (Blau 1964). The present analysis departs from the earlier one in important ways, however, because my conception of the nexus between macrostructures and exchange processes has changed greatly in the quarter of a century since the 1964 book was written. There I considered the analysis of exchange processes in interpersonal relations as the basis on which a macrostructural theory should be built, which is similar to the approach of the microfoundation of macrostructures I just criticized. Moreover, I treated cultural values as the central concept for transforming the analysis of exchange processes into an analysis of macrostructural conditions.

My present theoretical orientation has fundamentally changed in both of these respects. I view the primary task of sociology to be the analysis of how the macrostructural conditions in their environment limit the choices of individuals, not the analysis of how the social interaction in interpersonal relations affects the larger social structure. And I conceptualize macrostructure not in terms of common value orientations but in terms of the population structure defined as the population's distributions along various lines and the relationships of the different dimensions of these distributions. The two changes in my approach are related. A cultural conception of society in terms of prevailing values and norms could attribute a society's culture to the social interaction and practices of its members and subgroups. But it is hardly conceivable that contemporary people's relations and actions create society's population composition, whereas it is plausible that various aspects of the population structure, such as its ethnic diversity or economic inequality, affect interpersonal relations.

TRANSITION REVERSED

The Foundations of Sociology, by Coleman (1990a), is a major theoretical contribution, although I do not agree with two of its basic premises. The first with which I disagree is the assumption of rational-choice theory that all human behavior can be explained in strictly rational terms (which is not to say that rational choice exerts no influence, and aspects of it are implicit in my theory of social exchange). The second is his claim that it is fallacious to seek to account for social phenomena and relations on the basis of antecedent sociostructural conditions, because all social phenomena must be explained in terms of the decisions and actions of individuals. The discussion here is confined to one topic, albeit one of central significance for the theory and directly related to the second premise, namely, Coleman's analysis of the transition from the level of individual action to that of social structure.

Coleman (1990a: 2) states at the outset that the principal task of the social sciences is the explanation of social phenomena, not that of the behavior of individuals. This describes my orientation exactly, but what is meant by the "explanation of social phenomena" departs sharply from it. Since the rational behavior of individuals is the foundation of macrophenomena, according to Coleman, explaining how macrophenomena develop requires a three-step procedure: (1) ascertaining how the antecedent social condition influences individual values and motives; (2) tracing the effects of these individual motives on individual behavior; (3) and only then explaining the influence of social antecedent on social outcome as mediated by the rationally motivated behavior of individuals. Coleman is a methodological individualist but by no means a naive psychological reductionist. He emphasizes that the third step, determining the influence of interdependent individual behavior on social outcomes, must not simply aggregate individuals (and their behavior) but analyze their interdependence, both being essential elements of the resulting social system (pp. 300–313, 376).

This three-step scheme is initially developed by Coleman (1990a:

6–10) on the basis of a criticism of Max Weber's thesis in *The Protestant Ethic and the Spirit of Capitalism*. The thesis is that the emergence of capitalism cannot be explained on purely rational and economic grounds, because a necessary condition for its development is the Calvinist doctrine with its emphasis on "worldly asceticism." Coleman criticizes the proposition that the ethics of Calvinism is necessary for capitalist development as a shortcut that ignores the intervening steps in the causal sequence. An adequate explanation would require specifying (1) how the Calvinist doctrine affects individuals' religious beliefs; (2) how these beliefs motivate ascetic behavior in one's secular vocation; and (3) why such behavior by interdependent individuals is essential for the development of a capitalist system.[3]

In his criticism of Weber, Coleman's scheme replaces one causal nexus (structure-structure) by three (structure-motive, motive-behavior, and [interdependent] behavior-structure). His subsequent analysis, however, is largely confined to the third step—the influence of interdependent individual behavior on structural conditions. His first step, which is the focus of my theory—the limits structural conditions impose on individual choices and social relations—is hardly analyzed, and the same is true for the influences of motivation on individual behavior. Most of his attention centers on the third step—the transition from the behavior of interdependent individuals to various macrophenomena, such as collective action, legislation in a parliament, or the organization of a union. My critical discussion will also center on this transition, after summarizing some of Coleman's own analysis of cases of transition.

Coleman introduces the subject with a simple example of such a transition (1990a: 128–30). If an individual obtains a service from another, such as some advice or a loan, he feels obligated to reciprocate by exhibiting deference to the other and compliance with her wishes, which enhances her social status. Such recurring processes in a collectivity give rise to a stratified status structure. In a more complex example, involving economic assumptions and calculations (pp. 136–42), he uses data on homework, absences, and grades for every tenth-grade student in two schools to derive measures of the differentiated power structure and the variation in interests among students in the two schools. The illustrations

---

3. It seems strange to accuse Weber of ignoring motivated human behavior, inasmuch as his methodology (though a good part of his analysis is structural) represents the importance of *Verstehen* for social study—the need to interpret human conduct and social life in terms of a meaningful understanding of people's social values and motivations.

indicate how data on individuals can be used to derive attributes of social structure, albeit those of fairly small collectivities in these cases.

Of special interest is Coleman's (1990a: 381–84) analysis of how a commune—or any other committee or group that must decide on joint action—arrives at consensus. In contrast to formal organizations, there are no official procedures or decision rules, and votes are avoided because consensus is highly valued. To reach it, the members of the commune or group engage in often very lengthy discussions in which many related issues are aired and there is much give and take as individuals express and modify their opinions.

If the alternatives were limited in number, a vote (or series of votes) could resolve the issue, but even then a vote would ignore variations among individuals in the strength of their interest in different issues. Discussions take these differences into account. They do so by providing opportunities for a few persons who have a strong interest in one issue to give in on many other issues in exchange for getting support from many who do not have such strong interests in the matter of the minority's main concern. This is how minorities can win agreement on their major demands, but they do so at the price of supporting many individuals on issues of great interest to them.

Similar processes occur in legislatures, in this case not to reach consensus but to gain majority support for a bill that initially does not command a majority but is of great importance to a few members (Coleman 1966).[4] Legislators are voting on many issues, and though they may have some preference in most cases, their interest is not equally great in all. To gain support for the bills that are of greatest interest to them, they solicit the support of others who have little interest in the outcome of these bills, in return for which they support bills in which the others have much interest but they have little. (This is how small orthodox Jewish parties in Israel have been able to pass bills in the Knesset enforcing orthodox practices in a largely nonorthodox nation.)[5] Coleman (1990a: 386–87) suggests that these processes in which votes are weighted by the importance of and commitment to different issues yield outcomes that are morally superior to those that are decided by straight voting.

4. Coleman first developed the central ideas of *Foundations* in this impressive paper.

5. Another illustration is that for years Congress passed an oil depletion allowance that only a few legislators strongly favored, because these legislators succeeded in gaining the support of a majority who were weakly opposed in exchange for their support on bills the other lawmakers favored.

These examples may suffice to convey the imaginative analysis in which Coleman dissects the interdependent actions of individuals to show how they produce structural outcomes. It may be noted, however, that most of the structures he examines in detail are those of quite small collectivities. A commune or a parliament consists at most of a few hundred persons, whereas macrosociology tends to concentrate on populations of hundreds of thousands if not millions. To be sure, he also furnishes some examples of transitions producing large-scale systems as the result of the organizing endeavors of many interdependent persons, such as the organization of labor unions, the development of corporations, or the emergence of norms, described as "a prototypical micro-to-macro transition" (p. 244).

However, most of his detailed analysis, particularly that formulated quantitatively, involves very short-range transitions. Thus, the development of cooperative norms typically starts with bilateral monopoly (represented by an Edgeworth box) and goes on to three actors, and sometimes jumps from there to a perfectly competitive market (Coleman 1990a: 249–58, 328–35, 670–98). Moreover, in an ingenious simulation of an iterated prisoner's dilemma to study sanctions to enforce cooperative norms in groups varying in size from three to ten, Coleman (1990b) finds that the effectiveness of sanctions to sustain norms depends greatly on small group size. The tiny range in size is hardly a micro-macro transition, and the adverse effect of group size on cooperative norms fails to support his claim already mentioned that the "emergence of norms is in some respects a prototypical micro-to-macro transition" (Coleman 1990a: 244).

I fully agree with Coleman that sociologists must analyze the connections between the macrostructures of entire societies or communities and the daily relations and transactions in the multitude of settings in which our social lives actually take place. Whereas I agree with him on that, I think his linkage of the two is upside down and needs to be put right-side up. Population structures do not emerge from the interpersonal relations and conduct in innumerable face-to-face encounters (except that past ones may influence structural changes), not even if their interdependence is taken into account.[6]

---

6. This statement and the following analysis apply to macrostructures conceived in terms of people's distribution among social positions, but not only my specific version of it. Other examples of an equivalent conception of structure are Marx's class structure, Durkheim's division of labor, theories of segmented (originally, dual) economic sectors and labor

On the contrary, it is the social environment—the multidimensional composition of the population—that governs the life chances of individuals, both by supplying opportunities for and by imposing constraints on their cordial relations, conflicts, and social mobility. Since the macrostructure of a large society or community is far removed from the level of direct social interaction, the transition must be traced by analyzing whether and how macrostructural conditions penetrate through multiple levels to the microlevel of personal encounters and experiences and permeate the substructures on this lowest level. For instance, the impact of society's ethnic heterogeneity on people's life chances and social life depends on whether it penetrates into suburbs and neighborhoods or entails ethnic segregation of these substructures.

. . .

Let me illustrate that the micro-macro transition needs to be reversed into a macro-micro transition to represent the correct causal nexus. A widely used case, which Coleman (1990a: 300) himself criticizes, is the assumption in classical economics that laissez-faire capitalism develops because the independent actions of unrelated traders create perfect competition in a market. His criticism centers on the interdependence of individuals, which is both the source of social capital useful in competition and an impediment to the perfect competition assumed to exist by neoclassical economic theory.

My particular concern is not merely that individuals are interdependent but that complex institutional structures are required to create the framework within which economic transactions take place, including government commissions, courts to maintain law and order, legislatures, and stock exchanges. Capitalism is unthinkable except as a succession of innovations emerging in the context of a large number of already established institutions, and competition does not survive unless laws to protect it have been enacted.

The trading in a legislature of votes on one issue for votes on another is a very suggestive case of the micro-macro transition early analyzed by

---

markets, and the concept of market concentration. The analysis may not apply if social structure is conceptualized in cultural or interpersonal terms, such as in terms of "common-value integration" (Parsons 1937: 768), which implies that it is culturally determined (Parsons 1966: 113), or "rules and resources . . . produced and reproduced in interaction" (Giddens 1986: 25), or "interaction ritual chains" (Collins 1987: 195–98).

Coleman (1966). A very impressive paper, but is it really a micro-macro transition? Is it not the result of an election system like ours with campaigns financed largely by private contributions, which weakens party discipline and makes legislators indebted to large contributors? This is not typical of most Western democracies, where candidates' campaigns are financed for the most part by their political party or the government, and the consequent party discipline makes such trading unlikely. I consider it to be a macro-micro transition, reflecting the political structure's effect on individuals' conduct. (In the case of the Israeli Knesset, it is a multiparty structure with no party commanding an absolute majority.) Even the wide-ranging discussions in a commune are likely to turn into free-for-all shouting matches unless procedures and structures develop that regulate speaking time and order. I consider Coleman's insightful analysis of how the give and take in discussion groups and the trading of votes in legislatures improve equity by weighting votes by strength of commitment to presuppose a social structure that governs the limits of individual transactions. Hence, it indicates a macro-micro transition, not a micro-macro one.

In sum, population structures do not emerge as the result of the interpersonal relations and social processes in multitudes of small groups. At least, population structures in the sense in which the term is used here do not, for the actions and interactions of individuals cannot produce the composition of the population (except for future changes in it). The multidimensional space of broadly defined social positions among which people are distributed, which I term *population structure,* circumscribes the opportunities and constraints individuals experience in their social encounters and careers, provided that multilevel structural analysis ascertains how far various macrostructural properties penetrate into substructures.

In the long run, however, there is some feedback. Today's population structure limits the social relations and social mobility in its substructures, though even that influence determines only rates or probabilities and does not determine the acts of particular individuals. But the acts of individuals today exert some influence, though a small one in most cases, on tomorrow's population structure, that is, on changes in it. By voting, mating, marrying within one's group in some instances and outside in others, having fewer or more children, and in many other ways, persons influence the changes that occur in the population structure. The actions of persons in important positions—presidents, senators, executives of large corporations—naturally exert more influence on social change than the actions of other persons. These changes can be traced by analyzing historical trends. Such trends are discussed briefly in the next chapter.

A final question that should be raised is whether the difference between Coleman's analysis of transitions and mine of reversed transitions is one of perspective or whether the two imply empirical predictions that make it possible to decide between them. The macrostructural approach is essentially not a theory but a theoretical perspective, which I consider the most appropriate one for sociology, but many sociologists do not agree and employ other perspectives. The specific case of transition is somewhat different. Even in my view, there are feedback effects, as just mentioned, and some sociologists may consider, as Coleman apparently does, what I call reverse traditions to be mere feedbacks of micro-macro transitions. Specific empirical applications, however, are not mere perspectives but have testable implications. Take the trading of votes in legislatures. It should be possible to obtain historical evidence to ascertain whether differences in political structure, election financing, and parliamentary procedures have determined the trading of votes, as I suggest, or whether trading practices gradually evolved and formal structures and procedures were adopted to facilitate them, as Coleman implies. Empirical testing is also feasible for other forms of transition, though different research procedures—observation, survey, experiment—would be appropriate.

FORMULATION OF EXCHANGE THEORY

A fundamental difference between social life in small isolated communities and that in large complex societies is the declining significance of the groups into which one is born and the growing significance of reciprocated choices for human relations. To be sure, the significance of ascribed positions has by no means disappeared in contemporary complex societies. Most people's closest relations are with their parents and children. Other ascribed positions continue to exert a major influence on social relations, notably one's kin and the ethnic group and social class into which one is born. Yet, even for quite close relatives, except one's immediate family, the extent of social interaction and the intimacy of the relation are not ascribed but depend on reciprocal choices. Larger ascribed affiliations, like ethnic and class background, affect the likelihood of choice but do not predetermine who selects whom as close associate, which depends on reciprocated choices.

Thus, ascribed as well as achieved positions govern probabilities of association, which are generally higher for ascribed than achieved affiliations, but they do not determine specific associates (with the exception of parents and children), let alone the extent of social interaction and the closeness of the relation. Their probabilistic influences on ingroup associations are similar to those of a community's population structure. The population distributions in a community also influence only the probabilities of ingroup and intergroup relations of various kinds, but the specific dyads within which these probabilities find expression depend on mutual choices.

Dependence on reciprocated choice implies that, if I want to associate with someone, I cannot realize my goal unless I make him interested in associating with me. For our social relation to persist once it has been established, both of us have to sustain an interest in its continuation. To determine what brings these conditions about is the objective of exchange theory, which analyzes the processes that establish reciprocity in social relations and sustain it, and which thereby dissects the dynamics of social interaction.

Structural conditions impose limits on the exchange relations that can develop. The population structure of an entire society or large community, however, is far removed from the daily social life of individuals and hence does not affect it directly but indirectly. Multilevel structural analysis traces these indirect limiting influences. It discloses how macrostructural conditions are transmitted to successive levels and which ones reach the lowest level on which direct social interaction and exchange occur. It may indicate, for example, that society's racial heterogeneity penetrates into small substructures or that it is reflected in segregation of different races in different suburbs and neighborhoods with much homogeneity within them. The former situation would make intergroup relations more likely than the latter, but neither would determine which specific social relations occur.

Many, if not most, human gratifications are obtained in relations with other human beings. Intellectual stimulation and relaxing conversation, sexual pleasures and the enchantment of love, academic recognition and a happy family life, satisfying the lust for power and the need for acceptance—all of these are contingent on eliciting responses from others. Exchange theory analyzes the mutual gratifications persons provide one another that sustain social relations.

. . .

The basic assumption of the theory of social exchange is that persons establish social associations because they expect them to be rewarding and that they continue social interaction and expand it because they experience it to be rewarding. This assumption that two parties associate with one another not owing to normative requirements but because they both expect rewards from doing so implies that the exchange of rewards is a starting mechanism of social relations that is not contingent on norms prescribing obligations. If a person is attracted to others because she expects associating with them to be rewarding, she will want to associate with them to obtain the expected rewards. For them to associate with her, they must be interested in doing so, which depends, according to the initial assumption, on their expecting such association to be rewarding to them. Consequently, for the first person to realize the rewards expected from the association with others, she must impress them as a desirable associate with whom interaction will be rewarding.

Rewards thru exchng [handwritten margin note]

Individuals are often hesitant to take the first step for fear of rejection. A widely used early strategy is for people to impress others in whom they are interested with their outstanding qualities—their wit, charm, intelligence, knowledge of the arts—which implicitly promises that associating with them would be a rewarding experience. If the early steps are successful, they tend to become self-fulfilling prophecies. As each person puts his best foot forward, associating with him turns out to be an enjoyable experience. In due course, people start doing favors for one another. In a work situation, the more experienced may give their colleagues advice or help with a difficult job. Neighbors may lend one another tools. People who met socially may issue invitations to dinner or a party.

Most people enjoy doing favors for others, usually without any thought of return, at least initially. Nevertheless, a person who benefits from an association is under an obligation to reciprocate. If the benefits are recurrent—whether involving merely the enjoyment of the other's company or getting frequently needed advice about one's work from a colleague—the self-imposed obligation to reciprocate is sustained by the interest in continuing to obtain the benefits. It is further reinforced by the fear of not seeming ungrateful. Even when there is no initial thought of return, failure to reciprocate when the occasion arises invites such an accusation, which will be experienced though it remains unspoken.

Imagine a neighbor lends you her lawn mower in the summer, but when she asks you next winter to borrow your snow blower you refuse.

The neighbor and others who learn of your refusal undoubtedly will consider you ungrateful, and whether they do or not, you yourself will feel ungrateful and surely will be hesitant to ask to borrow her lawn mower again. The feelings and possible accusations of ingratitude indicate that favors freely given are not entirely free but create obligations in one's own mind to reciprocate as well as possible social pressures to discharge the obligations.

A fundamental distinction between social and economic exchange is that social exchange engenders diffuse obligations, whereas those in economic exchange are specified in an implicit or explicit contract. For economic transactions that are not immediately completed, like purchases in stores, the terms of the exchange are agreed upon in advance by both parties, and major agreements are formalized in a contract that specifies the precise nature of the obligations of both parties and when any outstanding debts are due. The favors in social exchange, by contrast, create diffuse obligations, to be discharged at some unspecified future date. If a couple give a dinner party, for instance, they have no agreement on when and where or even whether the guests will invite them back, though their relations may be weakened if they do not, or if they do so too late or too soon. The diffuseness of the obligations implies that large-scale social exchange is not likely to occur unless firm social bonds rooted in trust have been established.

In the absence of legal obligations to make a return for benefits received, the initial problem of new acquaintances is to prove themselves trustworthy in social exchange. This typically occurs as exchange relations evolve in a slow process, starting with minor transactions entailing little risk and requiring little trust. The mutual discharge of obligations and reciprocation profit both parties and prove them increasingly trustworthy as favors are regularly reciprocated. The growing mutual advantages gained from the association fortify their social bond. This may appear to be merely a by-product of social exchange, but it is, in fact, its most important product.

Implicit in discussions of social exchange is an element of rationality, if not calculation, which may give the impression that social exchange theory is simply a version of rational choice theory. However, this impression is misleading. To be sure, social exchange does imply some rational pursuit of rewards, but the prime benefit sought, once the friendship bond of mutual support and trust is clearly established, is the rewarding experience derived from the association itself. Any material benefits exchanged are incidental and of significance largely as tokens of the friendship.

. . .

I conceptualize processes of social association as occurring in the relation between two persons. Accordingly, the exchange theory just presented analyzes exchange processes in dyads, just as the intergroup relations analyzed in chapter 3 refer to rates of dyadic relations between members of different groups. Ekeh (1974) has criticized my and Homans's (1961) exchange theory as individualistic, ignoring the difference between my concern with social structure and Homans's psychological reductionism. His criticism centers on the analysis of dyadic exchange. He contrasts the concept of restricted or two-party exchange unfavorably with Lévi-Strauss's (1949) generalized or multiparty exchange. Ekeh (1974: 62–65) considers the latter (multiparty) exchange more Durkheimian, owing to its concern with structural integration, whereas he dismisses dyadic exchange as individualistic and thus lacking a structural focus.

There is good reason that I, as a structural sociologist, prefer restricted dyadic to generalized multiparty exchange. Generalized exchange refers to the prevailing practice that all members of a tribe or group freely provide benefits to other members without looking for any return from the person to whom the contribution is made. Since doing favors for others is socially expected, it is in effect a group norm. Conformity with this norm is the reason that all group members receive favors in the long run and solidarity is strengthened. My criticism of generalized exchange is that it is simply another name for conformity to group norms and consequently commits the tautological fallacy of explaining social conduct in terms of social norms demanding this conduct.[7] Generalized exchange thereby dispenses with the crucial insight of exchange theory that interpersonal relations are not contingent on social norms, because gradually expanding reciprocity supplies a mechanism for establishing and maintaining them and engendering trust to boot.

That my analysis of social exchange is confined to exchange processes that occur in dyads does not mean that the social context in which these processes occur can be ignored, since it does influence them. Actually, exchange processes are affected by several contexts of widening so-

7. Cultural theories that explain social patterns in terms of norms and values are prone to commit this tautology. It is the same fallacy as that of psychological explanations of behavior in terms of instincts to engage in such behavior.

cial circles. The most immediate social context is the groups to which the dyads belong, which exert two distinct influences on dyadic exchange.

First, a group's network structure defines the alternative opportunities for exchange relations various persons have and thereby affects the outcomes of persons in different network positions. (Exchange processes, in turn, may alter the network structure.) Experiments performed by Cook and her colleagues indicate that networks that provide alternative exchange partners to one person but not to others increase the bargaining power of this person in dyadic exchanges (see, for example, Cook, Gillmore, and Tamagishi 1983).

A second influence of the immediate social context is that it discourages failure to reciprocate for benefits received by social disapproval of such ingratitude. I realize that my reference to social disapproval, which implies social pressure, sounds as if I attributed exchange to group norms, for which I criticized the principle of generalized exchange. There is a major difference, however. If the practice of making a contribution freely to any group member without expecting a return from that member is explained by the cultural norm to do so, the *explicans* cannot explain the *explicandum*, because the two are redundant. But exchange is explained not by social pressures but by the returns it brings, including pleasant company or friendship as well as possibly tangible benefits. Social exchange, however, cannot prevail if trust, once established, is violated, and social disapproval discourages its violation. Social pressures do not explain—account for—reciprocal exchange, but they help to sustain it.

The influence of the wider social circles—the population structure of a neighborhood, community, or entire society—depends on the extent to which the population distributions of the encompassing social structure penetrate into the substructures of face-to-face groups. Many of the differences in society's population structure are the result of differences among rather than within substructures on successive levels. As a result, face-to-face groups are less differentiated than their encompassing social structures. Multilevel structural analysis discloses how much differentiation in various dimensions penetrates into the substructures of interpersonal relations. Greater homophily in segregated substructures promotes ingroup relations, but despite much segregation, some differentiation penetrates to the lowest level of interpersonal relations. Consequently, although ingroup relations prevail in daily social intercourse, intergroup relations also regularly occur.

The common occurrence of intergroup relations is revealed in a study by Marsden (1990) that applies my theoretical scheme to the egocentric face-to-face networks of a sample of the American population. He initially distinguishes a demand-side view of networks in terms of preferences for various kinds of associates from a supply-side view, like my theory's, in terms of opportunities for associating with diverse others. On the basis of previous research on the composition of families and work places, we know that families are more diverse in age and sex but less diverse in ethnic and religious affiliation than associates at work. Accordingly, Marsden hypothesizes more intergroup relations in respect to age and sex and fewer intergroup relations in respect to ethnic and religious affiliation between relatives than between fellow workers. The results support these hypotheses, which stipulate intergroup as well as ingroup relations even between close associates. Marsden concludes that my macrostructural opportunity theory is applicable to the study of the relations in microstructures, contrary to what I myself had stated.

I am pleased that the theory can be used in the investigation of face-to-face networks, which I had questioned. One should note, however, that confining network analysis to the supply-side approach would fail to take full advantage of the possibilities for analysis the small scope of these networks provides. In the study of large populations, analysis and research cannot proceed without ignoring the complexities of social life by having to aggregate specific observations into gross concepts and measures, like heterogeneity, intersection, or intergroup relations. The subtle processes that govern face-to-face relations are admittedly (but inevitably) obscured by such aggregations. The study of interpersonal relations and small networks can directly analyze these processes and thereby contribute to our understanding of them.

IMBALANCE IN EXCHANGE

A paradox of social exchange is that it gives rise to both social bonds between peers and differentiation of status. This was the case for the ceremonial exchange of gifts in nonliterate societies, and it is the case for exchange processes in advanced industrial societies. To start by exemplifying the former, the Kula ceremonial gift exchange of the Trobriand Islanders, as discussed by Malinowski (1961: 92), "provides every man within its ring with a few friends near at hand, and with some friendly allies in far away, dangerous, foreign districts." A few pages later he states that "among the natives of the Kula . . . wealth is the indispensable appanage of social rank" (p. 97). Probably the extreme case of the significance of social exchange for differentiation of status is the famous pot-latch of the Kwakiutl, a feast of reckless spending in which "status in associations and clans, and rank of every kind, are determined by the war of property" (Mauss 1954: 35).

A contemporary case of status differentiation resulting from social exchange was observed in the office of a federal government agency responsible for the enforcement of certain laws. The duties of the agents involved investigating private firms by auditing their books and conducting interviews, determining any legal violations and the action to be taken, and negotiating a settlement with the employer or a top manager. The work was quite complex, and agents often encountered problems. When they did, they were expected to consult their supervisor, but they tended to be reluctant to do so for fear of adversely affecting their annual rating by their supervisor. Instead, they usually consulted colleagues. Whereas officially prohibited, this practice was widespread and evidently tolerated. Although agents worked on different cases, one could observe all day long pairs or small clusters of persons in deep discussions, most of which dealt with problems of their cases. Lunch periods were filled with such discussions.

The observation of these consultations originally gave me the idea of social exchange. To cite the central passage (Blau 1955: 108):[8]

> A consultation can be considered an exchange of values; both participants gain something and both have to pay a price. The questioning agent is enabled to perform better than he could otherwise have done, without exposing his difficulties to the supervisor. By asking for advice, he implicitly pays his respect to the superior proficiency of his colleague. This acknowledgment of inferiority is the cost of receiving assistance. The consultant gains prestige, in return for which he is willing to devote some time to the consultation and permit it to disrupt his own work. The following remark illustrates this: "I like giving advice. It's flattering, I suppose, if you feel that the others come to you for advice."

The principle of marginal utility applies to these exchanges. Although most agents liked being consulted, for those frequently asked for

8. As indicated by the publication date, this was written long before the women's movement called attention to the implicit bias involved in referring to some unspecified person always by the masculine pronoun instead of using either he/she or even s/he (which I find deplorable) or alternating between feminine and masculine pronouns, as I have done in this book.

Advice @
work &
exchng

advice the gain in informal status of an additional consultation diminished and the cost in repeated interruptions of one's own work increased. As the most popular consultant said to me when asked about being consulted, "I never object, although sometimes it's annoying." The principle also applies to agents who frequently need advice, but in reverse, of course.

Repeated admissions of needing advice undermine one's self-confidence and standing in the group, particularly if an oft-interrupted consultant expresses some impatience or annoyance. To forestall such experiences, most agents establish partnerships of mutual consultation, reserving consulting the most expert colleagues for their most difficult problems. Since agents often have tentative solutions for their problems and need not so much an answer as assurance that theirs is correct, a colleague whose expertise is not superior to one's own can provide such support.

The most expert agents face a different dilemma: asking for advice or even for confirmation of their tentative solutions may well endanger their superior standing as experts. Making official decisions in a difficult case on one's own can easily raise doubts and questions in a person's mind, even an expert's. One way to cope with this situation is to stop going over it again and again in one's head and instead telling some colleagues about the interesting problems that have arisen in a given case and discussing how they might be solved, possibly over lunch if not in the office.

Such "thinking out loud" may well stimulate new associations and ideas one would not have come up with on one's own, particularly as the listeners are also experienced agents, who might raise objections if one is on the wrong track, and whose assent implicit in attentive listening and interested questions conveys approval. In contrast to asking for advice, telling colleagues about interesting problems in a case and how they might be solved enhances the respect of one's colleagues, though it is, in effect, a subtle form of asking colleagues to corroborate one's own provisional decisions.

. . .

To put the underlying principles of imbalanced and balanced exchange into general terms, rendering important services or providing valued benefactions is a claim to superior status. Reciprocation denies this claim, and excessive returns make a counterclaim, which can lead to a potlatch-like war of seeking to outdo one another to stay ahead. Failure to reciprocate by discharging one's obligations validates the claim and acknowledges the other's superiority in return for the benefits received and in the hope of continuing to receive them. Thus, the contingency that determines whether social exchanges lead to friendships between peers or superordination and subordination is whether benefits received are reciprocated or not. This, in turn, depends on whether one of the two parties has superior resources of the kind that are in contention (which was professional competence in the case of agents).[9]

In a seminal article, Emerson (1962) specified conditions in which balance in social exchange can be restored. I have slightly modified his scheme to conceptualize it as four alternatives to becoming dependent on a person's influence who has some services to offer that others need or want. First, they can give him something he needs or wants enough to reciprocate by satisfying their wishes, provided that they have resources that meet his needs. Second, they can obtain the needed benefits elsewhere, assuming that they have access to alternative sources of these benefits. These two possibilities, if recurring, result in reciprocal exchange relations between peers. Third, they can coerce him to give them what they want. This involves domination by force and is outside the purview of exchange. Fourth, they can resign themselves to do without what they thought they needed, which is Diogenes' solution for remaining independent.

If none of these four alternatives is available, the others become dependent on the supplier of the needed services and must defer to her to reciprocate for the benefits received lest she lose interest in continuing to provide them. Deference implies not only paying respect to another's superior ability, implicit in asking her help, but also deferring to her wishes in everyday intercourse. Thus, the social interaction among colleagues or in other groups that involves imbalances in social exchange gives rise to differentiation in the power to influence as well as in prestige, which is reflected in a stratified structure of informal status.

The illustration of instrumental assistance in a work group may have left the misleading impression that most social exchange involves instrumental benefits. Much of the social interaction, even among co-workers and still more outside a work situation, is social intercourse engaged in for its own sake. Hechter (1987: 33) states that people often join groups to pursue joint goods or common objectives, and he stresses that their

9. This analysis applies to processes of differentiation in informal status among persons whose formal status is essentially the same.

joint achievement and, particularly, the intrinsic gratifications obtained from social associations among fellow members are the sources of group solidarity.[10]

Workers who organize in order to bargain collectively with their employer for higher wages exemplify joint efforts to achieve a common objective. It is in the interest of the group as a whole if workers who devote more energy to and prove more adept in this endeavor are allowed to take the leading role in their organizing effort. Thus, superior status based on past services prompts other workers to acknowledge and submit to the leadership of the one who seems to be most effective in making contributions to organizing the nascent union. Informal leadership is legitimated by the social approval of the rest of the group, and this approval is the return for past services and for the future contributions the leader is expected to make to the welfare of the group by helping to organizing them.[11]

This fictitious description may well be idealized, but it is not completely inaccurate for the initial stage of workers getting together on their own to organize themselves for joint bargaining. To be sure, it is not applicable to formal positions of leadership, particularly not to the impersonal power their incumbents exercise. Thus, the description is not intended to depict the leadership of large national unions; indeed, it is designed as a contrast to them. Once a union has become a large, formal organization and its leaders have become persons of great power, a handful of workers with a grievance cannot on their own decide upon a course of action if the powerful leader is opposed. All they can do is organize a wildcat strike informally, as workers originally did, but now against both the union leadership and management. The point of this illustration is that the interpersonal power that develops in face-to-face relations is fun-

10. The achievement of joint goods raises the well-known free-rider problem (that persons may benefit from public goods without contributing to their production), which Hechter considers to have solved by distinguishing partly excludable goods from public goods. The former are not available to the entire public but only to group members. His major illustration is that one cannot enjoy the sociability in a group without having become a member and thus a contributor to that sociability. But this solution does not work for instrumental objectives, as indicated by the case next discussed in the text.

11. Workers who fail to contribute to the organizing efforts of the new union would also benefit from its success, which illustrates the criticism I made in the last sentence of the preceding footnote that Hechter's (1987) concept of partial excludability does not solve the freeloader problem for joint instrumental objectives.

damentally different from the impersonal power to dominate large numbers, even in the rare cases when the latter emerged from the former.[12]

IMPERSONAL POWER

Impersonal power on a large scale is fundamentally different from the power to influence others in interpersonal relations, which results from imbalance in exchange processes. Impersonal power does not emerge in face-to-face social interaction and exchange, and therefore its discussion does not, strictly speaking, belong in this chapter. The reason that it is discussed at all here is to bring out the contrast between the power of interpersonal influence and the impersonal power to dominate entire segments of society and large numbers of people. Perhaps *nonhuman power* would be a better term for the latter than *impersonal power,* though *nonhuman power* too may be misleading. It is exercised by persons, though by virtue of their formal positions in an organization that gives them control over large numbers of persons, and those who exercise it have no relations or contacts with those over whom it is exercised or even know them.

I refer essentially to what Weber (1978: 941–55) terms *Herrschaft,* which is best translated as *domination* (though the two are not perfectly synonymous). He distinguishes two main types of domination: economic power (p. 943), "domination by virtue of a constellation of interests (in particular: by virtue of a position of monopoly), and domination by virtue of authority, i.e., power to command and duty to obey." Weber apparently considers economic domination to consist primarily of power in market situations, but the concept is actually much broader. It includes, by implication, all influences exercised by using economic resources to create conditions that constrain people—either in their own interest or because they have no choice—to act in accordance with the decisions of the powerful. Domination by command authority entails authority transmitted by a chain of command, not merely direct authority over a few persons, like paternal authority.

Let me explicate why I claim that the two forms of domination

12. I am particularly critical of the inference made by conservative social scientists that the elite's domination of society's economy and government is earned as a return for the great contributions they have made to society. It is the counterpart of the assumption that oligopolistic corporations achieved their position in free competition.

require (and typically involve) absolutely no personal interaction with and often no knowledge of those over whom power is exercised. Economic domination entails using economic resources independent of how others will be affected. If the top executives of a large corporation decide to close a factory in one town and open one in another, the lives and livelihoods of thousands whom the executives have never seen are affected. Similarly, when rich investors or managers of large funds buy and sell large blocks of shares, their actions affect the fortunes of innumerable persons whom they do not even know.

Impersonal power by virtue of authority is not the exercise of power in an impersonal manner but, rather, its exercise over large numbers of persons through an administrative or military chain of command. Impersonal domination by means of authority is not exemplified by the power of the drill sergeant who directs the conduct of recruits by screaming curt and impersonal commands but by that of the commanding general whose orders, which may be given in polite language, are implemented by a chain of command. The commanding general's orders can move entire divisions or even armies to the front, away from it, or from one of its sectors to another, and these orders consequently determine whether huge numbers of soldiers will live or die. The executive orders of a president are another illustration of the impersonal domination exercised by authority over an administrative chain of command that often affects the lives and fortunes of millions. Neither the general nor the president is likely to have had contact with any of the large number of people whose fates their orders affect.[13]

The two major types of domination involve impersonal power of different kinds and degrees of impersonality. Both entail indirect power over others, in contrast to interpersonal power in the direct associations of people, and therefore make it possible to control very large numbers, sometimes many millions. Economic power is purely impersonal and is often, if not usually, exercised without any association with or knowledge of the people over whom it is exercised. This power may take many forms: monopolistic or oligopolistic domination of markets, leveraged buyouts, a mutual fund's large divestment of or investment in a com-

---

13. Both economic power and authority can also be used directly to prompt people with whom one associates to do one's bidding. You can pay people to work for you, and lieutenants can order their subordinates to shine their boots. What is distinctive about domination, however, is that it entails the exercise of power far beyond the persons with whom one has direct contact.

pany's shares, one-company towns, or the basic dependence of employees on their jobs, especially during periods of high unemployment.

Political authority is exercised through administrative organizations, which involve chains of command by managers and supervisors on many levels. The officials in the bureaucracies are themselves subject to the authority of a government[14] and exercise authority over the population at large, the ultimate subjects of the political authority of the sovereign (whether a democratic government or an absolute ruler). Bureaucrats are human beings, however, and political authority is contingent on their following orders throughout the chain of command. This makes political authority not so impersonal or reliable as the economic power to create conditions that force people (directly or in their self-interest) to act in accordance with the will of the dominant powers.

Major characteristics of bureaucracy are designed to minimize this difference. The emphasis on disciplined compliance, impersonal decisions, tenure with assured career advancement, and political neutrality serves to make officials as nearly impersonal a means of controlling people as are economic resources through which people's own interests can be mobilized to control them. But human beings do make decisions—and mistakes—of their own that recurrently divert the initial directives. There are, of course, also advantages in exercising power through people who can adjust decisions to varying situations. The point remains that economic and political control over many people is effected by mediating mechanisms that differ in the degree to which they are purely impersonal—nonhuman. The two types of power have in common, on the other hand, that they are both structural sources of power, in contrast to imbalanced exchange processes, which are the source of interpersonal power. Concentration of economic resources entails much inequality, and so does a bureaucratic hierarchy of authority. Both are structures of domination.

. . .

14. This is the case in theory, but in practice, Weber (1978: 991–92) stresses, bureaucracy's power position is normally "overwhelming. The political 'master' always finds himself, vis-à-vis the trained [top] official, in the position of a dilettante facing the expert. This holds whether the 'master,' whom the bureaucracy serves, is the 'people' . . . or a parliament . . . or an 'absolute' or 'constitutional' monarch." (Weber's failure to make any distinction between a democratic parliament and an absolute monarch, as well as the ironic quotation marks, are indicative of his conservative views.)

There are, of course, mixed and borderline cases. A prototype is the one when individuals use their informal relations and the obligations their associates have incurred to help advance their economic or political position. Public relations firms have virtually made a business out of establishing informal connections and utilizing—exploiting—them to strengthen their own or their clients' positions of power. To mention just a few other examples, interpersonal ties are taken advantage of to enhance impersonal power when members of a legislature obligate colleagues to get their votes for a leadership position; when lobbyists do personal favors for legislators in anticipation of influencing their future vote; when illegal insider trading, which rests on personal connections, enables a trader in a brokerage firm to become, in Stewart's words (1991: facing p. 94), "the most powerful man in American finance—and one of the richest, with earnings in one year of $550 million." [15]

That there are intermediate and ambiguous cases, however, must not let us confound the fundamental analytical distinction between the power to dominate large populations owing to economic control or political authority and the power to influence persons in direct social interaction. It is particularly deplorable when sociologists confuse this essential difference and use the process in which interpersonal power is differentiated to explain the superior wealth and power of persons in top positions as a return to them for their great, though unknown, contributions to society, which is the thesis of the functional theory of stratification (Davis and Moore 1945).[16]

Having great wealth or occupying positions of great political authority is not power but a source of it. This seems to imply that power should be observed when the source of it is used to exercise it. But persons who have great wealth or political authority need not always use that wealth or authority to influence people, since others might anticipate such persons' wishes and do what they expect them to want done. Dahl (1968: 405–15) supplies a good example. Since the president has the authority to make judicial appointments, a senator interested in such an appoint-

---

15. The reference is to Michael Milken of junk-bond fame.

16. It is no less erroneous in a democracy to confound the formal power of political authority with interpersonal influence and social approval of informal leadership. The endorsement of a candidate for president by the vote of many millions is completely different from the power a person achieves to influence another in imbalanced exchange in informal relations or from the power the informal leader earns in return for the contributions she has made in interpersonal relations to many others and to the group as a whole.

ment may well vote for bills the president favors without being asked to do so. If the president is impressed by such support, he may decide to make the judicial appointment the senator wants. This seems to indicate that the senator has influenced the president's decision, but it surely does not imply that she is more powerful than the president, for his power to make judicial appointments is what presumably affected her decision to support his bills consistently.

What the example from Dahl is intended to show is that power often is effective without its being overtly exercised. Cases of this are legion: a pupil bringing an apple to the teacher; the corporate political action committee making a contribution to a senator's campaign; a driver slowing down when passing a police car. A dramatic case is the power the majority has over an underprivileged minority regardless of how rare overt expressions of discrimination are. The reason the exercise of power is so difficult to study empirically or to analyze theoretically is that power often has effects without being explicitly exercised, indeed, without even a hint that it will be exercised. This is the reason that I have confined the discussion of impersonal power—domination—to the two major resources in which it originates and have not dealt with its exercise.

. . .

The parameter scheme, though designed for the analysis of structures of large population, can be applied to the structure of interpersonal networks, as Marsden's (1990) study shows. Since it is designed for macrostructural analysis, however, it is particularly applicable to the study of impersonal power or domination and its implications for the population, which are macrosociological phenomena. An important illustration is the concentration of a market's economic resources in one or a few firms, a form of inequality of economic power that interferes with free competition, which is extensively studied by economists and sociologists.

Mention of a few other cases of the application of parameters can help us to examine differences in resources or power. The distributions of wealth and income in society indicate the population's economic inequality, and its fluctuations—for example, its decline in the United States earlier in this century and its growth there in recent decades—govern the welfare of most people. The form of government is reflected in inequality in political power, which is substantial even in democracies and extreme in tyrannies. The dictator's decision to have his armies invade another country illustrate the latter; the democratic president's executive orders reflect the former. The intersection of different resources and forms of power lessens inequality. Generally, however, various resources and powers tend to be correlated and thus reinforce one another. Before examining another case of intersection, an apparent discrepancy between the analysis of domination and that of multilevel structural analysis in chapter 2 should be resolved.

The discussion of multilevel analysis stressed that the influence of parameters on interpersonal relations depends on their penetration into the lowest levels of substructures and on their not being deflected by segregation. The analysis of people's inequalities in power or resources, however, did not trace whether penetration to lower levels is impeded by segregation. The reason is that the degree of difference between people—between richer and poorer ones, for instance, or between more or less powerful ones—determines the parameter of extent of inequality in resources or power. On the other hand, how much society's inequality or heterogeneity in some dimension *affects* interpersonal relations is contingent on its penetrating to the level of face-to-face relations and on its not being prevented from doing so by segregation. In short, determining how much inequality exists in society does not require multilevel structural analysis but determining whether it influences interpersonal relations does.

A final form of intersection to be briefly noted, which was discussed in chapter 2, is the intersection of conflicts, which mitigates their adverse effects. Democracy depends on opposing political parties that are in contention over policies and elections, but the antagonism of political parties must not be so great that one seeks to destroy the other. Otherwise, democracy's survival would be threatened. Democracy's need for political opposition and its need for sufficient tolerance of opponents to prevent one another's suppression pose a dilemma, which is most pronounced if the same two camps confront each other on most issues, making animosity cumulative.

Crosscutting cleavages, which result from intersecting social affiliations, resolve this dilemma, as Lipset (1963) and Schattschneider (1975: 60–75) have pointed out. Multigroup affiliations with intersecting dimensions of social differences imply that the opposition camps on various issues will not be the same; that individuals supporting one side have associates that are on the opposite side; and that many are pulled by their various associates to opposite sides. As a result, as Lipset (1963: 77) puts it, "the chances for stable democracy are enhanced to the extent that groups and individuals have a number of crosscutting, politically relevant affiliations." In sum, intersection mitigates the adverse effects of different affiliations on intergroup relations, those of differences in power on inequality, and those of political cleavages on democracy.

CONCLUSIONS

Structure and process are often considered complementary concepts. In this chapter, the structural analysis on which this book is focused has been complemented by an analysis of social processes. Population distributions and their relationships govern social opportunities and constraints. But this only means that they determine the probabilities of certain social relations rather than others. Which individuals and dyads will give expression to the various rates governed by the population structure depends on their reciprocated voluntary choices, albeit choices limited by their social positions.

The social structure of the entire population, however, limits the interpersonal choices made in face-to-face relations only indirectly, not directly. Various forms of heterogeneity, inequality, and intersection compose the structure of the entire population. The respective forms of such differentiation in the entire population find partial expression in variations among substructures on several successive levels, and only the remaining differentiation penetrates into the lowest level, where interpersonal relations are formed. Differentiation among substructures implies relative homogeneity within them and promotes ingroup relations, whereas the more that differentiation penetrates to the lowest level, the more it furthers the intergroup choices of associates.

Interpersonal relations are maintained by processes of social exchange. The assumption is that persons are attracted to associate with others if they expect those associations to be rewarding. A person so attracted must communicate to the other that associating with her would be rewarding, since otherwise, by assumption, he would not be interested in associating with her. In short, for an association to be established, both parties must expect rewards from it, which gives both of the persons who are interested in associating with one another the incentive to prove themselves attractive associates.

As people get to know one another, they make implicit judgments about how rewarding that social interaction is compared to alternatives forgone; the more rewarding they consider it to be, the greater their efforts to make their company rewarding for their companions lest those companions lose interest in the association. The rewards derived from the social intercourse itself tend to be complemented by others—doing favors, attending events or playing golf together, extending some help. Every rewarding experience engenders obligations to reciprocate, and recurrent reciprocation promotes trust to do larger favors and strengthens the social bond.

Some rational choice is implicit in social exchange. All new social relations—except ascribed ones, into which we are born—start for a reason, superficial as it may be, like starting a conversation in a waiting lounge or asking for information. In social activities, the reward expected is largely the pleasure of socializing with a person who seems attractive or congenial. In a work situation, it may be a newcomer's need for assistance. Most casual contacts are soon forgotten, but those that both parties experience as rewarding are followed up, and a few slowly become close relations and friendships. Typically, there is an admixture of intrinsic rewards from the association itself and some extrinsic services or benefits, with the latter often playing a larger role in work situations. When the relation becomes closer and more intimate, increasing trust develops as both parties regularly discharge their obligations and prove themselves trustworthy. Once mutual trust has grown, great sacrifices may be made to help a friend or lover in need.

The social ties that develop in persisting social exchange are not merely its by-product but its primary social product. Even in work groups, where instrumental assistance is usually a significant element of social exchange, and certainly in nonwork groups, where the major rewards are those of sociability itself, social exchange is the foundation of people's social integration into their immediate social environment and thereby into their organizations, community, and society. In the terms of a well-known sociologist—a teacher, colleague, and friend of mine— the extrinsic rewards are the manifest function but social support and integration are the latent function of social exchange (Merton 1968: 73–138).[17]

Social exchange may not only cement peer relations but also generate

17. I was Merton's assistant when he wrote this essay on his functional paradigm (nearly half a century ago) and made extensive comments on it, which he all but ignored in the printed paper. My comments were not critical of functionalism, since I was not critical of it at the time, but I have become increasingly critical of this approach in recent years. I have repeatedly said in print that Merton is a structuralist and not a functionalist, increasingly so in his later writings. That he would become so was foreshadowed in this essay's concept of "structural constraint," which in effect denies any explanatory significance to functional analysis.

differentiation of informal status. Benefactors are not peers. A person who supplies important benefits to another makes a claim for superior status. Reciprocation invalidates this claim, but failure to reciprocate acknowledges it. Fraudulent deception [18] is the only way one can avoid any return for rewards received in social exchange. Otherwise, some form of reciprocation is inescapable in recurrent exchange lest the rewards cease. Rewards intrinsic to the association itself evidently are contingent on my continuing to participate and thereby also supply them; I cannot enjoy our game of chess unless I play it and you can enjoy it too. In case of extrinsic services, such as help or advice with one's work, repeated failure to reciprocate is also likely to result in the discontinuance of the benefits.

To be sure, it may be possible to obtain the benefits from another source or to do without them. But if one is unable or unwilling to do either and cannot reciprocate in kind, one must reciprocate by paying deference to the person furnishing the benefits. This deference is partly implicit in repeatedly asking a colleague for advice or help without ever being able to give any, but it is also likely to find expression in deferring to her wishes and complying with her requests to maintain her goodwill. Deference is an acknowledgment of another's superior status.

In a group situation, these processes of imbalanced exchange generate a differentiated structure of informal status. If the group has some instrumental objective they want to attain, they undoubtedly will seek to become organized for this purpose. For example, a group of friends may want to organize a club or unorganized workers may seek to establish a unit for collective bargaining. One of the group members with superior status whom the others respect may assume a leadership role in these efforts. The contributions this worker has made to the others may well incline them to accept him as their leader. In this situation, a secondary social exchange becomes superimposed on the original one. If the leader is successful in the organizing endeavor without antagonizing the rest by acting bossy or the like, the other workers are likely to express social approval of his leadership for his contribution to the common good and thereby to legitimate his leadership.

Impersonal power to dominate entire populations, Weber's *Herrschaft,* is fundamentally different from the interpersonal power by which

---

18. By fraudulent deception in this case I mean that one person convinces another that he supplies benefits to her in return for some that he receives without actually supplying them.

persons influence their associates. The former is based on economic and political resources, not on imbalanced exchange in face-to-face interaction. The two types of domination Weber distinguishes are economic control over markets and political authority through a chain of command. By impersonal power I do not refer to the formal, "impersonal" demeanor by which one exercises direct influence over another or others but to the domination of entire segments of the population without any contact with or even knowledge of the persons who are affected by one's domination. The prototype of economic domination is the monopolist in a market. Other instances are top executives of large corporations who buy and sell firms, or those who decide to close factories in one town and open them in others, which affects the livelihoods of many thousands whom they do not even know. The prototype of political domination is the dictator, whose decisions govern the lives of the country's population and who determines whether to invade another country. Other illustrations are not only the general whose command is implemented by thousands of soldiers he has never seen but also the democratic president who issues executive orders.

I must stress once more the distinction between the status structures in face-to-face groups and those in large populations, because it continues to be ignored by authors who explain population structures in terms of processes in small groups. Such interpretations implicitly deny the significance of power for society. Interpersonal relations are the outcomes of macrostructural conditions, which is the reason for including their analysis in a monograph on macrostructure. Macrostructural conditions and changes, however, must be understood in terms of the dominant economic and political powers in society at large, not by analogy to status structures in small groups.

SEVEN

HISTORICAL DEVELOPMENTS

T HE PRECEDING CHAPTERS HAVE presented a theoretical analysis of the significance for social life of differences in population structures, notably of the implications for various social relations and opportunities of different forms of heterogeneity, inequality, and intersecting differences among people. It is left to us to determine in this final chapter upon what antecedent conditions these differences in population structure depend. Attention centers on the impact of two historical changes on population structures—demographic trends and economic developments. Although these are not the only conditions that modify the structure of populations, they are of particular importance.[1]

Since population structure is conceptualized here as the distributions of a population among social positions in various dimensions, ascribed positions, which individuals cannot change, must be distinguished from achieved ones, from which persons can move to others. Demographic trends can directly influence the distributions of both kinds of social positions. Ethnic differences in fertility engender differences in ethnic heterogeneity, and class differences in fertility engender differences in inequality. Economic developments, on the other hand, influence achieved positions and distributions directly but ascribed ones only indirectly, mediated by their influence on demographic trends. Thus, fluctuations

---

1. Other important historical developments that influence a population structure are changes in the political system, in major institutions, and in the prevailing culture, such as the emergence of new major religions, as in the Reformation, and of radical political ideologies, as in the Enlightenment. Another type of influence on populations is that of various countries on one another.

173

in the rates of economic growth affect economic opportunities and inequality. But economic development can only influence ethnic heterogeneity indirectly by changing fertility differences among ethnic groups. The great importance of industrialization and economic development for people's opportunities and welfare is reflected in the emphasis on them in this chapter.

Demographic influences on population structures are examined in the first section, including those of differences among groups in fertility and mortality and the consequences of immigration, internal migration, and social mobility. The next section deals with the Industrial Revolution and the urbanization and industrialization it involved, including the improvements it effected as well as the catastrophic dislocation and impoverishment of many individuals it produced. The third section focuses on economic development. It analyzes the growing division of labor and the resulting changes in occupational distributions and opportunities. The final section deals with fluctuations in growth rates, such as the Kuznets curve, the logarithmic curve, and the recent U-turn. The significance of the decline in manufacturing and the expansion of services for these fluctuations is examined. In conclusion, questions are raised about the implications of the declining structural mobility for lower social strata and class conflict.

DEMOGRAPHIC TRENDS

Society's population distributions among ascribed positions, which cannot be changed by individuals, are governed by differences among segments of the population in demographic conditions—notably, fertility, mortality, immigration, and emigration. (Those of states or cities are also affected by internal migration.) Changes in distributions are the result of trends in these demographic differences. This does not mean, however, that demographic variations among subgroups of the population do not influence the population's structure in achieved positions. Achieved as well as ascribed differences among subunits are affected by their variations in demographic factors. Thus, race differences in fertility affect the population's racial composition, and socioeconomic differences in fertility affect its socioeconomic inequality. The racial differences in fertility, however, also increase socioeconomic inequality, owing to the economic differences between races.

The pronounced rural-urban difference in rate of natural increase (birthrate minus death rate) provides a dramatic illustration of the repercussions demographic trends have for social change. The rate of natural population increase has greatly declined with economic development and industrialization. Typically, however, this decline in natural population increase occurs only after a period of transition during which the population rapidly expands. This period of "demographic transition," as it is called, occurred in the nineteenth century in developed countries but is now in progress in less developed ones. The rapid population growth during the demographic transition is the result of increases in or diffusion of medical knowledge, which lowers mortality rates while fertility rates initially remain high. When fertility rates also decline in the long run, the rate of natural increase levels off and may ultimately stabilize.

A major reason for the decline in fertility in developed countries is the rural-urban difference in fertility and the resulting migration of large numbers from rural to urban places. This migration, in turn, is made possible by industrialization and improvements in farm productivity, which increase the need for a growing industrial labor force and reduce that for agricultural workers. Industrialization, therefore, leads to shortages of industrial labor in cities and a surplus of agricultural labor in rural areas, which provide strong incentives for children of farmers to move to cities to seek work in shops and factories. In highly industrialized countries, the proportion of the labor force who are farm workers has decreased dramatically. In the United States, for example, the agricultural labor force declined from a majority at the time of the Civil War to less than 3 percent in the 1980s. Although rural fertility has also declined, the population shift from rural to urban places has been primarily responsible for the decline in the rate of natural population growth.

Differences in rates of fertility among religious, racial, and other ethnic groups effect changes in the population's heterogeneity.[2] Thus, since Catholics have higher birthrates than Protestants, the religious heterogeneity of the American population is increasing. However, the same difference in fertility reduces the religious heterogeneity of cities where Catholics are in the majority. The case is parallel for ethnic differences. The higher birthrates of blacks than whites increase ethnic heterogeneity, but the same difference in birthrates reduces a city's racial heterogeneity

2. Strictly speaking, changes in rates of natural increase (fertility minus mortality rates) influence variations in heterogeneity. However, fertility differences generally exert the dominant influence on variations in natural increase, because mortality differences are typically less pronounced. Heterogeneity changes that depend mostly on mortality, which are exceptional, will be briefly examined later.

once whites are in the minority. Unidirectional changes do not have unidirectional effects on measures of dispersion. We shall encounter numerous such instances.

"That the poor have more children than the rich is a well-established fact" (United Nations (1953: 86). Class differences in fertility have been observed in Western, as well as many non-Western, populations at least since the turn of the nineteenth century. These differences imply that disproportionate numbers of children grow up in impoverished circumstances. In other words, there is more inequality among children than among adults, as Kuznets (1989: 342–49) has stressed. Strangely enough, the very class differences in fertility that intensify inequality also enhance structural opportunity for upward mobility.

The size of a country's population determines how much of the occupational services of various kinds is required at a given stage in economic development. Class differences in fertility imply that the middle class does not produce enough children to fill the demand for middle-class occupations and that the lower strata produce more children than are needed for low-status occupations. Indeed, research has shown that there has been much structurally generated opportunity for upward mobility in the United States (Blau and Duncan 1967; Featherman and Hauser 1978) and in other industrial countries during most of this century, at least until recently. To be sure, not all of this structural opportunity for occupational mobility is attributable to class differences in fertility. Most of it has been the result of changes in the occupational structure generated by economic growth. Yet class differences in fertility also contributed to opportunity for upward mobility.

Thus, a plausible inference is that class differences in fertility had opposite effects on inequality—increasing it, particularly the economic inequality among children, and also increasing opportunities for upward mobility, particularly that of children. These opposite effects help to explain paradoxical empirical observations. Although much upward occupational mobility occurred in the United States until recently, income inequality has not exhibited a consistent decline, at least not since the middle of the century. Maxwell (1990: 3) concludes from the data set available to him for 1947 to 1985 that "income inequality remained fairly constant until it began a slow upturn in the later 1960s that accelerated in the early 1980s."

Class differences in birthrates also have adverse effects on educational inequality, as reflected in the higher dropout rates of children raised in lower strata. In fact, empirical research reveals that children raised in large families, independent of their families' socioeconomic position, attain fewer years of schooling than those from smaller families (see, for instance, Blau and Duncan 1967: 298–307). These findings seem to imply that educational inequality is increasing.

Actually, however, educational inequality had declined. The negative influence on educational inequality of the larger number of children of poorer families is completely outweighed by the secular trend of rising levels of education. From 1940 to 1989, the education of persons (at least twenty-five years old) increased from 8.6 to 12.7 median years of schooling, which also reduced class differences in years of schooling (U.S. Bureau of the Census 1991a: 138). But reductions in educational inequality do not necessarily or even typically diminish occupational and economic inequalities, as we saw when reviewing Boudon's (1974) analysis.

Differences in mortality as well as fertility among various groups affect the population structure and changes in it. Most variations in mortality are less pronounced than those in fertility and consequently affect natural population trends less. Besides, several differences in mortality among groups parallel their differences in fertility and thus simply reduce the influence of differential fertility. The mortality rates of the poor are higher than those of the more affluent, for example, and the mortality of blacks is higher than that of whites. These differences in mortality simply reduce the effect of larger corresponding ones in fertility on the natural population increase.

An important exception is gender. The rate of mortality of women is lower than that of men, which implies that women have longer life expectancies than men. Hence, as an age cohort gets older, the sex ratio of its members and their sex heterogeneity are reduced. Except for family relations, people's social environment tends to consist largely of age peers. The older people get, therefore, the more homogeneously female does their non-kin environment of potential and actual social associates become.

· · ·

Two exogenous conditions influence a society's population size and structure: its natural increase, which has been discussed, and its net immigration (immigration minus emigration rate), to which we now turn. Endogenous conditions that alter a population's distributions and structure, but not its size, are people's internal moves, not only migration but also social mobility, such as occupational mobility, shifts in employment, or changes in industry.

Immigration and emigration are clearly quite different from fertility and mortality and have different specific consequences, but their principal influences in abstract structural terms—on heterogeneity or inequality—are parallel. The discussion here centers on immigration (referring to net immigration), which is of primary interest in countries like the United States, where the majority of the population—everybody except Native Americans and persons brought here by force as slaves—are either descendants of immigrants or immigrants themselves.

A large stream of immigrants arrived in the United States between the Civil War and World War I. The annual rate of immigration between 1851 and 1910 was 7.8 per 1,000 population (U.S. Bureau of the Census 1991a: 9).[3] Most of the immigrants came from Northern and Western Europe in the earlier and from Southern and Eastern Europe in the later part of the period. This steady flow of immigrants transformed a society fairly homogeneous in national descent into a very heterogeneous one. It also increased religious heterogeneity, because most of the early immigrants were Protestant and many, if not most, of the later ones were Catholic.

After World War I, legal restrictions reduced immigration greatly, though in the last few decades it has again increased somewhat (the annual rate per 1,000 U.S. population was less than 2.0 before 1970, it was 2.1 for 1971–80, and it was 2.7 for 1981–89 [U.S. Bureau of the Census 1991a: 9]). Many recent immigrants have been Asians, Mexicans, and other non-Europeans, creating an increasingly multicultural society. These changes in heterogeneity have undoubtedly contributed to the recent emphasis on multicultural education, and so has the dispersion of blacks throughout the country once many moved from the southern states, where they had been concentrated.

Although the United States has been a sanctuary for victims of political or religious persecution—at least, in the past—this country, with its vast frontier and expanding economy, has been for more people a haven of economic opportunity. It has attracted disproportionate numbers of the poor and of lower social strata, and while these immigrants did not find the promised "streets paved with gold," most of them improved their economic condition, despite being handicapped by having little education and little if any knowledge of English. In particular,

---

3. Computed from the data in table 5 (U.S. Bureau of the Census 1991a: 9), where annual rates are presented by decade.

a great many substantially improved the career opportunities of their children.

The occupational status of the foreign-born has been, on the average, inferior to that of Americans of native stock, which implies that the immigration of mostly poor people increased inequality, reinforcing the effect of class differences in fertility on it. However, both the occupational achievements and the opportunities for upward mobility of the children of immigrants, the second generation, were at least as good as, and for some subgroups better than, those of Americans of native parentage (Blau and Duncan 1967: 231–34). Thus, the immigration of persons of lower socioeconomic strata and the large number of children of persons of lower strata have paradoxical counteracting effects on inequality. The immigration of many poor persons, like the large families of poor people, raises economic inequality, but both also increase the demand for higher—as well as, of course, for lower—socioeconomic occupational services and thus provide opportunities of the next generation to improve their socioeconomic position, which reduces inequality.

Most immigrants have a number of characteristics in common that distinguish them from most non-immigrant Americans, which reduces the intersection of social differences in the population. All immigrants are by definition foreign-born, and most of those arriving in the large wave of immigration at the end of the nineteenth and the beginning of the twentieth centuries spoke hardly any or no English, were poor, and had little education. Many native-born Americans also were poor and had little education, but none of them had the entire combination of characteristics of the foreign-born. As a result, the immigrants' having become part of this country's population probably increased the consolidation and reduced the intersection of social differences in the population.

Internal migration redistributes the population in space. Migration from small towns to large cities reduces the spatial heterogeneity, and that from the metropolis to the suburbs increases its heterogeneity. Whereas internal migration does not affect the size or structural parameters of the entire population, it often affects both for various subunits. Migration to a state or city in excess of out-migration from it enlarges it. As increasing numbers of blacks migrated to northern cities, the racial heterogeneity of these cities increased, though once a city, like Gary or Newark, has a majority of blacks, the continuing in-migration of blacks, as well as moves of whites out of it into the suburbs ("white flight"), reduces its heterogeneity. The tendency of ethnic migrants to a city to settle in neighborhoods where people with the same ethnic background live increases the ethnic heterogeneity of the city but reduces that of its neighborhoods.

In terms of the conception of population structure as a multidimensional space of social positions among which people are distributed, the physical space where people are distributed is one of numerous social dimensions, albeit one of special importance. Migration is correspondingly conceived as one major form of social mobility, but there are other forms. Occupational mobility was discussed in chapter 4, theorems about mobility were presented in chapter 2, and the implication of economic development for career mobility is examined later in this chapter. A few other illustrations of social movements between positions are noted here to indicate the range of different kinds of social mobility.

Thus, change in marital status is a social move, from single to married, from married to divorced, or from married to widowhood. So is retirement from one's career. (The great significance of the status exit involved in widowhood and retirement is discussed in Z. Blau 1973: 209–45.) Intermarriage of spouses of different national descent is a more complicated case. The spouses move from single to married status, but their national descent does not change. However, if persons of a variety of national descent intermarry for several generations, national descent increasingly dissipates and the descendants ultimately consider themselves and are considered by others simply as Americans (see Alba 1985).

When a woman and a man whose religious affiliations differ marry, one of them often converts to the other's religion. Such conversions are a form of social mobility. Conversions that are not prompted by marriage also involve social movement from one religious affiliation to another. If many members of minority religions convert to the religion of the majority, religious heterogeneity declines. Although religion is largely an ascribed status attained at birth, it can be and sometimes is changed, which means that it is not entirely ascribed. National background and ethnic background are also essentially ascribed positions for which mobility from one to another can occur, as just exemplified, though in such cases it takes a number of generations.

The social mobility of many individuals is often not the result of independent decision but, rather, is precipitated by changes in substructures, organizations, or social conditions. For instance, if a corporation closes its factory in one town and builds another in a different town, many persons in the first town lose their job and must move to a new one or become unemployed, and many individuals in the second town have the opportunity to get a better job in the new factory than their old one. Consequently, the occupational structure of both places changes. If Congress passes a law that substantially raises the legal minimum wage, income inequality will diminish. A major stock market crash that adversely affects the portfolios of many wealthy persons is likely to reduce inequality in wealth. Revolutions that expropriate wealth do so more effectively.

Finally, there are two changes in organizations or associations that alter the population structure by changing the positions of large numbers without involving individual social mobility. One is the merger of organized collectivities to create a new, larger one, which reduces heterogeneity in the population. If two Protestant denominations, in the spirit of ecumenicalism, join to become a single church, religious heterogeneity is reduced. The merger of firms in an industry lessens heterogeneity and competition in the industry. A second change that affects heterogeneity without involving individual mobility is the opposite of the first: if a conflict in an organized collectivity leads to a split of its members into separate organizations, heterogeneity is increased. The division of a political party into several factions increases political heterogeneity. When a religious denomination divides into several sects, religious heterogeneity becomes more pronounced.

INDUSTRIAL REVOLUTION

The Industrial Revolution originated in England in the second part of the eighteenth century, and it transformed an agricultural into an industrial economy. Having started in England, it spread and led to corresponding industrial transformations, first in Western Europe, then in the United States, and industrialization has continued to expand throughout the world. The Industrial Revolution was not a political revolution that violently altered the nature of the political system, as the French Revolution did, but it set into motion historical processes that generated more profound and lasting changes in political as well as economic systems and in virtually all aspects of social structures and human lives.

To say that the Industrial Revolution occurred in the eighteenth century in England must not be interpreted to imply either that there were no preceding advances that led up to it or that the many subsequent industrial revolutions throughout the world merely adopted the English model and made no new contributions of their own. To be sure, England's industrial revolution was an important turning point, but it was made possible by earlier advances in knowledge and technology. It took advantage of scientific and technological innovations made in the six-teenth and seventeenth centuries and adapted them to improve produc-tion in agriculture as well as in industry, thereby initiating a new era of economic growth. Moreover, subsequent industrial developments did not simply follow England's lead but made their own contributions, of-ten surpassing England's both industrially and economically, the United States being an early and Japan the most recent case in point.

Industrial revolution involves the replacement of handicraft by manu-facture, human work by machine operations. Its foundation is that "in-animate power—in particular, steam—took the place of human and animal strength," in the words of Landes (1969: 1).[4] The mechanization of production started in England in the textile industry, first in cotton and then in wool, followed by that in coal and iron. The most important early innovation was the steam engine, which stimulated the change from handicraft to factory production and, later in the nineteenth century, the development of mass production.

The cotton industry provides a good illustration of the early stages in the mechanization of textiles, which applies to wool as well as cotton. Developments in the cotton industry indicate the interdependence of pro-duction processes and the productivity improvement effected by indus-trialization. The invention of the flying shuttle increased the speed of weaving, which enabled weavers to work much faster than could spin-ners, on whom they depended for the yarn they used. This bottleneck was overcome with the invention of the spinning jenny, which greatly increased the speed and productivity of spinning. The technological ad-vances of the English cotton industry enabled it to expand greatly, par-ticularly after Watt's invention of the steam engine led to the development of machine-operated looms.

An indication of this exponential growth with increasing mechaniz-ation is that the import of raw cotton to Britain increased nearly tenfold between 1760 and 1787, and it continued to increase at a rapid rate in the next half-century (Landes 1969: 41–42). Whereas the small-scale production in the eighteenth century was carried out in the homes of workers or in small shops of master weavers, the large-scale production in the nineteenth century took place mostly in factories. More and more, the machines set the pace of the production the workers had to follow.

---

4. My discussion of the Industrial Revolution in England is greatly indebted to Landes's *The Unbound Prometheus*.

Extensive industrialization, particularly large-scale machine production in factories, requires an industrial labor force. In preindustrial countries, however, the majority of people work in agriculture and are apparently needed on farms to feed the country's population. This implies that an agricultural revolution that raises the productivity of agricultural workers must occur to free enough workers for industrial employment. To be sure, the higher rural birthrates and urban mortality rates, which already existed, and the substantially higher urban than rural wages, made possible by the higher productivity of industrial than farm work, were strong incentives to migrate from farms to factory jobs in cities (Williamson 1991: 41–43). Yet as long as the majority, or nearly a majority, of the labor force was required in agriculture to provide the nourishment for the rest of the population, the labor force available for industry was limited.

The situation was remedied by an agricultural revolution, which started in the eighteenth century and was in full force in the nineteenth. Numerous practices were established that improved labor productivity in agriculture. Leaving land fallow every few years was replaced by constant tillage and crop rotation; new crops and new breeds of animals were introduced.

Another change that improved agricultural productivity, though at some human cost, was the enclosure of the common. The common was land that by tradition was left open for commoners to graze their cattle and sheep. Centuries ago statutes were enacted that permitted lords to enclose some common land, bifurcating it into some land for the lord's own use and some for the common use of the people. Early enclosures left most of the land for common use because the lord needed to prove that he had provided enough public land.

Increasingly strict enclosure laws, which enabled lords to enclose more of the common land, were enacted during the eighteenth century, reaching their peak near the end of the century in the midst of the Industrial Revolution. Enclosure raised productivity by making more efficient use of land than grazing does. Sheep could no longer freely roam on the common but had to travel in fold courses in which manure enriched the soil. Legumes, like turnips, and other new crops were introduced, with the result that crops for food and sheep for wool could be produced at the same time. Soon further improvements were made, such as selective breeding of livestock and better fertilization.

However, enclosures did not benefit most people, certainly not in the short run. The profits enclosure effected were the lord's; the costs it entailed were the common people's, who lost their livelihood as the result of expanding enclosures. In Polanyi's (1957: 35) blunt words: "Enclosures have appropriately been called a revolution of the rich against the poor. The lords and nobles . . . were literally robbing the poor of their share in the common, tearing down the houses which, by the hitherto unbreakable force of custom, the poor had long regraded as theirs and their heirs'."

. . .

The Industrial Revolution created a fundamental change in the economy from one dominated by agricultural to one dominated by industrial production. The extensive industrialization it effected required widespread urbanization, and expanding urbanization, in turn, depended on large-scale migration from rural to urban areas. Several conditions in eighteenth-century England promoted migration from agricultural work in rural to factory work in urban places, including higher rural than urban fertility and improvements in agricultural productivity, both of which engendered surplus labor in rural places. The two most important stimuli of urban migration, however, were probably the pull of the higher urban wages[5] and the push exerted by enclosures that deprived common rural people of their livelihood.

In the two centuries since, urbanization has expanded greatly in nearly all countries and increased at an accelerating rate. Moreover, the difference in urbanization and industrialization between highly industrialized and less industrialized countries continues to increase. Kuznets (1989: 47–52, 65–67) analyzes data that indicate that the larger the proportion of a country's labor force in agriculture, the smaller is the decline in the proportion of its labor force in agriculture (between 1950 and 1970, the period covered by his International Labor Office data). This implies, as he points out (p. 53), that the difference between less and more developed countries in the percentage of people in the agricultural labor force and hence in "per capita product" is widening.

The observed tendency for rural persons to be more likely to migrate to cities the more that rural persons have previously done so conforms to an implication of the macrostructural theory presented. The assumption introduced in chapter 3 (A-3) that associates in other groups (or places)

5. Machine production raised hourly productivity sufficiently to raise profits and still pay higher wages to attract workers.

facilitate mobility there implies that the larger the number of persons who have already migrated from farms to cities, the more likely are those remaining on farms to have friends or relatives in various cities, whose presence makes it easier and thus more likely for them to migrate to these cities. (Of course, other conditions also influence their chance of moving, such as the occupational opportunities that exist in various cities.) This inference can be tested by ascertaining, as it implies, that rural persons' probability of migrating to a city increases if they have associates there.

The progressive industrialization in Britain and other Western countries in the nineteenth century created great hardships and much misery for many common people. Although urban wages for unskilled workers considerably exceeded those of rural workers, the shift from farms to cities uprooted people from their traditions, institutions, and homes, often leaving them in dire straits. Work in agriculture gave even unskilled laborers control over their own specific movements and performance, but in mechanized factories machines dictated their every task, when and where each task had to be done, all day long. Moreover, as most farms in the nineteenth century were small, most farm laborers were in regular contact with their boss, whereas the laborers in large factories were several supervisory and managerial levels removed from the capitalist who owned the factory. To cite Landes (1969: 43) once more, "The introduction of machinery implied for the first time a complete separation from the means of production; the worker became a 'hand.'"

The effects of industrialization on the human condition were that people were torn from their communities, where they lived among kin and neighbors they knew, and were thrown into impersonal cities, where they knew at best a few persons. They had lost their social ties and now found themselves in unfamiliar surroundings. The lucky ones got jobs; the unlucky ones were unemployed. If they were lucky enough to find jobs, women and young children as well as men had to work long hours in crowded sweatshops. It is little wonder that these conditions bred poverty, alcoholism, crime, and vice.

The plight of much of the working class during the rise of both capitalism and industrialization in the nineteenth century was bad enough without overdramatizing it with nostalgic comparisons to a fictitious communal past. All too often, the horrors of the modern industrial world are contrasted with an imagined *Gemeinschaft* of rustic life in the villages of earlier centuries. However, peasants in past centuries hardly led an easy life of peaceful contentment among closely knit associates.

They had to put in long hours of work with primitive tools, were dominated by nobles and lords as well as large landowners, were threatened by bandits, and were often ruined by the many wars between principalities that destroyed their homes. In addition, the living standard of poor peasants was much lower than that of poor people in industrial societies today. Condemnation of the exploitation and deprivations of the many victims of the growing pains of industrialism and capitalism need not be justified by romanticizing the hard life of most common people in the past.

In terms of the parameter scheme, the large-scale migration from farms to factories in cities engendered multiple intersection of social origins and present social position. People moved from the places where their families had lived for generations to a variety of different places. The intersection of social origin and current social position actually involved numerous intersections: from one location to another; from a rural to an urban environment; from lifelong kin and neighbors to an impersonal environment filled with strangers and otherwise mostly recent acquaintances; occupationally, from farm to factory work. In all these and some other respects, the migrants' social origins intersect with their current social positions.

DIVISION OF LABOR AND GROWTH

The division of labor shapes an urbanized work force into implements for advancing industrialization and a capitalist economy, as pointed out in a book written in England in the middle of the Industrial Revolution. Adam Smith (1776)—whose warning against "dealers" who live on profit and have interests contrary to the public's was quoted in chapter 5—starts his classic *The Wealth of Nations* (1776) with an analysis of the division of labor and its importance for improving productivity and economic growth. Its first sentence reads, "The greatest improvement in the productive power of labour, and the greater part of the skill, dexterity, and judgment with which it is any where directed, or applied, seem to have been the effects of the division of labor." Smith continues with his famous illustration of the improvement in productivity the division of labor effects even in such a simple task as pin-making.

The great advantage of subdividing the manufacture of a product among different workers is that it simplifies each worker's task and makes it possible to carry out the various tasks simultaneously. Smith considers the need to perform various agricultural tasks in succession, depending on the season, a major reason that the division of labor and productivity had not progressed far in farming. He notes that the simpler tasks resulting from the division of labor improve dexterity, save time, and make the invention of machines to perform them more likely, all of which raise productivity.

Durkheim (1893) starts his monograph *De la division du travail social* by noting that the division of labor had not attracted sufficient attention for a theory about it to be developed until Adam Smith advanced one at the end of the eighteenth century. The sociological theory Durkheim developed a century later differs fundamentally from Smith's classical economics. Whereas both theories deal with functional consequences of the division of labor, they center attention on entirely different contributions it makes, one with its implications for the economy and the other with those for the social structure. Smith analyzes the division of labor's significance for raising productive efficiency and furthering economic development. Durkheim, in contrast, analyzes its significance for society's (organic) solidarity resting on interdependence after a population has become too large and diverse for the earlier (mechanical) solidarity resting on uniform moral convictions and repressive laws. In the process, Adam Smith laid the foundation of classical economics, and Durkheim that of structural sociology.

The analysis of the division of labor illustrates structural analysis so well because the concept of the division of labor is the prototype of a structural characteristic. Two requirements of structural properties have been emphasized (in chap. 1): (1) they must refer to emergent properties of populations, not to averages of their members (like average income); and (2) they must refer to differences among their members, which reflect the populations' interrelated subgroups. The division of labor meets these two criteria perfectly. It refers to the heterogeneity of occupational positions, which is not an average, and its transformation into indicators of occupational status provides a measure of occupational inequality, which is not a mean either. In addition, the division of labor is a perfect example of interdependent subunits.[6]

6. The analysis in *The Division of Labor in Society* best represents Durkheim's structural sociology and is the main reason that he is generally considered a structural sociologist by those critical of his approach, like Giddens (1986: 169), as well as those favorable to it, like the present author.

Finally, individuals cannot be described by a division of labor, which is the ultimate criterion of emergent population properties. To be sure, individuals have occupations, but an occupation is not a division of labor. Methodological individualists reject this conception because they claim that all characteristics of a population are ultimately the result of actions of its individual members. But this claim is disingenuous. Although individuals make decisions about their careers and occupations, these decisions do not determine society's (or General Motors') division of labor; on the contrary, the division of labor constrains the career decisions of individuals. The decline in manufacturing positions in the American division of labor has not been the result of individual choices to leave factories for poorer positions or unemployment.

The Industrial Revolution created the initial impetus for economic development; other conditions—notably, earlier scientific advances, improvements in agriculture, and urbanization—contributed to it; and the advancing division of labor provided a final thrust for economic growth. Kuznets (1971: 10–34) performed a comparative analysis of economic trends in developed countries since modern economic growth started, which was earlier for Britain and later for Japan but "concentrated between the 1830's and 1870's" (p. 303). He found that the average increase in "per capita product [was] about 2 percent a year." He stresses that this increase implies a fivefold rise over a century and predicts the continuation of such "growth over a long period" (p. 304). In the United States and other developed countries, high growth rates have indeed persisted in the twentieth century until recently, but they have tapered off and serious other economic problems have developed.[7]

. . .

The division of labor has been a driving force of the accelerating economic growth since the Industrial Revolution. Economic development, in turn, has become a major influence on the occupational structure that reflects a country's division of labor. The occupational structure governs people's career chances, the career opportunities in a population, and the constraints that limit its members' occupational choices. The division of labor, as manifest in the occupational structure, thus exerts major external constraints on people's life chances. This is another reason that

7. For the logistic curve portraying this pattern of economic growth, which will be discussed more fully below, see Sundrum (1991: 15–18).

Durkheim's study of the division of labor represents his major theoretical concern, namely, the external constraints social conditions ("social facts") impose on individuals. It also illustrates that external social constraints are primarily structural constraints.

Freedom/ Constraint of Occup. Structure

The occupational structure provides opportunities for upward social mobility, but it also limits these opportunities and thereby imposes constraints on the careers of people. Of course, it does not determine any individual's career—its success or failure—only the entire population's and various subgroups' probabilities of achieving mobility and of entering various occupations. The social structure also governs the opportunities in a population of establishing various social relations, such as marrying a spouse with certain ingroup and certain other outgroup characteristics. In other words, the influence of social conditions never indicates what happens to a given person, only the probabilities or rates of various social occurrences in a population or its different subpopulations. But the study of the influence of social conditions on rates of mobility between positions or rates of intergroup relations, for instance, and not what happens to one individual or another, is precisely the task of our discipline—sociology.

The division of labor, progressing with economic growth, increases occupational heterogeneity. An important component of this increase is the change from farm work, which is relatively little differentiated, to a great variety of jobs in cities. Whereas in the early stages of industrialization the unskilled newcomers to cities experienced much exploitation and hardship at work, continuing economic growth ameliorated the situation. Working conditions improved considerably, in good part as the result of union pressures, and the growing economy, with its increasingly complex machines and administration, needed more skilled personnel, a development that expanded the jobs in middle and contracted those in lower strata.

This change in the shape of the occupational pyramid created structural conditions that increased opportunities for upward mobility. It shifted the occupational distribution in a way that reduced inequality in occupational status. In the United States, for instance, the proportion of the labor force in the two highest-status occupational groups—the professional and managerial groups—expanded from 10 percent in 1900 to 26 percent in 1989. In contrast, the proportion in the three lowest-status occupations—household work, farm labor, and nonfarm labor—declined from 21 percent in 1900 to 12.5 percent in 1970, and the proportion in roughly equivalent low-status occupations had decreased by 1989 to less than 6 percent.[8]

These figures indicate that the changes in the division of labor in this century not only reduced inequality in occupational status but also improved opportunities for upward mobility. More than one in five of the youngsters who started to work at the end of the last century became laborers or worked in households, whereas only one in seventeen had to start in comparable menial jobs in recent years. Only one-tenth of the work force at the turn of this century had a professional or managerial job, but one-quarter do as we near the end of this century. To be sure, these opportunities are not equally distributed among the entire population. Family origins strongly influence occupational chances, and so do racial and other ethnic affiliations and gender. But this does not invalidate the point made that occupational opportunities have greatly increased, because social origins and other factors also influenced them a century ago, and in all likelihood no less than today. Yet recent changes do threaten these opportunities, as will be discussed presently.

Economic development and industrialization have greatly contributed to the rising levels of education. The economy's growing need for a literate and skilled labor force created pressures to raise people's education by various means, such as extending the years of compulsory schooling, building more schools, improving teacher training, and providing scholarships for college. At the same time, the rising efficiency in production made it possible for young persons to remain in school or training longer, because a smaller work force sufficed to provide the goods and services in demand. Fifty years ago, the median education in this country was about eight years, whereas now it approaches thirteen years—more than a high school education. Yet there are many high school dropouts and many of them are unemployed, which reflects the problems of education in a diverse society with an industrial labor market and a laissez-faire capitalist system.

8. The data, except those for 1989, were computed from U.S. Bureau of the Census (1975: 140–45), and the ranking of occupational groups is based on Duncan's (1961: 155) SEI. Several years ago, the census adopted new categories; those for the professional and managerial occupational groups are fairly comparable, though there were a number of specific changes (the proportion of them in 1970 from the 1975 publication source is 22.5 percent, which is also a large increase since 1900). The 1989 data are based on two categories in U.S. Bureau of the Census (1991a: 395–97), which seem more or less comparable to the three used for 1900–1970: "Handlers, equipment cleaners, helpers, and laborers" and "farm workers"; there is no entry for private household workers.

Although class differences in fertility increase educational inequality, since the children of poorer people leave school earlier than those from more affluent families, the pronounced increase in educational levels has overcome this effect and greatly diminished educational inequality. An increase in median income or wealth does not necessarily reduce inequality, because there is no ceiling and the income or wealth of the rich often rises more than that of most people, which is likely to enhance inequality. Since there is a maximum number of years of formal education that can be attained, however, a substantial increase in median education tends to reduce educational inequality.

Economic growth has improved both educational and occupational opportunities, and an individual's superior education improves her occupational opportunities. Yet rising levels of education in a population, which do reduce educational inequality, neither enhance occupational chances nor reduce inequality in occupational status. This is the paradox Boudon (1974) poses. The short answer to the implicit question is that the likelihood of getting a job in a certain field depends on the demand for persons qualified in this field and not on the supply of them.

As a matter of fact, a large supply of qualified applicants has the opposite effect: it reduces the chances of each one to obtain a job. This gets to the real issue Boudon raises. Every person has an interest in being better qualified than others, and employers have an interest in having as many highly qualified candidates as possible, which increases competition and lowers labor cost. The implication is that the pursuit of their own interests by prospective employees harms their own economic interests as job candidates and furthers the interests of employers for better qualified employees, possibly even at lower pay.

. . .

The division of labor played an important role in raising productivity, and capitalism did too (though probably not as much as classical economists claim),[9] since raising productivity by substituting machines for workers requires capital. The advantages of larger and more complex

---

9. Landes (1969: 79) disagrees with the importance widely attributed to capital formation for economic development. He notes that "economists and economic historians were wont to exaggerate the significance of capital formation as a motor of economic growth." A few lines later he specifies: "Whence these gains, then? They seem to derive from the quality of the inputs—from the higher productivity of new technology and the superior skills and knowledge of both entrepreneurs and workers" (p. 80).

machines stimulated the development of increasingly large manufacturing organizations, ultimately leading to the huge corporations discussed
in chapter 5. The development of the division of labor within organizations differs from that in society at large. The former is planned by managers to improve productivity, whereas the latter emerges as the result of
the decisions and actions of many people. It is of interest to compare
briefly the analysis of the division of labor of two major social theorists,
each of whom focuses on one of these two different forms of it.

Durkheim analyzes the division of labor in society at large, as we
have seen, and he emphasizes the contribution it makes to the solidarity and interdependence of the diverse parts of complex societies. Marx
(1906: 247–312, chap. 14) analyzes the division of labor within firms
and emphasizes that it is a means to exploit workers for the benefit of
capitalists and that its subdivision of jobs routinizes them and increases
the alienation of workers. Thus, Durkheim's analysis of the division of
labor in society considers it to have beneficial consequences, and Marx's
analysis of the division of labor in factories and other organizations
considers it to have adverse consequences, except, of course, for the
capitalists.

Both Marx and Durkheim, however, also discuss in short passages
the form on which they do not center attention, and in these discussions
they seem to agree with each other. Marx treats the division of labor
in society, which he contrasts briefly with that within manufacturing
firms, as a beneficial exchange among independent specialized producers
(1906: 385–92), which is not unlike Durkheim's evaluation. In Durkheim's brief analysis of pathological forms of the division of labor, which
he condemns, he essentially refers to practices that occur primarily within
manufacturing firms and other large organizations, such as "the anomic
division of labor," routine work "degrading the individual by making
him a machine," and "the forced division of labor."[10]

Thus, both Marx and Durkheim evaluate the division of labor
among independent producers in society positively but that imposed by
an organization management on workers negatively, but Marx virtually
ignores the former and Durkheim discusses the latter only in short last
chapters, as minor qualifications. Durkheim's overall emphasis is on the
great contributions and Marx's on the oppressive and exploitative consequences of the division of labor. As growing numbers of a popula-

10. These three citations are from Durkheim 1933: 353, 371, and 375. The first and
last are chapter headings.

tion are workers in large organizations, one may wonder whether the pathological forms Durkheim treats so casually are not of increasing significance.

CHANGES IN THE RATE OF GROWTH

To recapitulate the main points in a few words, the industrialization and division of labor initiated by the industrial revolution started a prolonged period of economic growth in Western countries. It completely transformed the economy and society of these countries, but this transformation was achieved at great cost borne by the common people, increasing numbers of whom suffered disastrous dislocations. Many of them were torn from their homes and neighbors and driven into the slums of unfamiliar cities, where most had to endure miserable lives of poverty and deprivation. In the long run, however, accelerating economic growth increased their chances of occupational mobility and, reinforced by workers' organizing themselves in unions, their standards of living.

A major transformation of the economies of developed countries appears to be taking place at present, which may well, once it has taken its course, have created as profound changes as the Industrial Revolution did. The greatly rising productivity in industrialized countries in the period of rapidly increasing economic growth seems to have sown the seeds of its own destruction. Just as improvements in agricultural productivity helped to free much of the work force for industrial work, improvements in industrial productivity, particularly in our age of automation, have helped free the largest portion of the work force for jobs in services.

The change that has occurred in the last thirty years is dramatically illustrated by the differences in the proportions of the American labor force between 1960 and 1990 engaged in three major groups of industries: agriculture, manufacturing, and services.[11] The labor force in agriculture continued to decline from 6.7 to 2.7 percent between 1960 and 1990. Manufacturing (durable and nondurable), which had greatly expanded in the nineteenth century and the first half of the twentieth,

11. The data for 1960 are computed from U.S. Bureau of the Census 1964: 1–223, table 91; the source for the 1990 data is U.S. Bureau of the Census 1991b. The three categories are: *agriculture* includes also forestry and fisheries; *manufacturing* includes durable and nondurable; *services* includes finance, insurance, and real estate; business; personal; entertainment; educational; health; other professional services; and public administration.

started to decline between 1960 and 1990 from 27.1 to 17.7 percent of the labor force, which is a reduction by one-third in thirty years. In sharp contrast, services (specified in note 11) increased by nearly one-half, from 30.1 to 44.4 percent.[12]

The end of the eighteenth century and the nineteenth century witnessed a change from an agricultural to an industrial economy, spurred by improvement in agricultural but particularly in industrial productivity. It appears that the end of the twentieth century and the twenty-first century will witness a change from an industrial to a service economy, spurred by industrial productivity. The long-term extreme decline in agricultural workers required to provide the needed sustenance for the population freed increasing proportions of the labor force to work in manufacturing and other industrial enterprises. By the same token, improvement of labor productivity in manufacturing is now reducing the labor force needed to provide all the products that are in demand, freeing increasing proportions of the work force for providing various services. This is reflected in the above figures on the great contraction of manufacturing and the great expansion of services. The very productive efficiency of manufacturing has obviated the need for part of its work force.

The enlargement of the work force that can provide services to the population is not a dire prospect, though the period of transition will be difficult. There are serious shortages of many important services even in developed countries, notably the United States, which would greatly benefit from expanded services in health, education, public welfare, rehabilitation, and other fields. However, this change poses a serious problem for economic growth. The much greater mechanization of manufacturing than services makes labor productivity much higher in manufacturing than in services, with the result that a shift from manufacturing to services reduces the rate of economic growth. This is not merely a threat for future economic development. It has already started to happen. We turn now to a discussion of fluctuations in economic growth and their implications for income inequality.

. . .

12. The following industries were not included: mining, construction, transportation, communication, wholesale trade, and retail trade. All but one of these employed less than 10 percent of the labor force in either year and changed by less than 1 percent between 1960 and 1990. The exception, in both respects, is retail trade, which increased during these thirty years, from 14.8 to 16.8 percent.

Kuznets (1955) explained the now well-known Kuznets curve of rates of economic growth on the basis of deductive theoretical reasoning. He started with the assumption that wages are, on the average, higher in industry than in agriculture, which is indeed the case, and made inferences about what the effects on inequality are as growing proportions of the labor force move from agricultural to industrial work. If everybody works in agriculture, there is little inequality. As increasing proportions of the work force shift to industrial work, wage inequality increases, because a small but growing proportion earn higher wages than the rest. Once nearly one-half of the population work in the better-paid jobs in industry, income differences are at their maximum, and further shifts of workers from low-income farm to higher-income industrial jobs reduce inequality. The implication he draws is that income inequality in early stages of industrialization, as long as the majority still work in agriculture, increases, but it decreases in later stages, when only a declining minority does, which is reflected in the upside-down U of the Kuznets curve.

The shift from agricultural to industrial work produced the declining rate of inequality after roughly the majority of the population had made such a shift, but the ultimate cause of this migration, of the higher wages prompting it, and of the resulting decline in inequality was the accelerating rate of economic growth. Kuznets predicted the continuation of this growth, as earlier noted, and so did neoclassical economic theorists. Indeed, an accelerating rate of economic growth prevailed in developed countries following their industrial revolution until fairly recently, when this rate slowed down. This trend produced a logistic curve of economic growth, with slow initial but then rapidly increasing growth until the middle of the century, followed by a decline in growth rate after 1960 (Sundrum 1991: 15–17).

These important changes in economic growth may be illustrated with a few data, starting with the accelerating rate of growth generated by the Industrial Revolution in England at the end of the eighteenth century. The decennial rate of growth there was 2 percent in the 80 years before 1780 and 13 percent in the 100 years after (Kuznets 1966: 64). It took other Western countries until the end of the nineteenth or the twentieth century to catch up, but by that time most of them were experiencing decennial rates of growth of more than 20 percent, and so did the United Kingdom (Kuznets 1966: 352–53).

The rapid economic growth, which reached an average of 4.9 percent annually in sixteen developed countries in the third quarter of this century (Sundrum 1991: 23), "plunged downward to half the previous level"

(p. 279) in the mid-1970s, to 2.25 percent annually for the same countries in 1973–86 (p. 25). As a matter of fact, the latter growth rates were substantially below those of less developed countries in the 1970s (based on all less developed countries with a population of more than 1 million), which were 4.4 percent (p. 24). An important reason for this downturn in economic growth in the most industrialized countries is the lower productivity of the service sector, which has expanded, whereas the more productive manufacturing sector has contracted.

The logistic curve no longer does justice to the most recent changes in growth rates and their economic consequences for people. The image used in Harrison and Bluestone's (1988) *The Great U-Turn* is more appropriate. After a long period of growth and prosperity the United States has entered one of decline and prolonged recession. The change from accelerating rates of economic growth for scores of years to decelerating ones in the last two decades has already been discussed. Other indications of the economic U-turn are pointed out by Harrison and Bluestone. Earnings have regularly increased (in constant dollars) since the middle of the century, so that people have come to expect a somewhat rising standard of living, but earnings have decreased since 1973 (pp. 4, 112–13, 119). The proportion of poor people declined until the early 1970s, but it has risen since then (pp. 122, 135).

The most important change is in income inequality. There is some disagreement about whether this change qualifies as a U-turn, but there is no disagreement on the recent trend. The question is whether income inequality declined or merely fluctuated before 1970, since different measures do not reveal exactly the same trend. The most plausible inference is that there was some decline in inequality earlier, as the Kuznets curve implies, but family inequality merely fluctuated and remained fairly constant from the mid-1940s to around 1970, as Maxwell (1990) concludes. Whatever measure is used, however, full agreement exists that income inequality has increased at least since 1980. A most carefully designed recent study by Blackburn and Bloom (1987: 580) finds an increase in family income inequality from .39 in 1980 to .43 in 1987,[13] and there are indications that it has further risen since.[14]

---

13. Their analysis uses the Gini index for families, adjusted by weights from the Social Security Administration, which take into account not only number of persons in the family but also other factors, such as age composition.

14. The regressive changes in taxation Reagan introduced and other policies of his have undoubtedly contributed to the increase in income inequality, but the fundamental source

Kuznets's theoretical model of the upside-down U curve in income inequality during industrialization can be applied to explain the U-shaped curve in recent income inequality. His principle, it will be remembered, is that shifts of lower-paid farm to higher-paid industrial work initially increase income inequality, but when nearly one-half of the working population have made this change further shifts from farm to factory work reduce it. By the same token, the expansion of service jobs, as long as it results—directly or indirectly—from the contraction of lower-paid farm jobs, helps reduce inequality. But once much of the expansion of service jobs is the result of moves from higher-paid manufacturing or even managerial jobs, inequality increases. If at the same time the income of the highest-paid segments of managerial and professional workers rises, as has been the case, the increase in inequality is still more pronounced.

. . .

The Industrial Revolution created catastrophic disruptions of social institutions and human lives and great hardships for common people. But in the long run the accelerating rate of economic growth to which it gave rise contributed to people's welfare, notably by raising standards of living and opportunities for social mobility. The current change from an industrial to a service economy, in the United States and other developed countries, reinforced by the economic crisis of the 1980s, also engendered disastrous dislocations of established careers and social relations and untold miseries for many people. Will this change also benefit the economy and people's welfare in the long run? So far, it has not, but we are still in the early stages of developments in information technology (computers and various electronic equipment for services). The early stages of a predominantly service economy, far from furthering economic growth, have decelerated the rate of growth and, far from promoting mobility opportunity, have restricted it.

People in the United States and other industrialized countries have experienced much opportunity for upward occupational mobility during most of this century. But these opportunities for upward mobility have come to an end, for they were the long-run contributions of the Industrial Revolution—the high productivity and accelerating rate of growth it

---

of such a major change in long-term trends must, in my opinion, be a change in the economic infrastructure.

generated. These contributions have begun to fall off, however, with the deindustrialization implicit in the transition to a service economy. Structural mobility has diminished (Hout 1988), and some predict it will diminish further in the next few years (Krymkowski and Krauze 1992). The standard of living of the middle as well as the working class has also decreased, while poverty, unemployment, and homelessness have increased, as has economic inequality. Whereas the expansion of high-status occupations in the period of rapid economic growth generated structural opportunities for upward mobility, the period of a slowdown in this growth and an expansion of low-status service occupations has engendered structural constraints fostering downward mobility.

A democratic society differs from a feudal one in that, in the former, people do not have to stay in the station in which they were born for their entire lives but have opportunities to move up the social ladder. There are basically only two ways in which substantial upward mobility can occur in a population (if we ignore the influence on mobility chances of class differences in fertility and immigration, which have been declining). One is by means of structural mobility, which means that the expansion of high strata and the contraction of low ones create opportunities for upward mobility. The other is by means of circulation mobility, or fluidity, which refers to those movements from social origins to occupational destinations that are independent of any difference between (change in) the occupational distribution of parents and that of their children, the current population.

Circulation mobility reveals the fluidity of the occupational structure, that is, how little occupational achievements depend on family origin. However, circulation mobility is zero-sum: it requires as much downward as upward mobility. As a matter of fact, circulation mobility increases the risk of downward mobility of the children of the upper class disproportionately. Since circulation mobility requires the same *numbers* to move down as move up, it raises the small upper strata's probability of declining much more than the much larger lower strata's probability of rising.

If the higher and middle strata no longer expand, thereby generating structural mobility (and if differential fertility and immigration decline to the point where they are inconsequential), people in lower socioeconomic strata and their offspring are condemned to spend their lives in those strata unless the occupational structure can be made more fluid. This would necessitate reducing the substantial influence social origins, including ethnic as well as class background, exert today on occupational

chances, which is the major reason circulation mobility is currently limited. In principle, it should be possible to restrict at least the material
advantages children from higher strata now enjoy and improve those
of children from lower strata, though the more intangible social and
psychological class differences cannot easily be eradicated in the short
run. Even equalizing the material factors that affect career opportunities
would not be easy, however.

Endeavors to promote circulation mobility threaten the interests of
the most powerful groups in society. The powerful members of the upper
class would surely oppose with all their might any social or political
movement that sought to reclaim opportunities for the underprivileged
by instituting measures to restrict the advantages of upper-class offspring
and thereby to reduce inequality of career chances. Enhanced circulation
mobility would increase the risk of downward mobility of the higher
strata as it improved the opportunities of upward mobility of the lower
ones. Hence, endeavors to make the occupational structure more fluid
would intensify contrasting class interests and create a situation ripe for
serious class conflict.

We are clearly not yet confronted with such a class conflict in the
United States, but we may well be so in the twenty-first century if present
trends continue. Class conflict becomes violent only under certain conditions. We may make inferences about these conditions from a study of
violent rebellions by the Tillys (1975: 4–8, 243–45). They specify three
conditions increasing the likelihood that rebellions will turn to collective
violence. A breakdown of established traditions and social relations, and
firm social solidarity of the group protesting the status quo constitute two
of those conditions. But the most important condition is that a power
struggle ensue as the protesting group that mobilizes for collective action
to effect major reforms encounters repression by its opposition, typically
representatives of the government. The implication I draw is that future
class conflict may turn into violent confrontations if traditional opportunities have been disrupted and if a solidarity has developed among the
various elements of the protest movement, but then only if the efforts of
the protesters to mobilize opposition to the status quo encounter repression by the establishment.

These are, of course, mere conjectures. I do not know how likely it
is that intensified class conflict will develop, nor what the probability is
that it will become violent. I am convinced, however, that we are at the
threshold of a major transformation, in the United States and many other
countries. Symptoms of this impending transformation are the recent

economic crises and dislocations in the developed countries, the violent ethnic conflicts in many parts of the world, and the impending development of predominantly service economies in the most developed countries. The last is the source of the decelerating rate of economic growth and the consequent decline in structural mobility, which is the basic reason for the likely intensification of class conflict. There is an alternative possibility, however.

Industrialization in its earlier stages involved increasing routinization of work to save labor costs, as exemplified by the many jobs on assembly lines, but ultimately growing routinization made it possible for machines to replace many workers on routine jobs, as indicated by the decrease in unskilled laborers. That the growth of services has also been accompanied by increasing routinization to save labor costs is exemplified by the replacement of waiters and waitresses by countermen and counterwomen. The more routinized a job becomes, however, the easier it should be for machines to perform it, whether it involves nonmanual or manual work. Automation has occurred on a large scale in manufacturing, and the computer and other developments in high technology may also make it likely in many of the economy's expanding service industries.

. . .

Indeed, automation in the services has already started to expand. Before explicating this statement, I must point out that many studies of its increasing mechanization define the service sector more broadly than I did in reporting its growth (pp. 193–94). In addition to the industries I included (specified in note 11), the board definition often used also includes in the service sector transportation, communication, utilities, and trade. By either definition, it is the fastest growing sector of the United States economy.

From 1967 to 1990 employment in the service industries (broadly defined but excluding that in nonprofit and government organizations) more than doubled, from 32 to 67 million, while employment in manufacturing dropped despite the growth in the labor force. The industries in retail trade and personal and business services expanded most and "combined accounted for more than 75 percent of the employment growth in service industries" (Kronemer 1993: 44–45). As a matter of fact, services have become the dominant sector of the economy. By the 1980s, the service sector accounted "for 71 percent of the country's GNP and 75 percent of its employment" (Quinn 1988: 16). This rapid growth of service industries has been accompanied by increasing investments in information technology.

Firms in the service sector have become increasingly capital inten-sive, and most of their capital investments have been in information technology. "As a result, the broad segment of the economy that can be classified as service providers now owns about 84 percent of the total U.S. stock in information technology items" (Roach 1988: 118). Service-providing industries spent more than twice as large a proportion of their capital budget on information technology than goods-producing indus-tries did (in 1985; earlier, the discrepancy was even greater [see Roach 1988: 124–25]). Except for communications, with its large telephone system, fully 49 percent of all service industries' investments in informa-tion technology was in computers (p. 132).

The large amount of capital devoted to information technology had three major advantages for firms in many of the service industries, as Quinn (1988: 26–27) points out. It promoted the development of larger companies that effected substantial economies of scale. These economies sometimes bred what he calls "economies of scope," using the same tech-nologies to provide a wider variety of services. A third advantage is that computer technology facilitated handling complex tasks economically. The resulting gains in efficiency enabled a number of corporations in var-ious service industries to improve the productivity of their operations, and even to handle complex, large-scale operations that had before defied endeavors to cope with them effectively. Quinn provides some illustra-tions of interest.

Coordination of a large number of transactions has been carried out with the aid of computers and other electronic facilities in banks, airline companies, mail order houses, and credit-card companies. Electronic sys-tems and devices performed the work of many thousands of clerks and their supervisors in these and other firms, and the transactions in the largest of them had become so complex that they became feasible only with the development of modern information systems. The stock market and big trading houses in securities were being overwhelmed by the huge and rapidly growing number of transactions (up to 500 million shares a day) when they solved the problem by installing automated trading sys-tems. These are now complemented by networks of decentralized trading offices throughout the United States and, indeed, among nations.

The empirical results we have reviewed leave no doubt that the large-scale introduction of information technology in service industries has automated many operations, made it possible to perform tasks that were once impossible, and often improved efficiency. The important questions still to be answered are whether introducing information technology has improved, or will eventually improve, productivity in the service industries as much as technological advances improved productivity in manufacturing; and whether it has improved, or has prospects to improve, opportunities for structural upward mobility by eliminating the most routine and expanding the more challenging occupational positions in the service industries.

Kronemer (1993: 45–46) presents data showing that productivity gains in services have been substantial, yet not so large as those that have occurred in the same period in manufacturing. Productivity rose between 1973 and 1990 in "89 percent of the measured industries in the manufacturing sector" and in 69 percent of those in the service sector. When a longer period is examined using another, perhaps more reliable, measure (GDP per 1,000 employees), productivity in services also is observed to have risen considerably but neither as much nor as consistently as that in manufacturing. Productivity so measured increased in total services (except government) by more than two-thirds from 1948 (2.03) to 1973 (3.47) but then remained nearly constant to 1983 (3.54), whereas productivity in total goods doubled from 1948 (1.72) to 1973 (3.49) and continued to rise to 1983 (4.19).[15] Apparently information technology improved productivity in the service sector greatly, but the technological advances in manufacturing improved its productivity still more.

The answer to the first question raised above is that the large investment in information technology by the service sectors has improved productivity substantially. It has not, however, raised service productivity as much as manufacturing productivity has been increased simultaneously by technological progress. Besides, after some increase the rate of service productivity has actually declined in the 1980s (Roach 1988: 133). The reason may be, Roach (1988: 135–36) surmises, that computers and electronic devices are so new that managers have not yet learned how best to utilize them for various services or what technology is most appropriate for which services. They also have yet to determine the services for which perhaps no appropriate technology so far exists, or for which maybe none could exist (like infant care).

The other question raised above is whether the past and probable

15. Computed from Kendrick 1988: 101, table 2.

future increase in service productivity will eliminate routine low-grade jobs and expand occupations entailing more education and income, thereby renewing opportunities for structural mobility. No definite answer to this question is, of course, possible, but projections about the changes in the occupational structure between 1990 and 2005 permit some inferences. Silvestri and Lukasiewicz (1991) computed projections of the employment distribution among nine major occupational groups in 2005 and compared it with that in 1990. The four highest-ranking occupational groups[16] (compare the figures in the first with those in the next four rows in the last column of chart 1, p. 65) all increased their share of the labor force. If this is indicative of a growing trend, it would suggest that the growth in services and their productivity could renew in the long run opportunities for structural mobility, though this is obviously mere conjecture.

CONCLUSIONS

This book has presented a macrosociological analysis of the influence of population structures on people's occupational opportunities, their social relations, and their organizational participation. The focus on structural analysis has explicitly ignored cultural influences, not because they are unimportant, which they undoubtedly are not, but because a theoretical analysis must maintain a conceptual focus and not attempt to deal with all possible influences. My focus is clearly on the influences of a population's composition in various respects on social life, which does not imply that cultural factors do not also exert influences on it. Cultural traditions legitimate forms of social organization and structure and thereby perpetuate them by transforming them into institutions that last for generations.

Cultural institutions have not been analyzed in this study, however, as its focus has been on the influence of the existing population structure on people's opportunities and their limitations. Population structure is defined as a population's distribution among social positions in all dimensions. These distributions exhibit various forms of heterogeneity, of inequality, and of intersecting social differences. At the core of this analysis is my attempt to develop a formal theory of the effects of these

16. These are as follows: executive, administrative, and managerial; professional specialty; technicians and related support; marketing and sales.

population distributions on social relations, centering attention on intergroup relations. This theory is presented in chapter 2. The major propositions, derived from an assumption about contact opportunities, are theorems about the effects the distributions of people, which I call structural parameters, have on rates of intergroup relations. Tests of empirical implications of these and related theorems are supplied in chapter 3.

A theory of occupational opportunities, which is not formulated as rigorously as that of intergroup relations, is presented in chapter 4. I analyze there the influence of the occupational structure, which reflects society's division of labor, on chances of social mobility. This analysis takes into account not only the structural influences on social mobility of the matrix of occupational origins and destinations but also those of the internal changes in positions within this matrix. Two other topics discussed in chapter 4 are the nexus of economic sector and labor demand, and the relationship of structural and circulation mobility.

In chapter 5, I examine the encompassing population structure as the social context of the organizations and other substructures within it, particularly how the recruitment of members and growth are affected by the composition and distributions of the larger population. The chapter's second half centers on firms and large corporations, which exert such a dominant influence in contemporary society. After reporting studies of their political influence and the significance of interlocking directorates, I review recent mergers that have made firms owned by large corporations serve as intersections of markets and corporations.

Chapter 6 is devoted to the micro-macro issue, and I modify my earlier position that micro- and macroanalysis cannot be combined in one theory. First, however, I analyze Coleman's idea of a micro-macro transition and argue that his conception is upside down and must be reversed to put it right-side up. Microstructures are not the foundations of macrostructures but their ultimate expression in face-to-face relations, which integrate a population's diverse subgroups by promoting intergroup relations, the more so the more the diversity penetrates into face-to-face groups. Social exchange in dyads is analyzed to explain how it sometimes engenders bonds between peers and at other times engenders differences in social status. Interpersonal power over associates in direct social interaction is contrasted with the impersonal economic and political power to dominate many thousands or millions of people by means of control over resources or of authority implemented by a chain of command.

This last chapter asks what the conditions are that influence the various forms of heterogeneity, inequality, and intersection in a population, which heretofore have been taken as given in analyzing their social consequences. The answer in most general terms is that historical antecedents influence current population characteristics. Two historical developments are examined to trace how they affect the current population structure: demographic trends and economic developments. For example, differences in fertility among ascribed groups, such as ethnic or religious groups, affect heterogeneity. The higher birthrates of the poor than the affluent increase inequality. So did the higher birthrates of the many poor immigrants to this country about a century ago, but the resulting lopsided occupational distribution improved opportunities for upward mobility of the second generation, the immigrants' children.

The Industrial Revolution was the catalyst of modern economic development. It gave rise to the division of labor and increases in urbanization as well as to industrialization. Earlier, these developments primarily benefited the aristocracy and the rising bourgeoisie but seriously disrupted the traditional life of common people and created great hardships for them. In the long run, however, the accelerating rate of economic growth it promoted improved ordinary people's standards of living and their opportunities for upward mobility.

The progressing division of labor and its repercussions for the occupational distribution played a major role in the expansion of occupational opportunities. The higher wages paid for industrial work as compared to agricultural work provided people with incentives to migrate from farm to urban jobs. At first, migration to the better industrial jobs increased inequality, but once nearly one-half of the farm workers had moved to jobs in cities, further moves reduced it, which is reflected in the inverted U of Kuznets's curve of income inequality.

Recently, however, the rate of growth has decelerated, turning into a logistic and ultimately a U-shaped curve. This is manifest in disruptive changes in the economy and in the lives of many, if not most, people. Indications of the economic crisis in the United States are a huge national debt, an unfavorable balance of trade, and a change of emphasis in the largest corporations from production to financial speculation. Consequences for the people, except for the rich, who are getting richer, are reduced standards of living; diminished opportunities for upward mobility; growing unemployment, poverty, and homelessness; and increasing economic inequality.

The expansion of higher occupational positions engendered by changes in the division of labor with increasing industrialization generated much structural mobility during most of this century. The recent expansion of services and decline of manufacturing have reduced productivity, the source of economic growth, and greatly diminished structural upward mobility. Restoring opportunities to the lower strata in the absence of structural mobility would require instituting measures that would dramatically increase circulation mobility, which is independent of family background. Circulation mobility is zero-sum, however, and consequently against the interests of the higher strata, which raises the specter of increasing class conflict.

These are both dire prospects—a stagnant society with little career opportunity or one torn by class conflict. But these are not the only alternatives. Another possibility might be a second industrial revolution that transformed service industries as the original one transformed manufacturing. Recent decades have witnessed great advances in information technology—such as computers, electronics, and automation—and service industries have invested significant capital in this technology. Although these investments have effected substantial improvements in the productivity of services, the increase in service productivity has so far been neither as great nor as consistent as the concurrent increase in manufacturing productivity. The reason for the recent decline in service productivity is probably that computers and electronic systems are so new that managers have not yet learned how to use them to best advantage, nor have they as yet acquired sufficient experience to know which ones are most appropriate for which services.

If this inference is correct and the recent slowdown in the growth of service productivity is temporary and reflects the problems of adjusting operations to a new technology, productivity in services could be expected to accelerate after a period of transition, as that in manufacturing did. Achieving greater service productivity might well involve substituting electronic for human operations and reserving for human beings as far as possible the more complex and interesting tasks that cannot be automated. If such changes occurred, they would redistribute the labor force. Increasing demand for employees with substantial training and skills would expand the higher socioeconomic strata, and shrinking demand for routine work would contract the lower strata.

Such a redistribution of the occupational structure would restore structural mobility. Projections of the occupational distributions in 2005 imply some shift along these lines that could be the beginning of a trend that would re-create structural mobility. This is sheer speculation, however, and even if it ultimately proves correct it would be preceded by a long period of transition with much unemployment, major disruptions of people's lives, and untold miseries, just as happened after the original Industrial Revolution. In the long run, however, the advances in information technology may revitalize the economy and, by stimulating greater structural mobility, improve the opportunities of the lower strata and raise their standard of living.

In closing, let us briefly view the impending service economy from another perspective. Instead of asking whether technological advances can raise productivity in services and economic growth, we now ask what new contributions expanding services themselves can make. When a declining proportion of the labor force could supply enough farm products to meet the needs of the entire population, more industrial workers became available to produce material goods. When later a declining proportion of workers sufficed to produce all the material goods in demand, more employees became available to satisfy the great need for various services in developed countries. The American case clearly illustrates the need for better services.

For the United States fails to provide to all citizens many services other Western countries do. We do not supply free health care to everybody. We restrict higher education, except for a few scholarships, to those who can afford it. Still more important is the need for remedies for the deplorable state of American public education. Above all, our welfare system needs to be reorganized to supply adequate allowances for all the poor, and particularly to furnish trained social workers and other specialists to help restore normal lives and work opportunities to the many youngsters in the slums whom our neglect has condemned to a life of drugs, crime, and vice. The expanding services furnish a golden opportunity to enrich human life by providing intangible services. Since most of these service jobs require considerable education and are middle class, the expansion of services may even further structural mobility.

Why just worry about economic growth and the material benefits it can bring? We can reorient our thinking instead and perhaps give up some material goods in exchange for better services of all kinds. Trading more riches for a richer life is a good bargain.

BIBLIOGRAPHY

Alba, Richard D. 1985. *Italian Americans*. Englewood Cliffs: Prentice Hall.

Althauser, Robert P., and Arne L. Kalleberg. 1981. Pp. 119–49 in I. Berg (ed.), *Sociological Perspectives on Labor Markets*. New York: Academic Press.

Anderson, Arnold C. 1961. "A Skeptical Note on the Relation of Vertical Mobility to Education." *American Journal of Sociology* 66: 560–70.

Averitt, Robert T. 1968. *The Dual Economy*. New York: Norton.

Bales, Robert F. 1950. *Interaction Process Analysis*. Cambridge, Mass.: Addison-Wesley.

Barnett, Larry D. 1962. "Research in Interreligious Dating and Marriage." *Marriage and Family Living* 24: 191–94.

Baron, James N., and William T. Bielby. 1980. "Bringing Firms Back In." *American Sociological Review* 45: 737–65.

Bavelas, Alex. 1950. "Communication Patterns in Task-Oriented Groups." *Acoustical Society of America* 22: 725–30.

Bealer, Robert C., Fern K. Willits, and Gerald Bender. 1963. "Religious Exogamy." *Sociology and Social Research* 48: 69–79.

Beck, E. M., Patrick M. Horan, and Charles M. Tolbert. 1978. "Stratification in a Dual Economy." *American Sociological Review* 43: 704–20.

Bell, Daniel. 1974. *The Coming of Post-Industrial Society*. London: Heineman.

Blackburn, McKinley L., and David E. Bloom. 1987. "Earnings and Income Inequality in the United States." *Population and Development Review* 13: 575–609.

Blalock, Hubert M. 1969. *Theory Construction*. Englewood Cliffs: Prentice Hall.

Blau, Judith R. 1993. *Social Contracts and Economic Markets*. New York: Plenum.

Blau, Judith R., and Peter M. Blau. 1982. "The Cost of Inequality." *American Sociological Review* 47: 114–29.

Blau, Peter M. 1955. *The Dynamics of Bureaucracy*. Chicago: University of Chicago Press.

———. 1960. "Structural Effects." *American Sociological Review* 20: 41–45.

———. 1964. *Exchange and Power in Social Life*. New York: Wiley.

———. 1970. "A Formal Theory of Differentiation in Organizations." *American Sociological Review* 35: 201–18.

———. 1977. *Inequality and Heterogeneity*. New York: Free Press.

Blau, Peter M., and Otis Dudle Duncan. 1967. *The American Occupational Structure*. New York: Wiley.

Blau, Peter M., and Danching Ruan. 1990. "Inequality and Mobility in Urban China and America." *Research in Stratification and Mobility* 9: 3–32.

Blau, Peter M., Danching Ruan, and Monika Ardelt. 1991. "Interpersonal Choice and Networks in China." *Social Forces* 69: 1037–62.

Blau, Peter M., and Joseph E. Schwartz. 1984. *Crosscutting Social Circles*. Orlando: Academic Press. (B&S.)

Blau, Zena S. 1973. *Old Age in a Changing Society*. New York: Franklin Watts.

Boudon, Raymond. 1974 (1973). *Education, Opportunity, and Social Inequality*. New York: Wiley.

Boulding, Kenneth E. 1955 (1941). *Economic Analysis*. New York: Harper.

Bourdieu, Pierre. 1984 (1979). *Distinction*. Cambridge, Mass.: Harvard University Press.

Braithwaite, Richard B. 1953. *Scientific Explanation*. Cambridge: At the University Press.

Breiger, Ronald L. 1974. "The Duality of Persons and Groups." *Social Forces* 53: 181–90.

———. 1990. "Social Control and Social Networks." Pp. 453–76 in C. Calhoun, M. W. Meyer, and W. R. Scott (eds.), *Structures of Power and Constraint*. Cambridge: University Press.

Burma, John H. 1963. "Interethnic Marriage in Los Angeles, 1948–1959." *Social Forces* 42: 156–65.

Burt, Ronald S. 1982. *Toward a Structural Theory of Action*. New York: Academic Press.

———. 1983. *Corporate Profits and Cooptation*. New York: Academic Press.

———. 1992. *Structural Holes*. Cambridge, Mass.: Harvard University Press.

Calhoun, Craig. 1991. "Indirect Relationships and Imagined Communities." Pp. 95–121 in P. Bourdieu and J. S. Coleman (eds.), *Social Theory for a Changing Society*. New York: Westview Press.

Calhoun, Craig, and W. Richard Scott. 1990. "Introduction: Peter Blau's Sociological Structuralism." Pp. 1–36 in C. Calhoun, M. W. Meyer, and W. R. Scott (eds.), *Structures of Power and Constraint*. Cambridge: University Press.

Cartwright, Dorwin, and Frank Harary. 1956. "Structural Balance." *Psychological Review* 63: 277–93.

Chandler, Alfred. 1990 (March/April). "The Enduring Logic of Industrial Success. *Harvard Business Review* 68, no. 2: 130–40.

Coleman, James S. 1966. "Foundations for a Theory of Collective Decisions." *American Journal of Sociology* 71: 615–27.

———. 1982. *The Asymmetric Society.* Syracuse: Syracuse University Press.

———. 1990a. *Foundations of Social Theory.* Cambridge, Mass.: Belknap/Harvard University Press.

———. 1990b. "Rational Action, Networks, and the Emergence of Norms." Pp. 91–112 in C. Calhoun, M. W. Meyer, and W. R. Scott (eds.), *Structures of Power and Constraint.* Cambridge: University Press.

Collins, Randall. 1987. "Interaction Ritual Chains, Power and Property." Pp. 193–206 in J. C. Alexander, B. Giesen, R. Muench, and N. J. Smelser (eds.), *The Micro-Macro Link.* Berkeley: University of California Press.

Cook, Karen S. 1982. "Network Structures from an Exchange Perspective." Pp. 177–99 in P.V. Marsden and N. Lin (eds.), *Social Structure and Network Analysis.* Beverly Hills: Sage.

Cook, Karen S., Mary R. Gillmore, and Toshio Tamagishi. 1983. "The Distribution of Power in Exchange Networks." *American Journal of Sociology* 89: 275–305.

Coser, Lewis A. 1984. "Introduction." Pp. ix–xxiv in Emile Durkheim, *The Division of Labor in Society.* New York: Macmillan.

Coser, Rose L. 1975. "The Complexity of Roles as Seedbed of Individual Autonomy." Pp. 237–64 in L. A. Coser (ed.), *The Idea of Social Structure.* New York: Harcourt Brace Jovanovich.

Costner, Herbert L., and Robert K. Leik. 1964. "Deductions from Axiomatic Theory." *American Sociological Review* 29: 819–35.

Cronbach, Lee J. 1951. "Coefficient Alpha and the Internal Structure of Tests." *Psychometrika* 16: 297–334.

Dahl, Robert A. 1968. "Power." *International Encyclopedia of the Social Sciences.* New York: Macmillan and Free Press.

Davis, Kingsley, and Wilbert E. Moore. 1945. "Some Principles of Stratification." *American Sociological Review* 10: 242–49.

Doeringer, Peter B., and Michael J. Piore. 1971. *Internal Labor Markets and Manpower Analysis.* Lexington, Mass.: Heath.

Duncan, Otis Dudley. 1961. "A Socioeconomic Index for All Occupations." Pp. 109–38 in A. J. Reiss (ed.), *Occupations and Social Status.* New York: Free Press.

Durkheim Émile. 1893. *De la division du travail social.* Paris: Alcan.

———. 1933. *The Division of Labor in Society.* Glencoe: Free Press.

Easterlin, Richard A. 1978. "What Will 1984 Be Like? Socioeconomic Implications of Recent Twists in Age Structure." *Demography* 15: 397–421.

———. 1980. *Birth and Fortune.* New York: Basic Books.

Eccles, Robert G., and Harrison C. White. 1986. "Firm and Market Interfaces of Profit Center Control. Pp. 203–24 in S. Lindenberg, J. S. Coleman, and S. Nowak (eds.), *Approaches to Social Theory.* New York: Russell Sage.

Edwards, Alba M. 1943. *Comparative Occupational Statistics for the United States, 1877–1940.* Washington: GPO.

Ekeh, Peter P. 1974. *Social Exchange Theory.* Cambridge, Mass.: Harvard University Press.

Emerson, Richard M. 1962. "Power-Dependence Relations." *American Sociological Review* 27: 31–41.

———. 1972. "Exchange Theory." Pp. 38–87 in J. Berger, M. Zelditch, and B. Anderson (eds.), *Sociological Theory in Progress.* Boston: Houghton Mifflin.

———. 1976. "Social Exchange Theory." *Annual Review of Sociology* 2: 335–62.

Evans-Pritchard, E. E. 1972 (1940). *The Nuer.* New York: Oxford University Press.

Featherman, David L., and Robert M. Hauser. 1978. *Opportunity and Change.* New York: Academic Press.

Featherman, David L., F. Lancaster Jones, and Robert M. Hauser. 1975. "Assumptions of Mobility Research in the United States." *Social Science Research* 4: 329–60.

Feld, Scott L. 1981. "The Focused Organization of Organizational Ties." *American Journal of Sociology* 86: 1015–35.

Fligstein, Neil. 1990. *The Transformation of Corporate Control.* Cambridge, Mass.: Harvard University Press.

Ganzeboom, Harry B. G., Ruud Luijkx, and Donald Treiman. 1989. "Intergenerational Class Mobility in Comparative Perspective." *Research in Stratification and Mobility* 8: 3–84.

Ganzeboom, Harry B. G., Donald J. Treiman, and Wout C. Ultee. 1991. "Comparative Intergenerational Stratification Research." *Annual Review of Sociology* 17: 277–302.

Gibbs, Jack B., and Walter T. Martin. 1962. "Urbanization, Technology, and the Division of Labor." *American Sociological Review* 27: 667–77.

Giddens, Anthony. 1986 (1984). *The Constitution of Society.* Berkeley: University of California Press.

Golddthorpe, John H. 1980. *Social Mobility and Class Structure in Modern Britain.* Oxford: Clarendon Press.

Goodman, Leo A. 1979. "Muliplicative Models for the Analysis of Occupational

Mobility Tables and Other Kinds of Cross-Classification Tables." *American Journal of Sociology* 84: 804–19.

———. 1984. *The Analysis of Cross-Classified Data Having Ordered Categories.* Cambridge, Mass.: Harvard University Press.

Gouldner, Alvin W. 1970. *The Coming Crisis of Western Sociology.* New York: Basic Books.

Granovetter, Mark S. 1973. "The Strength of Weak Ties." *American Journal of Sociology* 78: 1360–80.

———. 1974. *Getting a Job.* Cambridge, Mass.: Harvard University Press.

———. 1985. "Economic Action and Social Structure." *American Journal of Sociology* 91: 481–510.

Hannan, Michael T., and John Freeman. 1989. *Organizational Ecology.* Cambridge, Mass.: Harvard University Press.

Harrison, Bennett, and Barry Bluestone. 1988. *The Great U-Turn.* New York: Basic Books.

Harrison, Roderick J. 1988. "Opportunity Models." *Research in Stratification and Mobility* 7: 3–33.

Hauser, Robert M., John N. Koffel, Harry P. Travis, and Peter J. Dicksinson. 1975. "Structural Changes in Occupational Mobility among Men in the United States." *American Sociological Review* 40: 585–98.

Hechter, Michael. 1987. *Principles of Group Solidarity.* Berkeley: University of California Press.

Heider, Fritz. 1958. *The Psychology of Interpersonal Relations.* New York: Wiley.

Hodson, Randy, and Robert L. Kaufman. 1981. "Circularity in the Dual Economy." *American Journal of Sociology* 86: 881–87.

Homans, George C. 1961. *Social Behavior.* New York: Harcourt, Brace & World.

Hout, Michael. 1988. "More Universalism, Less Structural Mobility." *American Journal of Sociology* 93: 1358–1400.

Kalleberg, Arne L., and Ivar Berg. 1987. *Work and Industry.* New York: Plenum.

Kendrick, John W. 1988. Pp. 99–117 in B. Guile and J. B. Quinn (eds.), *Technology in Services.* Washington: National Academy Press.

Knight, Frank H. 1921. *Risk, Uncertainty and Profit.* Boston: Houghton Mifflin.

Kronemer, Alexander. 1993. "Productivity in Industry and Government, 1973–91." *Monthly Labor Review* 116, no. 7: 44–50.

Krymkowski, Daniel H., and Tadeus K. Krauze. 1992. "Occupational Mobility in the Year 2000." *Social Forces* 71: 145–57.

Kuznets, Simon. 1955. "Economic Growth and Income Inequality." *American Economic Review* 45: 1–28.

———. 1966. *Modern Economic Growth.* New Haven: Yale University Press.

———. 1971. *Economic Growth of Nations*. Cambridge, Mass.: Belknap/Harvard University Press

———. 1989. *Economic Development, the Family, and Income Distribution*. Cambridge: Cambridge University Press.

Landes, David S. 1969. *The Unbound Prometheus*. Cambridge: Cambridge University Press.

Laumann, Edward O. 1973. *Bonds of Pluralism*. New York: Wiley.

Lazarsfeld, Paul F., and Herbert Menzel. 1969 (1961). "On the Relation between Individual and Collective Properties." Pp. 499–516 in A. Etzioni (ed.), *A Sociological Reader on Complex Organizations*. New York: Holt, Rinehart & Winston.

Lévi-Strauss, Claude. 1949. *Les structures élémentaires de la parenté*. Paris: Presses Universitaires de France.

———. 1963. *Structural Anthropology*. New York: Basic Books.

Lieberson, Stanley. 1969. "Measuring Population Diversity." *American Sociological Review* 34: 850–62.

———. 1987 (1985). *Making It Count*. Berkeley: University of California Press.

Lipset, Seymour Martin. 1963 (1960). *Political Man*. Garden City: Doubleday.

Lipset, Seymour M., and Reinhard Bendix. 1959. *Social Mobility in Industrial Society*. Berkeley: University of California Press.

Lipset, Seymour M., and Hans L. Zetterberg. 1956. "A Theory of Social Mobility." *Transactions of the Third World Congress of Sociology*, 3: 155–77.

Locke, Harvey J., George Sabagh, and Mary Margaret Thomes. 1957. "Interfaith Marriages." *Social Problems* 4: 329–35.

McPherson, J. Miller. 1981. "Voluntary Affiliation." Pp. 325–51 in P. M. Blau and R. K. Merton (eds.), *Continuities in Structural Inquiry*. London: Sage.

McPherson, J. Miller, and James R. Ranger-Moore. 1991. "Evolution of a Dancing Landscape." *Social Forces* 70: 19–42.

McPherson, J. Miller, and Lynn Smith-Lovin. 1986. "Sex Segregation in Voluntary Associations." *American Sociological Review* 51: 61–79.

Malinowski, Bronislaw. 1961 (1922). *Argonauts of the Western Pacific*. New York: Dutton.

Marsden, Peter V. 1987. "Core Discussion Networks of Americans." *American Sociological Review* 52: 122–31.

———. 1990. "Network Diversity, Substructures, and Opportunities for Contact." Pp. 396–410 in C. Calhoun, M. W. Meyer, and W. R. Scott (eds.), *Structures of Power and Constraint*. Cambridge: University Press.

Marx, Karl. 1906 (1873). *Capital*. New York: Humbolt.

Mauss, Marcel. 1954 (1925). *The Gift*. Glencoe, Ill.: Free Press.

Maxwell, Nan L. 1990. *Income Inequality in the United States, 1947–1985*. New York: Greenwood.

Merton, Robert K. 1948. "Social Psychology of Housing." Pp. 164–217 in Wayne Dennis (ed.), *Current Trends in Social Psychology*. Pittsburgh: University of Pittsburgh Press.

———. 1968 (1949). *Social Theory and Social Structure*. New York: Free Press.

Merton, Robert K., Patricia S. West, and Marie Jahoda. 1951. "Patterns of Social Life." New York: Columbia University Bureau of Social Research. (Mimeographed.)

Messner, Steven F., and Scott J. South. 1986. "Economic Deprivation, Opportunity Structure, and Robbery Victimization." *Social Forces* 64: 975–91.

Mintz, Beth, and Michael Schwartz. 1985. *The Power Structure of American Business*. Chicago: University of Chicago Press.

Mizruchi, Mark S. 1989. "Similarity of Political Behavior among Large American Corporations." *American Journal of Sociology* 95: 401–24.

———. 1992. *The Structure of Corporate Political Action*. Cambridge, Mass.: Harvard University Press.

Moreno, J. L. 1934. *Who Shall Survive?* Washington: Nervous and Mental Disease Publishing Co.

Newcomb, Theodore M. 1961. *The Acquaintance Process*. Holt, Rinehart & Winston.

Nielsen, François. 1985. "Toward a Theory of Ethnic Solidarity in Modern Cities." *American Sociological Review* 50: 133–49.

O'Brien, Robert M. 1987. "The Interracial Nature of Violent Crime." *American Journal of Sociology* 92: 817–35.

Parsons, Talcott. 1937. *The Structure of Social Action*. New York: McGraw-Hill.

———. 1966. *Societies*. Englewood Cliffs: Prentice-Hall.

Piore, Michael J. 1975. "Notes for a Theory of Labor Market Segmentation." In R. Edwards, M. Reich, and D. Gordon (eds.), *Labor Market Segmentation*. Lexington, Mass.: Heath.

Polanyi, Karl. 1957 (1944). *The Great Transformation*. Boston: Beacon Press.

Popper, Karl R. 1959 (1934). *The Logic of Scientific Discovery*. New York: Basic Books.

Quinn, James B. 1988. "Technology in Services." Pp. 16–46 in B. Guile and J. B. Quinn (eds.), *Technology in Services*. Washington: National Academy Press.

Roach, Stephen S. 1988. "Technology and the Service Sector." Pp. 118–38 in B. Guile and J. B. Quinn (eds.), *Technology in Services*. Washington: National Academy Press.

Rytina, Steven. 1987. "Paths to Plausible Inference." Unpublished manuscript.

———. 1989. "Life Chances and Continuity of Rank." *American Sociological Review* 54: 910–28.

Rytina, Steven, Peter M. Blau, Terry Blum, and Joseph Schwartz. 1988. "Inequality and Intermarriage." *Social Forces* 66: 645–75.

Sampson, Robert J. 1984. "Group Size, Heterogeneity, and Intergroup Conflict." *Social Forces* 62: 618–39.

Schattschneider, E. E. 1975 (1960). *The Semisovereign People.* Hinsdale, Ill.: Dryden.

Schlussel, Yvette R. 1986. "Market Structure, Organizational Size, and Individual Outcomes." Ph.D. dissertation, Columbia University.

Schwartz, Joseph E. 1990. "Penetrating Differentiation." Pp. 353–74 in C. Calhoun, M. W. Meyer, and W. R. Scott (eds.), *Structures of Power and Constraint.* Cambridge: University Press.

Silvestri, George, and John Lukasiewicz. 1991. "Occupational Employment Projections." *Monthly Labor Review* 115, no. 11: 64–94.

Simmel, Georg. 1923 (1908). *Soziologie.* Leipzig: Duncker & Humblot.

Simon, Herbert A. 1962. "The Architecture of Complexity." *Proceedings of the American Philosophical Society* 106: 467–82.

Simpson, E. H. 1949. "Measurement of Diversity." *Nature* 163: 688.

Skvoretz, John. 1990. "Social Structure and Intermarriage." Pp. 375–96 in C. Calhoun, M. W. Meyer, and W. R. Scott (eds.), *Structures of Power and Constraint.* Cambridge: University Press.

Smith, Adam. 1776. *An Inquiry into the Nature and Causes of the Wealth of Nations.* London: Strahan and Cadell.

Snyder, David, and Edward L. Kick. 1979. "Structural Position in the World System and Economic Growth, 1955–1970." *American Journal of Sociology* 84: 1096–1126.

Sørensen, Aage B. 1992. "The Structural Bases of Social Inequality." Paper presented at the Annual Meeting of the American Sociological Association.

South, Scott J., and Richard B. Felson. 1990. "The Racial Patterning of Rape." *Social Forces* 69: 71–93.

South, Scott J., and Steven F. Messner. 1986. "Structural Determinants of Intergroup Associations." *American Journal of Sociology* 91: 1409–30.

State Statistical Bureau, China. 1990. *Statistical Yearbook of the People's Republic of China, 1990.* Beijing: Zhongguo Tongji Chubanshe (Chinese Statistical Publication House).

Stewart, James B. 1991. *Den of Thieves.* New York: Simon & Schuster.

Stewman, Shelby, and Suresh K. Konda. 1983. "Careers and Organizational Labor Markets." *American Journal of Sociology* 88: 637–85.

Stinchcombe, Arthur L. 1975. Pp. 11–33 in L. C. Coser (ed.), *The Idea of Social Structure.* New York: Harcourt Brace Jovanovich.

Strodtbeck, Fred L., Rita M. James, and Charles Hawkins. 1958. "Social Status in Jury Deliberation." Pp. 379–88 in E. E. Maccoby, T. M. Newcomb, and E. L. Hartley (eds.), *Readings in Social Psychology.* New York: Holt, Rinehart & Winston.

Sundrum, R. M. 1991. *Economic Growth in Theory and Practice*. New York: St. Martin's Press.

Thomas, John L. 1951. "The Factor of Religion in the Selection of Marriage Mates." *American Sociological Review* 16: 487–91.

Tilly, Charles, Louise Tilly, and Richard Tilly. 1975. *The Rebellious Century*. Cambridge, Mass.: Harvard University Press.

Tocqueville, Alexis de. 1980 (1835). *Democracy in America*. New York: Knopf.

Tolbert, Charles, Patrick M. Horan, and E. M. Beck. 1980. "The Structure of Economic Segmentation." *American Journal of Sociology* 85: 1095–1116.

Turner, Jonathan H. 1986 (1974). *The Structure of Sociological Theory*. Chicago: Dorsey Press.

Tyree, Andrea, and Judith Treas. 1974. "The Occupational and Marital Mobility of Women." *American Sociological Review* 39: 293–302.

United Nations, Department of Social Affairs, Population Division. 1953. *The Determinants and Consequences of Population Trends*. Population Studies, N.17. New York: United Nations.

U.S. Bureau of the Census. 1964. *U.S. Census of Populations: 1960:* 1960. Vol. 1. *Characteristics of the Population*. Part 1. United States Summary. Washington: GPO.

———. 1975. *Historical Statistics of the United States, Colonial Times to 1970*. Washington: GPO.

———. 1991a. *Statistical Abstracts of the United States*. Washington: GPO.

———. 1991b. *Census of Population and Housing: Summary Tape File 3* (United States) (machine readable data files), prepared by the Bureau of the Census. Washington: The Bureau.

Useem, Michael. 1984. *The Inner Circle*. New York: Oxford University Press.

Van Buren, Mark. 1991. "Ethnic Intermarriage." Unpublished manuscript.

Wallace, Michael, and Arne L. Kalleberg. 1981. "Economic Organization of Firms and Labor Market Consequences." Pp.77–117 in I. Berg (ed.), *Sociological Perspectives on Labor Markets*. New York: Academic Press.

Warner, Lloyd, and Paul S. Lunt. 1941. *The Social Life of Modern Community*. New Haven: Yale University Press.

Weber, Max. 1978 (1922). *Economy and Society*. Berkeley: University of California Press.

Wellman, Barry. 1988. "Structural Analysis." Pp. 19–61 in B. Wellman and S. D. Berkowitz (eds.), *Social Structures*. Cambridge: Cambridge University Press.

White, Harrison C. 1970. *Chains of Opportunity*. Cambridge, Mass.: Harvard University Press.

Williamson, Jeffrey G. 1991. *Inequality, Poverty, and History*. Cambridge: Blackwell.

Wilson, William J. 1987. *The Truly Disadvantaged*. Chicago: University of Chicago Press.

Wright, Erik O., Cynthia Costello, David Hacken, and Joey Sprague. 1982. "The American Class Structure." *American Sociological Review* 47: 709–26.

Zerubavel, Eviatar. 1991. *The Fine Line*. Chicago: University of Chicago Press.

Author Index

Subject Index